S

Illustrator® CS4 FOR DUMMIES

Cheat Sheet

D0752301

Getting Familiar with the Illustrator Workspace

Control panel

Menu bar · Arrange Documents · Help

Selection tool · Go to Bridge · Workspaces · Panels

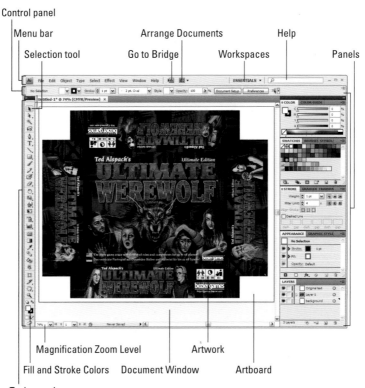

Magnification Zoom Level · Artwork

Fill and Stroke Colors · Document Window · Artboard

Tools panel

Nifty Illustrator Tips and Tricks

- ✔ Press X to toggle between Fill and Stroke, and Shift+X to swap fill and stroke colors.
- ✔ Zoom in quickly by choosing a magnification zoom level from the lower left (look for "74%" on the image here).
- ✔ An asterisk (*) in the Document tab means that the document has not been saved since you made changes.
- ✔ Quickly get more screen real estate by clicking the double arrows at the top right of the stack of panels.
- ✔ Pause the cursor over any Illustrator element (button, tool, panel, and so on) to see the name of that element.

For Dummies: Bestselling Book Series for Beginners

Illustrator® CS4 FOR DUMMIES®

Selecting and Moving Shortcuts

To Do This	Mac Shortcut Key	Windows Shortcut Key
Activate Selection tool last used (Select, Direct Select, or Group Select)	⌘+any tool (except Selection tools)	Ctrl+any tool (except Selection tools)
Toggle between Select and Direct Select (or between Select and Group Select)	None	Ctrl+Tab
Add to or subtract from selection	Shift+click with any Selection tool	Shift+click with any Selection tool
Select All	⌘+A	Ctrl+A
Deselect All	Shift+⌘+A	Shift+Ctrl+A
Move selection in 1 pt increments	Any arrow key	Any arrow key
Move selection in 10 pt increments	Shift+press any arrow key	Shift+press any arrow key
Constrain movement to 45° angles	Shift+drag with any Selection tool	Shift+drag with any Selection tool

Type Shortcuts

To Do This	Mac Shortcut	Windows Shortcut
Align text to left, right, or center	Shift+⌘+L, R, or C	Shift+Ctrl+L, R, or C
Justify text	Shift+⌘+J	Shift+Ctrl+J
Increase font size	Shift+⌘+. (period)	Shift+Ctrl+. (period)
Decrease font size	Shift+⌘+, (comma)	Shift+Ctrl+, (comma)
Select entire word	Double-click word	Double-click word
Select entire paragraph	Triple-click a word in the paragraph	Triple-click a word in the paragraph

For Dummies: Bestselling Book Series for Beginners

Illustrator® CS4

FOR

DUMMIES®

Illustrator® **CS4**
FOR
DUMMIES®

by Ted Alspach

WILEY

Wiley Publishing, Inc.

S

Illustrator® CS4 For Dummies®

Published by
Wiley Publishing, Inc.
111 River St.
Hoboken, NJ 07030-5774
www.wiley.com

WILEY

About the Author

Ted Alspach is the author of more than 30 books on graphics, design, and Web publishing, including *Illustrator CS4 Bible* (Wiley.). Ted is also the designer of more than a dozen board games and expansions, including *Rapscallion, Seismic, Start Player,* and *Ultimate Werewolf.* Ted spent eight years at Adobe Systems, Inc. working on both Illustrator and the Creative Suite.

Dedication

To all the people who are brave enough to engage in the use of Illustrator for the first time — may this book serve as a guide to the wonders of vector graphics and the power of infinite editability and scalability.

Author's Acknowledgments

Thanks to everyone at Wiley for helping to work toward another great edition of this book!

Publisher's Acknowledgments

We're proud of this book; please send us your comments through our online registration form located at www.dummies.com/register/.

Some of the people who helped bring this book to market include the following:

Acquisitions, Editorial, and Media Development

Sr. Project Editor: Paul Levesque

Executive Editor: Bob Woerner

Sr. Copy Editor: Teresa Artman

Technical Editor: Chad Perkins

Editorial Manager: Leah Cameron

Editorial Assistant: Amanda Foxworth

Sr. Editorial Assistant: Cherie Case

Cartoons: Rich Tennant (www.the5thwave.com)

Composition Services

Project Coordinator: Erin Smith

Layout and Graphics: Claudia Bell, Stacie Brooks, Carl Byers, Carrie A. Cesavice, Melanee Habig, Stephanie D. Jumper, Brent Savage, Christine Williams

Proofreader: Betty Kish

Indexer: Sherry Massey

Publishing and Editorial for Technology Dummies

Richard Swadley, Vice President and Executive Group Publisher

Andy Cummings, Vice President and Publisher

Mary C. Corder, Editorial Director

Publishing for Consumer Dummies

Diane Graves Steele, Vice President and Publisher

Composition Services

Gerry Fahey, Vice President of Production Services

Debbie Stailey, Director of Composition Services

Contents at a Glance

Table of Contents

Introduction

*W*elcome to *Illustrator CS4 For Dummies*. You're reading this book because you want to find out more about Adobe Illustrator. That's a very smart move because Adobe Illustrator is the industry-standard graphics software. Not only does it outsell all its competitors combined (what few of them that have not yet been crushed by the awesomeness that is Illustrator), it's also the most powerful graphics-creation tool ever created. With Illustrator, all you need to produce graphics like the best you've seen in print or on the Web is knowledge and artistic ability. Artistic ability is a challenge that you can handle on your own. The other half — knowledge — is what this book is all about.

Like a tragic hero, the great power of Illustrator is also its terrible curse. With its 30+ panels, 70+ tools, and scores of menu items, its sheer depth is enough to make the most hardened graphics expert go shaky in the knees. Don't be fooled by Illustrator's vastness, however, because you will find a unique, consistent logic underlying it all. After you master a few basics, all the rest falls nicely into place.

The mission of this book is to get you past Illustrator's intimidation factor and into its Wow! factor. I take you from being befuddled and mystified by Illustrator's nigh-infinite options to creating the kinds of graphics that others look at and say, "Wow, how did you do *that*?"

About This Book

This book is written to make your journey into Adobe Illustrator flexible and self paced. Each chapter is as self contained as possible. You can hop in anywhere you want, with a minimum of flipping to other parts of the book to find out what you missed. If your goal is to find out more about the Pencil tool, for example, you can skip everything else and go directly to Chapter 8 without getting hopelessly lost. On the other hand, if you're determined to find out as much about the program as possible, you can read the book from cover to cover. I organized the book so that the chapters move from simple to more complex concepts. The early chapters make a good base for understanding the latter ones.

Use this book as both a reference book and an on-site trainer for Adobe Illustrator. To find out more about a specific feature, look for it in the index or the table of contents. To get a more in-depth feel for the feature, follow the step-by-step instructions that accompany the information on the major features.

By and large, people get more out of doing than out of reading about doing. Adobe Illustrator is a classic case-in-point. Don't bother to memorize anything in this book. Instead, pick up a concept, work with it in Illustrator for a while, and then come back to the book when you're ready for something new. Above all, have fun with it! Adobe Illustrator is one of the coolest programs on the planet. With a little practice, you can be creating illustrations that knock your socks off.

Note: Because I realize that some folks use PCs and some folks use Macs, I try to offer commands for both Windows and Macintosh platforms. Occasionally I offer information specific to one platform or the other, including keyboard shortcuts. While you journey through this book, you'll see that many figures (those that show you what you see on-screen) are a mixed bag of all things Mr. Gates and Mr. Jobs.

What You Don't Need to Read

I love to think that you pore over each and every word I write. I also realize that you have a life. Feel free to skip any information that seems far afield from what you need to know. The stuff that no one should ever *really* have to know (but which is nonetheless utterly fascinating) is clearly labeled with a Technical Stuff icon. You'll also run across some bonus material placed in a sidebar — a gray shaded box — that I fill with cool-to-know-but-not-imperative stuff.

Foolish Assumptions

I'm going to make just the following two basic Foolish Assumptions about you, Gentle Reader:

- **You have time, patience, and a strong desire to master Adobe Illustrator.** Illustrator has a steep learning curve at the start; but after you get the basics, you find the program pretty straightforward. Getting over that first hump is going to take a little endurance and can get pretty frustrating at times. Be patient with yourself and the program. All shall be revealed in the fullness of time. Until then, this book is intended to help you get over that initial learning hump.

- **You have access to a computer with Adobe Illustrator CS4 on it.** This hands-on book isn't meant to be read like a novel. If this is your very own copy of the book, attack it with highlighters and sticky notes, scribble in some marginalia, or even force it open until it lies flat on your desk. Then — after you collect all the loose pages and glue 'em back in — you can have both hands free to work at the computer while you follow along.

How This Book Is Organized

In this book, you find 18 chapters organized in five parts. Each part reflects a major Illustrator concept; each chapter chomps a concept into easily digestible morsels. The whole thing is arranged in a logical order, so you can read straight through if you're so inclined. Or you can jump in at any point to find the exact information you need. To help you do that, here's an overview of what you can find in each of those five parts.

Part 1: Driving People Crazy — Illustrator's Bum Rap

Here's where you get the absolute basics of Illustrator. What it is, what it does, and why it's worth the effort. The wonders of blank pages, paths, and the beguiling Pen tool all make their debut here. By the time you finish this part, you have a good overview of the entire program.

Part 11: Drawing and Coloring Your Artwork

This part is where the fun begins — you roll up your sleeves and start creating illustrations. Whether or not you can draw using old-fashioned paper and pencil (ewww — how 20th century), wait'll you see what you can create with Illustrator!

Part 111: Taking Your Paths to Obedience School

With Illustrator, you can really unleash your creativity. Unfortunately, unleashed creativity often results in an unruly mess. This part looks at how to tame the mess through changing parts of graphics, organizing graphics into separate layers, and using many other techniques that prove that organization and creativity are not mutually exclusive. You don't even need a smock.

Part 1V: Practically Speaking: Type, Print, and Files

Illustrator is truly a wondrous modifier of written characters, so I devote this part to working with type, and then getting your creations to print. I cover everything from the most basic formatting to complex type treatments. Stick around here, too, for the skinny on posting your art to the Web and moving files in and out of Illustrator.

Part V: The Part of Tens

No *For Dummies* book is complete without its Top Ten lists, and this book is no exception. Here are lots of tips to help you use Illustrator more effectively, ways to customize Illustrator (chrome hubcaps optional), and some very snazzy techniques that will make you the envy of your friends and raise you to "nemesis" level with your enemies. Save this part for dessert.

But that's not all!: Bonus chapters

I tried and I tried but no matter how hard I squeezed, I just couldn't fit everything into this book. (Kind of like how some people pack a steamer trunk for a weekend getaway lark.) Rather than try to skimp on all I wanted to show you, I put two extra-cool chapters on the Web for you. These two chapters cover putting your art on the Web and techniques for creating some killer effects. Check 'em out at www.dummies.com/go/illustratorcs4.

About All Those Little Icons

Scattered throughout this book you find some nifty little icons that point out bits of information that are especially useful, important, or noteworthy.

Remember helps you remember to remember. The information you find at these icons is stuff that you use on a regular basis in Illustrator. Write it down on your hand so that you can refer to it at any instant. Just don't wash that hand! Or better yet, bookmark the page or remember the advice you find there.

Look to these icons for utterly fascinating techno-trivia that most people never need to know. This information is the kind you can drop into a conversation at a party to remind people how much smarter you are than everyone else. (Assuming that you plan to go home alone, that is.)

This bull's-eye points out information that can help you do something faster, easier, or better; save you time and money; or make you the hero of the beach. Or at least make you a little less stressed during a production crunch!

Watch out! This impending-explosion icon means that danger lurks nearby. Heed it when directed to those things you should avoid and what things you must absolutely never do.

Road Signs along the Way

You will see some special ways I make text look in this book, such as bold print or shortcut keys or paths for how to find things. Here's a quick legend for the road signs you should watch for.

When I ask you to type (enter) something — in a text box, for example — **I make it bold**. When you see a construction like this — Choose Edit⇨Paste — that means to go to the Edit menu and choose Paste from there. Keyboard shortcuts look like Ctrl+Z (Windows) or ⌘+Z (Mac).

Where to Go from Here

Illustrator is a graphics adventure waiting for you to take it on. This book is your guide for that adventure. If you're ravenous to know everything now, you can rush through the text as fast as you can, starting with Chapter 1 and charging right through to the end. Or you can take your time, pick a point that interests you, explore it at your leisure, and then come back to a different place in the book later. Whatever works best for you, this book is your ready-willing-and-able guide for the journey. All you have to do is start your computer, launch Illustrator, turn the page, and let the adventure begin.

Part I
Driving People Crazy — Illustrator's Bum Rap

The 5th Wave   By Rich Tennant

"Frankly, I'm not sure this is the way to enhance our color graphics."

*H*ere you meet the main character of the book: Adobe Illustrator. You get a look at its illustrious past, its remarkable powers, its place in the universe, and (most importantly) why it will make your life approximately a million times better than it was before you used it. You probe the difference between vectors and pixels. You hover above the various parts of Illustrator and watch what they do. By the end of this part, you uncover a straightforward, easy-going, and ultimately quite logical program behind the layers of complexity that make up the exterior of Adobe Illustrator.

Introducing the World of Illustrator

In This Chapter

▶ Getting a look at how graphic artists use Illustrator

▶ Becoming familiar with the Illustrator interface

▶ Noting some Mac and Windows differences

▶ Creating new documents

▶ Saving your artwork

▶ Printing Illustrator documents

▶ Bailing out of a document (and Illustrator itself)

The first time you run Illustrator, you'll probably think that Adobe *Intimidator* would be a more appropriate name than Adobe *Illustrator*. The program's dozens of tools, hundreds of commands, and more than 30 panels can transform confident, secure individuals into drooling, confused, and frustrated drones.

The situation doesn't have to be that way, of course. Sure, all that stuff is scary. Even more frightening to some is the prospect of facing the giant white nothingness of the Document window — the endless possibilities, the confusion over where to start. This chapter helps you get past that initial stage and move forward into the mystical state of eagerly awaiting (instead of fearing) each new feature and function.

From Humble Origins to Master of the Graphics Universe

As its box proudly proclaims, Adobe Illustrator is the "Industry Standard Graphics Software." The software didn't always enjoy that standing, though. Illustrator evolved from a geeky math experiment into the graphics power-house it is today.

A brief history of Illustrator

Until the mid-1980s, computer art was limited to blocky-looking video games, spheroid reflections, and the movie *Tron.* Then something happened to change all that (in addition to Jeff Bridges' refusal to make a sequel) — namely, *PostScript,* a computer language created especially for printers. Adobe created PostScript specifically to help printers produce millions of teeny-tiny dots on the page, without running out of memory. (Graphics files were notoriously huge relative to the teeny-tiny computers of the day.)

In 1987, Adobe released Illustrator 1.1, which was designed primarily to be a *front end* for PostScript: that is, a way to make its capabilities actually usable. At that time, the concept of artwork scalable to any size *without loss of quality* (one world-beating advantage of creating art within Illustrator) was brand new. Illustrator gave companies the opportunity to have electronic versions of their logos that could be printed at *any* size.

In the 20-plus years since version 1.1, Adobe Illustrator has become the Web-ready, giant application that it is today. Millions of people around the world use Illustrator and its thousands of features (big and small) meet a wide variety of graphics needs. Oddly enough, the one aspect of Illustrator that hasn't changed is the perceived intimidation factor. Version 1.1 had several tools, many menu items, a neurosis-inducing Pen tool, Bézier curves, and that way-scary blank page when you started it up. The most recent version still has nearly every feature that 1.1 did and has added a staggering array of new features, but it still has that way-scary blank page. Illustrator 1.1 was a playful little kitten compared with the beast that is Illustrator CS4!

The new features in Illustrator CS4 include:

- **Multiple Pages:** Don't search for "Multiple Pages" in the list of new Illustrator features when you're looking at the official Adobe documentation. In their infinite wisdom, they have named this feature "Multiple Artboards," but you and I know the truth, so we'll call it what it is: multiple pages in Illustrator,

- **Super-Smart Smart Guides:** Little lines and hints that appear as you work, helping you to align your drawings automatically. Beware: After you start using them, you'll never be able to go back to the, er, "dumb" Smart Guides from previous versions.

- **Streamlined, Shiny User Interface:** The first thing you'll notice are those funny little tabs above your document windows. When you're done being distracted by that, however, you'll find that the panels and tools and control panel are all optimized to magically work just the way you expect them to, with automatically-resizing panels and options that exist only when it makes sense that they do. And did I mention it's shiny?

Illustrator's place in the cosmos

Professional graphic artists have a Tools panel of programs that they use to create the books, magazines, newspapers, packaging, advertisements, and Web sites that you see every day. Any professional will tell you that you need the right tool for the job to do the job well. The right tools (in this case) are software products: drawing programs, paint programs, and products for page layout and Web-authoring. *Drawing programs,* such as Adobe Illustrator, are the best tools for creating crisp, professional-looking graphics (such as logos), working with creative type effects, and re-creating photographs from line drawings. *Painting programs* (often called *image editing programs*), such as Adobe Photoshop, provide tools to color-correct, retouch, and edit digital photographs and re-create "natural media" effects, such as hand-painting. Page layout programs, such as Adobe InDesign or QuarkXPress, enable you to combine graphics that you create in drawing and paint programs with text for print publishing. You can use Web-authoring tools (such as Macromedia Dreamweaver or Adobe GoLive) to combine graphics, text, sound, animation, and interactivity for presentation on the World Wide Web.

Although each tool performs a fairly specific (if wide-ranging) task, there is some crossover between applications. For example, Illustrator has some limited image editing capabilities, but very few people ever use them. Because you can edit images with complete control and freedom in Photoshop, why use the wrong tool for the job? InDesign enables you to run type along a curve, but Illustrator has so many tools for creative type effects that you'd be silly to do them anywhere else.

By using Illustrator on its own, you can create an astonishing variety of graphics and type effects. When you combine it with paint, page layout, video, and Web-authoring programs, you have the tools you need to create print and Web publications that match the quality of anything you see in the stands or on-screen today.

Illustrator is the *de facto* standard in graphics creation. Although there used to be several competing programs out there (FreeHand, which is now gone forever; and CorelDRAW, which stumbles on, somehow unaware that no one is paying attention), Illustrator is used more than 20 times as much as any competing products combined. This is mainly because it's the gold standard in several ways, from feature breadth and depth to tight integration with other standard applications and formats, including Photoshop, Flash, and PDF.

Adobe has products in the other categories: Photoshop, InDesign, Flash, After Effects, and Dreamweaver. One benefit of using Illustrator is that it works very well (as you might expect) with the other Adobe products, most of which have a similar interface and way of working. If you know one Adobe product well, chances are that you'll have an easy time of figuring out other Adobe products.

Illustrator excels at creating and editing artwork of all types. In fact, you can use Illustrator to create and edit nearly anything that didn't start out as a photograph — and thanks to Live Trace, you can even do that! For more about the differences between photographs and artwork created with Illustrator, see Chapter 2.

Starting Up Illustrator and Revving It a Little

To get Illustrator running, double-click the application's icon (Mac) or choose Illustrator from the Start menu (Windows). (The first method also works in Windows, if you're a Mac user who happens to be using Windows. Don't worry; I won't tell a soul. Honest.)

The Illustrator startup process displays the *splash screen* — an image to look at while the program is cranking up. It's a lovely shade of orange, quite like the sunset that has set on Illustrator's competitors over the years. And you can't miss the giant *Ai,* which stands (of course) for Adobe Illustrator (and also happens to be the two-letter file extension of native Illustrator files).

As Illustrator continues the startup process, the block of orange disappears and is replaced by the Welcome screen, as shown in Figure 1-1. The Welcome screen gives the following options to start using Illustrator.

- **Open a Recent Item:** Here, you'll see a list of the most recent files you've opened up in Adobe Illustrator. This is a great way to get right back to work where you last left off, without having to search for your files. *Note:* At the bottom of the list is an Open folder icon; clicking that icon brings up a standard Open dialog box, which you can use to navigate to any file you want.

- **Create New:** Here is a list of common file structures to get you started. You can also click the From Template folder to load a predefined template for items such as business cards, CD labels, and other stuff you probably don't want to have to start making from scratch. Clicking any of the predefined file structures (such as Print Document) displays the New Document dialog box, as shown in Figure 1-2.

- **Getting Started, New Features, Resources, and Illustrator Exchange:** Technically, this part of the Welcome screen doesn't get you started in Illustrator, but it can help you get started thinking about how you can best use Illustrator. Each of these items is a link that takes you to various Adobe-sponsored Web pages with useful information. Good when you're really really bored.

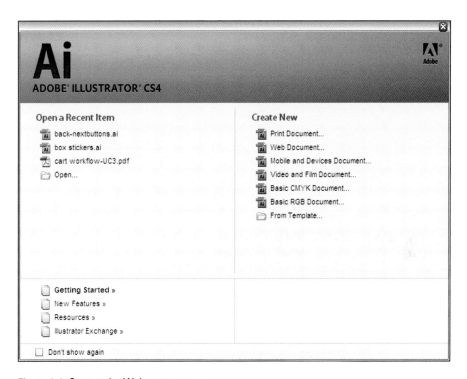

Figure 1-1: Start at the Welcome screen.

Figure 1-2: The New Document dialog box.

If you mark the Don't Show Again check box, this handy Welcome screen will never bother you again. But because the Welcome screen is actually pretty handy, don't check that box! If (say, in a fit of rebellion) you do dismiss the Welcome screen "forever," you can get it back at any time by choosing Help➪Welcome Screen from the main menu. And then you should clear the box, like I mentioned, so this doesn't happen again.

Before you start a new document, you have to answer a few questions in the New Document dialog box about the name, page size, units of measurement, orientation, and color mode that you plan to use. If you've gotten to this dialog box via one of the links under Create New on the Welcome screen, it will be prepopulated with the appropriate values, which you can simply accept by clicking OK. The next few sections discuss the various fields and options in the New Document dialog box.

What's in a Name (field)?

You can give your new document a name in the Name field. If you don't, Illustrator names it Untitled-1, and every new document you create is titled sequentially — Untitled-2, Untitled-3, and so on, until you quit the program. When you relaunch, you'll be right back at Untitled-1. If you don't give a name to the new document, you get another chance when you save it. The advantage to naming your document is clarity: If you ignore my advice and accumulate a bunch of unsaved files (*not* recommended!), you can't tell them apart. Besides, when you see the true name of the document in the title bar (at the top of the document), you don't forget what you're doing.

Artboard options

You can set up a document so that it has more than one artboard right from the start by increasing the Artboard number to anything greater than "1." After you do that, a bunch of other options become available, such as the space between artboards, how they're laid out, and the number of columns you'd like the artboards to appear in. Most of the time, however, you'll just leave this at 1 and pretend you never even saw these settings.

Page size, units, and orientation

You set your page size by choosing a predefined size from the Size drop-down menu or by typing values into the Height and Width fields. Your page size truly matters only when you're printing your document directly out of Illustrator. Otherwise, it just exists as a point of reference — a guide to show you how far things are apart from each other. One great thing about

Illustrator: For the most part, size doesn't matter (no, really). When you create graphics for the Web, you can determine the size of the graphic when you save it. When you're creating graphics for print, most of the time, you'll be creating graphics to be imported into page layout applications, such as QuarkXPress or InDesign. In the latter case, although it's always best to size your image in Illustrator, you can scale the graphic to the size you need it in your page layout. In either case, the Web browser or page layout application recognizes your Illustrator drawing, ignoring the page size.

Page size is good for two things: proofing and conceptualization. Often, you'll want to print your artwork on paper directly from Illustrator to get an idea of what it looks like. In this case, set the Size to the size of paper loaded in your printer. While creating graphics, keep in mind the size of the page or browser window that you're creating for: In this case, set the Height and Width to whatever the target output is. For example, if you're creating for the Web, you might want to set the size to 1024 pixels x 768 pixels, which is a fairly standard minimum size for computer screens, to help you visualize the final artwork. Actually, you can change the size of the artwork to be anything you want, at any time, and that's one of the great things about creating in Illustrator. In addition, you can change the "bleed" amount of a document, which is how much stuff that doesn't fit on your artboard will still print. This is great for when you have backgrounds that go to the edges of the page. (Having this extra "bleed" area results in better looking edges.)

By default, Illustrator measures image size in *points* (1 point [pt] = $\frac{1}{72}$ inch). If that unit of measurement is unfamiliar to you, be sure to select a different unit from the Units drop-down menu in the New Document dialog box. Your ruler also changes units (when you choose View➪Show Rulers) to the type you selected. And although it won't change the ruler units, you can also type the unit of measurement along with the number when you specify values for page size in the Height and Width fields. When you open a new document, it comes up showing a width in points: say, for instance, 612 pt. If you want to specify a width of 10 inches or 30 centimeters, just type (respectively) **10 in** or **30 cm** in the Width field. If you don't know the standard abbreviation for a unit of measurement, you can type the whole word out (for example, **10 inches** or **30 centimeters**). Illustrator understands what you mean and does the conversion for you. And it will do so wherever you enter a unit of measurement, not only in the New Document dialog box. Smart, very smart!

CMYK or RGB?

CMYK or RGB? In Illustrator, this question is a bit more significant than the ubiquitous question, "Paper or plastic?" To understand why you have to answer Illustrator's question, you need a little more history and some tech-nobabble. (Sorry, I'll try to keep this brief.)

Illustrator has been around for a long time, back when putting color images on the Web was impossible, and interactive multimedia was little more than a buzzword. In those days, the main reason for creating documents in color on the computer was so you could print them in color. Color printing almost always uses a *CMYK* process — for *c*yan, *m*agenta, *y*ellow, and blac*k* inks (the *k* stands for black because RGB has dibs on *b,* which stands for *blue*). These four colors, blended in different amounts, produce the full range of colors you see in printed material. So back then, Illustrator used only CMYK colors because nobody needed to do anything in color besides print.

Then along came interactive multimedia — in effect, the "lights, camera, sound, and action" for computer users. Shortly after that came the Web. Because images used for multimedia and the Web appear only on the computer screen, a need emerged for RGB images. *So what's RGB, already?* Okay, I'm getting to that: Computer screens create the colors you see by using electrons to make a coating of phosphors glow *r*ed, *g*reen, or *b*lue (hence, RGB) in different intensities. If you're creating content for multimedia applications or for the Web, you need RGB images that look good on-screen. You probably don't give two hoots about CMYK. So Illustrator, trying to please everyone, added the capability to create colors in RGB.

Unfortunately, this new feature didn't quite please everyone. In fact, it upset some people quite a lot and left a wake of money wasted, deadlines blown, marriages ruined, lives lost, and empires crushed. (Well, okay, that's a little exaggeration, but *only* a little.) CMYK and RGB just didn't get along.

Printing in color meant using the standard four-color printing process: Every image had its own percentage of cyan, magenta, yellow, and black, so four sets of films were made (one for each of those colors), and the final printed image combined the colors. Each set consisted of only four single-color plates (C, M, Y, and K), and that's all you'd expect to print out. However, if your Illustrator file contained any RGB elements (even a few pixels' worth), you had big trouble: Three additional films would print out — frequently at a cost of $100 or more per film — for every page that contained any RGB colors. If you weren't paying attention, one mistake like that could cost thousands of dollars. And a lot of people weren't paying attention because they'd never had to worry about RGB colors in an Illustrator file before. (You can bet they did after that!) To prevent this sort of uproar from happening again, Adobe wisely removed the capability to combine CMYK and RGB colors in the same document. That's why you have to specify CMYK *or* RGB before you start a new document. Sure, it's a hassle, but you're so much better off having this hassle now rather than spending money for it later!

So which do you choose, CMYK or RGB? You might think it safe to assume that RGB is for multimedia or the Web and CMYK is for print. Okay, that's a safe assumption, but not necessarily the *best* assumption. If you aren't sure where you're going to output, pick RGB. You can always change to CMYK later if you're required to, and you'll be able to print directly to color printers just fine that way.

For the sake of your creativity, choose RGB when

- ✓ **You're creating for the Web or for multimedia.** In this situation, you're always creating work that's going to be viewed in RGB, and you have no practical reason whatever to use CMYK.

- ✓ **You're creating for print BUT do not need precise CMYK colors.** If you don't have to specify exact CMYK values while you work, choose RGB. (You can convert to CMYK by using the File➪Document Color Mode command *before you print.* Just don't forget to, okay?) I know that approach sounds like asking for trouble, but I can give you three good reasons for using RGB this way:

  - *Some of Illustrator's coolest features (including many Photoshop filter effects) work only with RGB color.*

  - *When you work in RGB, you can use the full range of colors — millions of them — that are possible on the computer.* CMYK supports only mere thousands of colors. If you're creating content for both print and the Web, creating the image in RGB gives you the maximum color range possible in both CMYK *and* RGB.

  - *Some desktop inkjet color printers print well in RGB.* For example, Epson six-color printers print a wider range *(gamut)* of colors in RGB than in CMYK.

For the sake of accuracy, choose CMYK when

- ✓ **You need precise CMYK colors.** Some artists who create for print use a swatch book of printed CMYK colors. They use only the specific CMYK colors they see in the book because they feel (and rightly so) that this is the only way to get a good idea of what that color will look like when it finally prints. If your designs have to meet such specific requirements, you should always work in CMYK. Some companies specify the exact CMYK colors they want in their publications. If you're working on a project for one of those companies, use CMYK.

✔ **You're creating for grayscale or black-and-white print.** In RGB, shades of gray exist by default as blends of red, green, and blue. If you're printing with black ink, this blending is a hassle because you always have to work with three colors instead of one. In CMYK, however, you can create shades of gray as percentages of black ink, ignoring all other colors (which you might as well do if they won't be visible anyway).

After you answer the three magic New Document questions (name, page specs, and color choice), click OK and behold: A blank page opens, inviting you to realize your creative potential, as shown in Figure 1-3. You're ready to start illustrating. If blank-page syndrome doesn't faze you and you want to dig into the good stuff right away, thumb over to Chapter 2.

Of course, you can also mess around with the Raster Effects setting and preview mode, but doing so will make your life difficult. My advice is to keep these as the default settings.

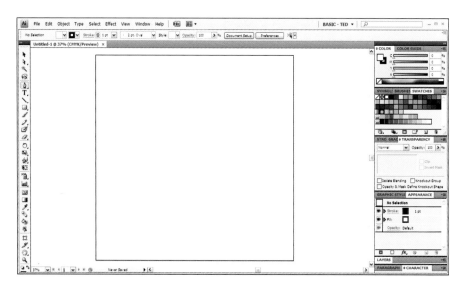

Figure 1-3: Your first blank page. Awe inspiring, isn't it?

Exploring the Illustrator Workspace

Between figuring out what the 250+ menu items actually do and rearranging panels (until you have a tiny little area on your document in which you can actually work), you might find the Illustrator environment a bit daunting. (If you do, you're far from alone.) And that's *after* the good people at Adobe took out an entire menu from the product for CS4 (the Filter menu, whose time has long past). The next sections are an overview of all the stuff that's preventing you from getting any work done. (That stuff is what the geeks call the *UI.*)

Illustrator tool time

The Illustrator Tools panel (that alien artifact in Figure 1-4) is the place where most people start when they use Illustrator. After showing you a whole bunch of tools, some odd-looking buttons, and a gang of giant square things, the Tools panel (as shown in Figure 1-4) pretends that's all there is to it. Actually, the Tools panel has over 50 hidden tools. Select most tools in Illustrator by clicking (once) the tool you want in the Tools panel. The cursor then changes to either something that looks like the tool, or in the case of special tools (Rectangle, Ellipse, and others), a cross-hair cursor.

The tools live in *toolslots,* which are subdivisions within the Tools panel. Many toolslots contain more than one tool, as indicated by a small black arrow in the bottom-right corner of the toolslot. To access a hidden tool, click and hold the mouse pointer on a tool in its toolslot. You then see a bunch of other (usually related) tools materialize by the toolslot that you clicked (as shown with the Pen tool in Figure 1-4). Use those other tools by dragging to the tool you want to use and then releasing the mouse button.

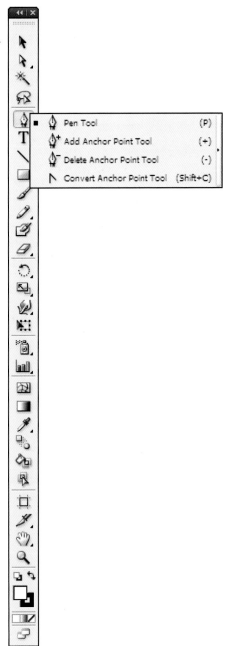

Figure 1-4: The Illustrator Tools panel.

Drag over to the little bar to the right of the hidden tools in the toolslot and let go of the mouse button when the little bar becomes highlighted. A separate little window appears, containing all the tools from the toolslot. You can drag this window off the Tools panel and place it anywhere on the screen. This procedure can save your sanity if you're constantly switching between two tools that share a toolslot, such as the Pen tool and the Convert Direction Point tool. To get rid of this toolslot window, click the tiny white Close box (Mac) in its upper-left corner or the X (Windows).

When you pause the mouse pointer over any tool, the name of the tool appears, followed by a letter. Well, no, the letters aren't grades given to the tools for their usefulness; the letters let you know which keys to press if you want quick access to the tools. (For instance, press the P key on your keyboard to get the Pen tool or R to get the Rotate tool.)

As you gaze at the Tools panel, notice that it doesn't have a Close or Expand box along its top. One possible explanation for this is that you go to the Tools panel for just about everything you do in Illustrator, and it's almost impossible to work without it. If you really want to, though, you can hide the Tools panel by selecting Tools from the Window menu at the top of the screen. To bring back the Tools panel, go to the Window menu again and select Tools.

You can hide the Tools panel temporarily — along with your other panels — by pressing the Tab key. Although this feature can be unsettling if you don't know about it (if you hit the Tab key by accident, everything disappears except your graphics and the menu bar!), it's still mighty useful, especially if you're working on a small computer screen. You can work with everything hidden, press the Tab key when you need to, select the tool or panel item you need, and then get back to work unfettered by the things you aren't using. This approach is a lot faster than selecting to show or hide the Tools panel from the Window menu whenever you want to do something different.

Panels to suit any artist

Illustrator has a ton of panels in addition to the Tools panel. You might think of a panel as something more closely associated with a painter than an illustrator, but nonetheless, Illustrator has about 30 of them. Like with a painter's palette that holds the paints she uses most, an Illustrator panel provides quick access to the most frequently used commands and features. The contents of panels are organized according to what they do. For example, the Character panel contains commands to format individual pieces or big chunks of text, and you use the Color panel to create and change colors. Although Illustrator has dozens of panels, you rarely need to have them all open at once. When entering text, for example, you want the Character panel open, but you probably don't need the Gradient panel open because the Gradient panel controls only, um, gradients. (Go figure.)

You open a panel by choosing it as a menu item. These all live in the Window menu (such as Window➪Colors). To close a panel, click the X in its upper-right corner.

Fortunately, Illustrator can both tab and dock panels to keep them more organized, giving you a wee bit of space in which you can actually draw and edit your artwork. *Tabbing* lets you stack panels in one area so they overlap like index cards. *Docking* connects the top of one panel to the bottom of another so that both panels are visible but take up as little space as possible.

By default, Illustrator displays the panels shown in Figure 1-5, docked along the right edge of the screen. Notice that some of the panels are grouped into sets and offer you several tabs. (For instance, the Stroke, Gradient, and Transparency panels are tabbed together in one set.) Initially, you see only the Stroke panel; the Gradient and Transparency panels are hidden behind the Stroke panel. To see either of those panels, click the tab for the one you want to view.

You can combine panels by any method that you feel works for you. To move a panel from one set to another, click and drag that panel's tab from one set into another — or out by itself (which creates a new tab group). Illustrator doesn't limit you; you can combine any panel with any set. You can even put all of Illustrator's panels into one set if you really want to. I don't advise doing so, though, because the tabs would all overlap so you couldn't tell what's what.

Another way to use panels is to reduce them to their icon view by clicking the double triangle at the top of the stack of docked panels. Doing this results in a column of very nice looking icons, which initially have little (if any) meaning

Figure 1-5: The default set of panels when you start Illustrator.

to you, as shown in Figure 1-6. (The Appearance panel here is temporarily showing because I clicked its icon.) Clicking an icon displays its associated panel, allowing you to make changes to various settings; as soon as you're done in that panel, it snaps closed, leaving you a ton of valuable screen space.

Many Illustrator panels have their own menus, which pop up when you click the triangle in the upper-right corner of the panel, as shown in Figure 1-7.

Items in the panels' pop-up menus relate specifically to each panel. This makes them easy to ignore and easy to figure out — after you master the individual panel, that is.

Menus with the finest cuisine

Illustrator menus are organized fairly well. Some menus are immediately obvious. For example, you find commands having to do with type under the Type menu, and commands for viewing your document under the View menu. Other menus are a little less intuitive and make sense only after you start using them. For instance, after you realize that *any one on-screen "thing" in Illustrator is an object,* you discover that items in the Object menu relate to objects. Other menus take a little more work and experimentation to understand. Believe it or not, all these menus are arranged to make figuring out and using Illustrator as easy as possible.

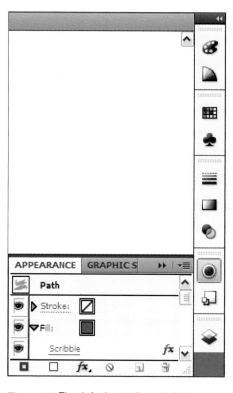

Figure 1-6: The default set of panels in icon view.

Figure 1-7: Panels also have their own menus.

To use an item in a menu, drag down to that item and release. Something should happen when you do that (no explosions or tsunamis, as far as I know), depending on which menu item you select. Even the way a menu item appears on a menu can be a handy tip. For example, consider the following characteristics:

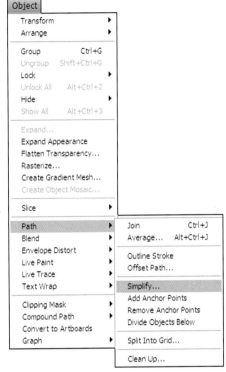

- **Submenus:** Many of Illustrator's menus have several submenus in them, indicated by a little triangle to the right of the menu item. To access a menu item in a submenu, drag down to the title of the submenu and then over to the item you want to use. (See Figure 1-8.)

- **Keyboard commands:** Most menu items in Illustrator have keyboard shortcuts (key combi-nations listed at the right) that can activate them.

- **More info needed:** An ellipsis (. . .) indicates that when you click the item, a dialog box appears, requesting additional input from you.

Figure 1-8: The Path submenu in the Object menu.

- **Unavailable commands:** A grayed-out menu item means Illustrator won't let you do anything with that item just now.

Mac and Windows issues spring eternal

Okay, I know some loyalties in this area are fierce. Can't we all just get along for a while? Regardless of which system you use or like, you work in Illustrator pretty much the same way. A few small differences are important enough to mention, however, especially if you jump between the two systems:

- **The .ai extension:** Windows users often need filename extensions after their filenames or the system refuses to look at the files. The Illustrator file extension is .ai. That's right, as in *aieee!* but without the *eee!* Most file types (on Windows systems) have three-letter extensions;

Illustrator uses two. Windows folks should save Illustrator documents with the `.ai` extension for maximum compatibility with all flavors of Windows. Having the wrong extension on the file can cause problems. If you were to put `.aif` on there, for example, Windows would try to open the file as a sound file, fail, and give you an error message!

Windows users are accustomed to using two- and three-letter filename extensions. Mac users don't have to, but they really should get in the habit of doing so. For starters, that keeps the peace when you send files and lets you instantly identify what the file is. Illustrator lets you save files in an alphabet soup of file formats, such as PDF (`.pdf`), TIFF (`.tif`), EPS (`.eps`), or JPEG (`.jpg`). Each of these formats has its own unique properties and purposes. When you see `.eps` on a file, chances are good that it's a graphic created for use in a page layout program. When you see `.gif`, you know it's a graphic created for display on the Web. File extensions can tell you a lot about your files even before you open them.

✐ **Right-click versus Control-click:** While in Illustrator, Windows users can right-click most places in Illustrator to display a contextual menu (see Figure 1-9). Mac users who don't have a right mouse button can press the Control key while clicking the mouse button. Contextual menus (clever creatures!) are context-sensitive: They recognize what the mouse is near when you click and give you options you can apply. For example:

Figure 1-9: A contextual menu appears when you right-click (Windows) or Control-click (Mac).

- Control-click (or right-click) the Ruler, and a contextual menu shows up, offering to help you change the Ruler's unit of measurement.

- Control-click (or right-click) text, and you can change the font, size, and a slew of other options.

- Click a path, and up come the options related to paths, and so on.

All the items found in contextual menus appear in the regular menus, too, so you never really *have* to use contextual menus. They're among those little luxuries (like a steering wheel–warmer on a cold day) that make Illustrator so nice to use.

Defining the Document Area

Illustrator uses a traditional art board as a metaphor; it's what you see when you create a new file (as shown in Figure 1-10). You have the page you're working on (the *Artboard*), and the table the page sits on (the *Scratch area,* which traditional artists will recognize as a *Pasteboard*). When you create a new document, the Artboard appears as a rectangle in the middle of a white expanse. The actual size and shape of the Artboard depends on what you enter for height and width when you create a new document.

Artboard

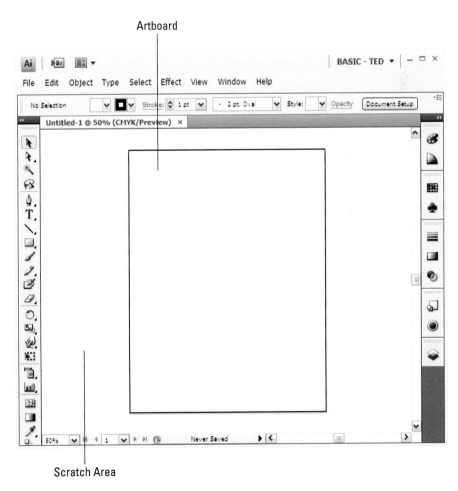

Scratch Area

Figure 1-10: The Artboard and the Scratch area: the first two rather boring elements you meet when you create a new Illustrator file.

The Artboard serves as a guide to show how large your artwork is (relative to the page size you chose when you created the document). Many people find it easier to create with a specific page size in mind. If you come from a traditional graphic arts background, you might find the idea of an Artboard and Pasteboard (or Scratch area) reassuring. You can create elements and leave them in the Scratch area, ready for you to grab and add to the artwork you're creating on the Artboard. As to how the Artboard affects your art — well, it doesn't. It's only a guide to help you get your bearings. Elements in the Scratch area still print if you print to large enough paper. If you save your Illustrator artwork as an EPS (Encapsulated PostScript) to bring it into a page layout program (or as a GIF to use on the Web), anything in the Scratch area is saved with it.

If you don't find the Artboard useful as a guide, you can hide it altogether by choosing View⇨Hide Artboard.

For printing a document, you might find the Page Tiling feature a little more significant than the Artboard. Illustrator smartly recognizes the printer that your document is selected to print to and creates a Page Tile (a rectangle), which is the size and shape of the largest area that the selected printer can print. You can recognize the Page Tiling feature by a thin, dotted line that appears just inside the Artboard if you set page size to the size of your printer paper.

Most printers show a printable area slightly smaller than the page size. Anything outside these guides doesn't print. Even so, remember that this guide is based on *your* printer; what's inside someone else's printable area might not be the same.

Opening Existing Documents

To open any existing Illustrator document, choose File⇨Open from the main menu and then select the document you want (using the Windows Open dialog box shown in Figure 1-11; Mac dialog boxes look a little different).

Another way to open a document is by double-clicking the file itself. If you double-click an Illustrator file when Illustrator isn't running, the program launches for you automatically. (Glad it's not a missile.)

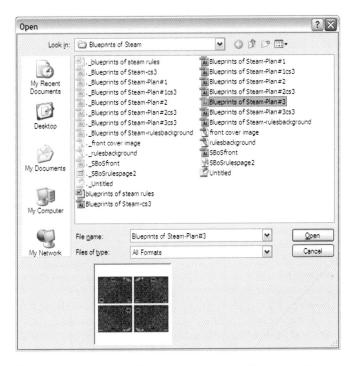

Figure 1-11: Use the Open dialog box to select the file you want to open.

Viewing Illustrator Documents

Illustrator provides versatile options for viewing documents, including controls for zooming, scrolling, and hiding (or showing) certain document features. You can zoom to the smallest areas of your artwork and make changes so minute that they aren't visible to the human eye (and maybe feel better knowing that your graphic is microscopically perfect). Or, to get a good feel for your artwork's effect in the real world, view your document at the actual size it prints. Or you can view your on-screen objects as their "skeletons" of essential points and paths, with no strokes or colors to distract you from the true essence of your artwork. A view of any phase is available, from points-and-paths to perfect printout. Bottom line: You have to see what you're doing to know what you're doing. Illustrator offers that capability.

Zooming in and out of artwork

You can view your artwork at actual size (approximately its size when it prints), much larger, or much smaller. Changing the zoom amount changes only the image's on-screen appearance — not the image's actual size, how it prints, or its appearance in another application. Zooming is like using binoculars to watch a neighbor violate the bylaws of the homeowners' association. Those unapproved maple saplings (and the sap who's planting them) don't actually change size; you just zoom in on them from a discreet distance.

The Zoom tool

The Zoom tool is the magnifying glass at the bottom of the Tools panel. When you click the Zoom tool and move it over the document, a plus sign appears in the center of the magnifying glass. Clicking the Zoom tool makes the details of your artwork appear larger in the document window. You can click until you zoom in to 6,400 percent (64 times larger than actual size). *Note:* If you print while zoomed in, the image still prints at actual size. Figure 1-12 shows a document viewed at actual size and zoomed in to 400 percent.

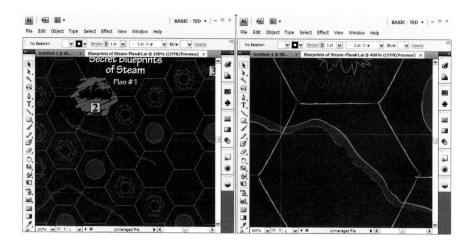

Figure 1-12: Two views of the artwork: actual size and zoomed to 400 percent.

The Zoom tool is actually two tools in one. When you hold down the Option key (Alt on Windows), the magnifying glass contains a minus sign. Holding down the Alt or Option key and clicking your image with the Zoom tool causes your image to appear smaller. You can zoom out as far as 3.13 percent (where everything is really tiny). Figure 1-13 shows the art from Figure 1-12 as it would look at 25 percent of its actual size.

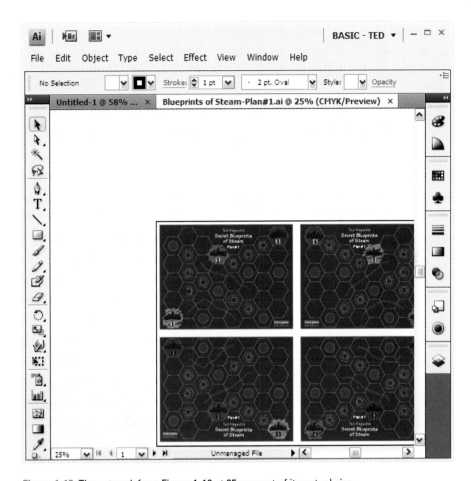

Figure 1-13: The artwork from Figure 1-12 at 25 percent of its actual size.

Speed zoom ahead

Zooming is something Illustrator users do often enough to warrant the multitude of keyboard commands associated with this function. In order of usefulness, the following items represent some of the most useful speed-zoom techniques:

- **Use any tool to Zoom In.** Press ⌘+spacebar on a Mac (Ctrl+spacebar on Windows), and the tool you're using changes to the magnifying glass with a plus sign in it. Click the area where you want to zoom in. After you release the keys, the Zoom tool switches back to the tool you were previously using. This shortcut is *really* handy.

- **Use any tool to Zoom Out.** Press ⌘+Option+spacebar on a Mac (Ctrl+Alt+spacebar in Windows), and the tool you're using changes to the magnifying glass with a minus sign in it. Click the image to zoom out.

After you release the keys, the Zoom tool switches back to the tool you were using. This shortcut is as handy as the temporary Zoom In tool.

✔ **Go to Actual Size:** Press ⌘+1 on a Mac (Ctrl+1 in Windows) to return to actual size. You can also double-click the Zoom tool to do this.

✔ **Go to Fit In Window view:** Press ⌘+0 on a Mac (Ctrl+0 in Windows) to zoom to the level at which your page fits into the window. You can also double-click the Hand tool to do this.

✔ **Zoom in and out.** Press ⌘++ (plus) on a Mac (Ctrl++ [plus] in Windows) to zoom in one level or ⌘+– [minus] on a Mac (Ctrl+– [minus] in Windows) to zoom out one level.

✔ **Activate the Zoom In tool.** Press Z to change to the Zoom In tool. If you actually read to the bottom of this list, geekiness from someone you know is starting to rub off on you. I strongly advise taking a few days off — away from your computer (and from said geek).

✔ **While Zooming:** Press the spacebar to move around the current marquee (the dotted lines).

Scrolling around your document

You can use the scroll bars to move around your document, but they limit you to moving horizontally or vertically — and only one of those directions at a time. If you're really cool (and you know you are), you can use the Hand tool to move around your document in any direction.

To use the Hand tool, choose it from the Tools panel. Then click and drag anywhere in the document. The artwork moves in the direction you drag. At first, this action might seem slightly awkward — ah! but power corrupts. After a few minutes of pushing your art around, you'll never want to go back to those nasty scroll bars.

You can use any tool as the Hand tool. To change a tool into the Hand tool, hold down the spacebar while you click the tool. Then click and drag just as you would with the Hand tool. Let go of the spacebar, and the tool you were using returns to its original form. This trick works with any tool except the Text tool. If you have the Text tool active, press ⌘+spacebar on a Mac (Ctrl+spacebar on Windows).

Looking at the guts of your artwork

Typically, what you see in your Document window is pretty much what's going to print (the view in Preview mode). However, what you see isn't what the printer and Illustrator look at. Instead, they see all your Illustrator artwork and objects as a series of outlines, placed images, and text (the view in Outline mode). If you want to view your document in this skeletal form, choose View⇨Outline. Outline mode is a great diagnostic tool: It helps you understand how a document was made. Figure 1-14 shows artwork in both Preview and Outline modes. Outline mode also makes it easier to select objects that are very close together.

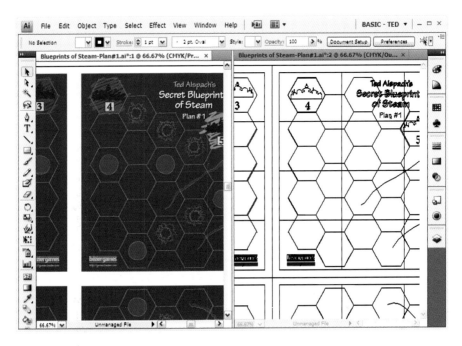

Figure 1-14: Art in Preview mode and Outline mode.

Notice that in Preview mode, things like the scribbly swashes between the numbered cities and the squiggles and circles don't show up. That's because those are all Illustrator Effects, which aren't objects that are defined by paths and lines and points and such, but instead are applied to different objects. You can learn a lot about documents by viewing them this way.

Using Templates

Few things in life are as frightening as a blank page staring you down. Knowing this, the good folks at Adobe have supplied hundreds of templates to get you started quickly and easily. *Templates,* such as the filmy one shown in Figure 1-15, provide you with a stylish yet fully customizable starting point. Because you can change so much in each template, from colors to fonts to objects, your use of a template is sure to be different than your buddy Larry's use of it. And, as evidenced by his questionable wardrobe, Larry has absolutely no design sense whatsoever.

To use a template in Illustrator, select the From Template option (under Create New) in the Welcome screen that I talk about earlier in the chapter, or choose File➪New from Template. The template opens up as an untitled document. Don't be concerned about writing over the template; you're actually opening a copy of the original file.

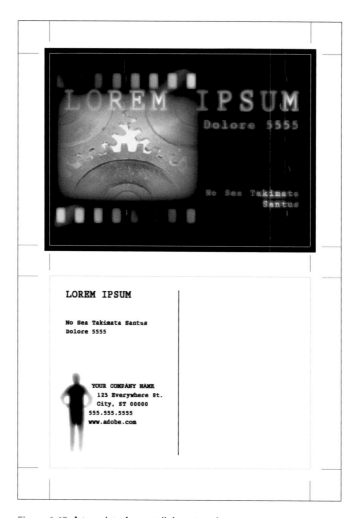

Figure 1-15: A template for a stylin' postcard.

Saving Illustrator Documents

The instant you accomplish something you like, you should save it. And you should save every few minutes, even if you haven't done something you like. If you don't, you lose all the work and have to re-create it if you crash, accidentally quit, or accidentally shut off the power supply to your computer. Unlike applications such as Microsoft Word or Adobe InDesign, Illustrator has no auto-save feature. Anything you don't save is lost. Just remember that old TLA (three-letter acronym), SOS: Save Often, Silly! Saving takes only a second, and it saves not only your artwork but also your time and sanity.

To save a document, choose File⇨Save. If you haven't yet saved the document, the Save As dialog box (as shown in Figure 1-16) appears. Reward its promptness by naming your file something appropriate, witty, and deep. Or type something hurried-but-meaningful, such as **gasdfoiu** or **jkl23**, so you can challenge yourself later to figure out what that @#*! document is. (Just kidding.)

Figure 1-16: Name your masterpiece in the Save As dialog box.

If you've already saved your document, the Save command updates the existing file. If you're not sure whether you previously saved a document, look at the title bar. If it reads Untitled-1, you probably haven't saved. (Only someone with a creepy sense of humor would pick *Untitled-1* as a title just to befuddle the rest of us.) Illustrator is incredibly smart, so much so that it's unsettling when it comes to saving files. Whenever you make a change, a little asterisk (*) appears to the right of your file name, telling you that you haven't saved the files since you made changes. As soon as you smack good ol' ⌘+S on a Mac (Ctrl+S on Windows), the asterisk goes away.

Changing Your Mind

One of Illustrator's most powerful features is likely strikingly familiar: the Edit⇨Undo command that gives you a way to take back the goof you just made. And in Illustrator, choosing Edit⇨Undo can be a multiple undo, making you the Master of Time! You can take your artwork back through time, step by step, all the way to when you first opened the document! If you make a mistake (or several), just choose Edit⇨Undo (or press ⌘+Z on a Mac or Ctrl+Z on Windows) repeatedly until you get back to the way things were before they went so wrong. To redo the last thing you undid, choose Edit⇨Redo (or press ⌘+Shift+Z on a Mac or Ctrl+Shift+Z on Windows). (A time machine with a reverse gear — way cool.)

Imagine creating with wild abandon — moving points, changing colors and line thicknesses, and deleting paths — because in Illustrator, you can change your mind after the fact. Think of what you could obliterate from time: the misplaced stroke that looks like a bad tattoo, the missed goal that kept your team from the playoffs, the blind date that went so horribly wrong. Well, okay, it only works in Illustrator. At least it works somewhere.

You can take a graphic back to the way it was when you first opened it, with one exception: If you close a file and then reopen it, you can't go back to anything you did before you closed the file. You can, however, save a file and then go back to things that happened before you saved it — if you left the file open after you saved it. In that case, the only thing that can't be undone is the Save command: You still have a file on your hard drive that exists exactly as it did when you hit Save. This method can be useful if you have to create multiple revisions of the same document.

Printing Illustrator Documents

If your computer is connected to a printer, you can print just about anything you create in Illustrator. Before you print, however, make sure that your artwork is within the Page Tiling boundaries (that dotted gray rectangle that shows up when you choose View⇨Show Page Tiling). Only items within these boundaries print. The dotted lines on the page indicate the trim area; if your image is outside the dotted lines, it won't print.

To print your artwork, choose File⇨Print. The Print dialog box appears (see Figure 1-17). Click OK; soon a sheet of paper emerges from your printer with your artwork on it.

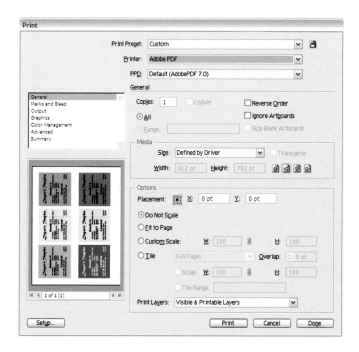

Figure 1-17: The Print dialog box has more options than Illustrator 1.1 had in the entire program.

Closing Documents and Quitting Illustrator

To close an Illustrator document, choose File⇨Close. The document closes without a fuss. If you haven't saved before closing, a dialog box appears, asking whether you want to save changes made to your artwork. To quit Illustrator, choose File⇨Quit (Mac) or File⇨Exit (Windows). If you haven't saved before quitting, a dialog box appears and asks whether you want to save your changes. (Consistent good manners — aren't they wonderful?)

Following the Righteous Path

In This Chapter

▷ Understanding how paths and pixels work

▷ Knowing the differences between paths and pixels

▷ Determining when to use paths and when to use pixels

▷ Using PostScript printing and paths

▷ Creating paths

*B*eing new to Illustrator typically means being new to paths. *Paths* are the heart and soul of Illustrator — its primary way to create graphics. Nearly all computer-generated graphics are either pixel-based or path-based (also known as *vector-based* — more on that later). Getting a firm grip on the differences between the two graphics types can help you create graphics of any type.

Pixel-based images (created in Adobe Photoshop as well as by scanners and digital cameras) use a fixed grid of tiny colored squares (kind of like tiny mosaic tiles) to create images on your screen. Your computer monitor's *resolution* is a measure of how detailed an onscreen image can be, based on how many pixels the screen can provide per square inch. To give you an idea of how small these pixels are, every square inch of an average monitor contains as many as to 9,216 pixels. Even so, monitors have a relatively low resolution; they don't use many pixels per inch compared with high-resolution printing, which can require 90,000 pixels in a square inch or more.

In spite of their astonishing quantity, pixels work just like mosaic tiles (or like the dots in a Seurat painting). Because images are a bit less distinct from farther away, putting together squares of different colors results in a smooth picture when seen from a distance; the individual squares are, in effect, invisible. The more squares used to create a square inch of the image — that is, the higher the resolution — the smoother and more realistic the picture is.

In addition to their staggeringly small size, the range of colors that pixels can have is equally astonishing. A single pixel can display only one color at a time, but that color can be any of 16.7 million.

Path-based (often called *vector-based*) graphics are much simpler — and in some ways, easier to comprehend — than their pixel-based cousins. Think of an image in a coloring book: A shape is defined by a line. Inside the line, you can add color. By using this simple method of shapes and color, you can create just about any picture you can imagine. In Illustrator, the shapes can be any size and complexity, and the lines can be as thick or as thin as you want, or even invisible. And the shapes can be filled with an astonishing variety of colors, patterns, and gradients (even pixel-based images), but the same basic coloring-book principle applies.

Whether Paths or Pixels Are Better

You choose between paths and pixels for different reasons. Paths are better for some things, pixels are better for others, and each approach has its strengths. The key to determining whether to use paths (which Illustrator creates) or pixels (from a program, such as Photoshop) is to be familiar with the capabilities of each method. Figure 2-1 shows path-based artwork next to pixel-based artwork.

Figure 2-1: Path-based artwork (left) and pixel-based artwork (right).

Paths are generally better for type, logos, and precision graphics. Pixels are generally better for photographs, painting-style illustrations, complex backgrounds, textures, and simulated lighting effects. Quite often, however, the proper combination of paths and pixels results in the best final illustration possible. Determining what combination to use is a lot easier when you're hip to the advantages and drawbacks of both paths and pixels.

Paths: The ultimate flexibility in graphics

Paths are used to define any shape from a simple square or circle to the shape of South America. Because paths are merely the *outline* of these shapes — not the shapes themselves — they take up very little storage space. A path-based square that measures 15 x 15 feet takes up no more room in your computer than a 1 x 1–inch path-based square.

How can such a large square and such a tiny one both occupy the same amount of computer memory? Through math, mostly. Looking at how Illustrator draws a square can help you make sense of this. To Illustrator, a square is simply a set of four locations — one for each of four points (the *corners*) — as well as any Fill or Stroke information (what color the square is). Where the points are doesn't matter. What does matter is that you have four of 'em and that they make a square when you connect the dots.

What about complex outlines? A semi-accurate representation of regions in the United States of America with a limited amount of detail probably needs dozens of points to define the shape of the continent. In this case, there's nary a straight line anywhere: From point to point, it's nothing but curved lines. And because they need more information to describe them, those curved lines take up about twice as much disk space as straight lines do. Even so, a tiny, little 1-inch-high illustration of the U.S. can be enlarged to 15 feet tall and still have exactly the same file size because the illustration still has exactly the same number of points. Only the math that determines the location of those points has been changed to put them farther apart.

Figure 2-2 shows a regional U.S. map next to an orange square that physically appears to be about three times as large as the U.S. (well, three times as large as the illustration of the U.S.). Which one is bigger in terms of file size? The U.S. map is. It has more detail and, therefore, more points.

What's so cool about paths is something I previously allude to: You can make paths much larger or smaller in physical dimensions without increasing the file size or losing image quality. You can rotate a path, flip it *(reflecting),* skew it *(shearing),* or distort it in a number of ways without changing the file size or detail. (Here's the secret reason why: *All you're really changing is the location of the points.*) This near-effortless scalability makes Illustrator the perfect choice for creating logos that appear on business cards, letterheads, Web pages, various documents, banners, billboards, or signs.

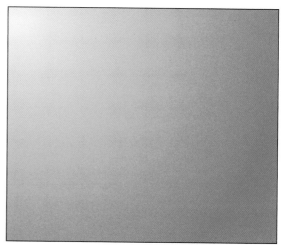

Figure 2-2: The map shape is a larger Illustrator file than the square because more points are used to define the shape.

Pixels: Detail and realism to spare

Pixel-based images are used for photographs because the fine "random" naturalistic detail is virtually impossible to create in a path-based image. Digitized photographs represent the majority of the pixel-based images in use today. The rest are mostly Web graphics and other onscreen images.

Even a low-resolution pixel-based image can have 5,184 squares of color per square inch, each of which can be any of 16.7 million different colors. In a path-based image, every different color (with a few exceptions) must be defined by a separate path. To equal the number of different colors that you can create in a pixel-based image, you'd have to draw so many paths that . . . well, imagine covering a basketball with confetti, one piece at a time. For this reason, pixel-based images are the hands-down choice over path-based graphics if you're re-creating the continuous tones and irregular patterns found in nature, such as an outdoor scene with a lot of grass, trees, and furry animals.

On the other hand, paths are far superior to pixels if you want to maintain the quality of a graphic image despite enlarging and reducing its size. Think what you have to do to increase the size of artwork made with mosaic tiles. You have to increase the number of tiles unless you can enlarge the tiles that are already there. But if you did that, the tiles would be obvious from a distance.

Same deal with pixel images. You have to add more tiles (pixels), or you see the pixels you already have showing up onscreen as big squares. And when you add pixels, you make the file size larger while reducing the quality (the worst of both worlds) because you can't get away with just tossing in any old pixels.

An artisan may be able to add tiles to a mosaic and preserve its image quality, but a computer is just guessing about what tiles to add (in geek-speak, a process called *interpolation*). There's just no way to enlarge a pixel-based image without reducing the quality. Check out Figure 2-3 if you don't believe me. Look what happens when I scale up the image on the left to become the image on the right — look at all those nasty pixels!

Likewise, shrinking the image means throwing away pixels, which also degrades the image because it then has fewer pixels available for showing detail. In technical circles, changing the number of pixels in an image is *resampling*.

Figure 2-3: The original image (left) and scaled up (right).

An image with thousands of pixels can be displayed on-screen or printed much larger — and with high quality — than an image with only 900 pixels. Of course, all those pixels take up a whole lot more storage space on your hard drive. Path-based images have no such limitations.

How Paths and Pixels Compare

This is it — the definitive answer you've been looking for: Use pixels for photographic manipulation. File sizes are large but indeed smaller than if you try to create the same photographic image by using paths. Pixel-based graphics that need to print or display at large sizes require larger file sizes than the same graphics printed or displayed at smaller sizes. Use path-based graphics to create any type of graphics; their file sizes are typically much smaller than their pixel-based counterparts, and you can always create pixel-based graphics from the path-based ones at a multitude of sizes and resolutions. A path-based graphic can be displayed or printed at any size, from microscopic to billboard, without any change in file size, yet always at maximum quality. And the best part is that path-based graphics are easily edited, unlike their "every single pixel is a color" pixel counterparts.

A comparison of path and pixel documents

The best way to show advantages of each format is to take a look at the same graphic created with both paths and pixels. The illustration shown in Figure 2-4 is a logo, created with paths, for the internationally renowned comic strip Board 2 Pieces. The idea here is to use this logo on all manufactured goods associated with Board 2 Pieces as well as on signs, brochures, and other places.

Figure 2-4: A logo for Board 2 Pieces, created with paths.

One thing you notice right away is that the logo is pretty much all text. Paths represent text fairly well. A big advantage in creating this logo with paths is its scalability: You can enlarge or reduce it to virtually any size without changing the image quality. Compare Figure 2-4 (which weighs in at 188K) with Figure 2-5, which shows a pixel-based version of the logo (tipping the scales at 1.2MB). (Looks like a clone, doesn't it? Looks can be deceiving.)

Figure 2-5: The same Board 2 Pieces logo, created with pixels.

If you use a high-enough resolution, the pixel-based logo looks as good as the path-based, but its file size is 1.2MB (almost ten times the size of the path-based logo). Maybe that isn't a problem if you have a hard drive the size of New Jersey, but watch what happens when you change the size of the logo. If you enlarge the path-based version (as in Figure 2-4) by 500%, you get the image in Figure 2-6.

All I had room for in Figure 2-6 was a smidgen of the logo — the whole thing would be over 20 inches square — but note how the edges remain perfectly smooth and crisp in the path-based version. And the file size is still only 188K! On the other hand, if you enlarge the pixel-based version, you get the image on the right. Notice the dreaded jagged edges. Worse, the whole logo at this size would become the Giant File That Ate New Jersey — over 25MB in size — more than 100 times the file size of the path version!

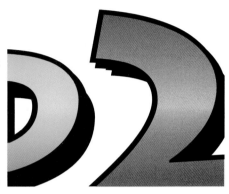

Figure 2-6: A section of the Board 2 Pieces logo, enlarged to five times its original size.

It is very difficult to create artwork approaching photographic realism with paths, but it can be done. An image of Venus, shown in Figure 2-7, was created entirely within Illustrator and consists entirely of paths.

Figure 2-7: A close up of Venus.

Although it's difficult, you can achieve surreal photo-realistic effects with Illustrator, such as Venus's eye, shown zoomed in at several times its original size in Figure 2-8.

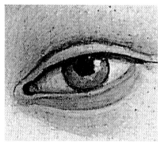

Figure 2-8: The vectors-only version of Venus's eye, compared with the original Botticelli painting at the same level.

When to use paths and when to use pixels

In Table 2-1, check out some attributes that are best created with paths and some that are best created with pixels.

Table 2-1	What Paths and Pixels Are Especially Good For
Use Paths If Your Artwork Contains	*Use Pixels If Your Artwork Contains*
Large amounts of type	Photographs
Geometric shapes	Complex naturalistic textures
Thin lines	Soft-edged random details

Often, for best results, you might have to combine pixels with paths (or vectors) in the same piece of art. Fortunately, Illustrator is a perfect tool for doing that. The File➪Place command enables you to bring pixel-based artwork into Illustrator to combine it with vector-based artwork.

Paths and Printing

Illustrator sends paths directly to printers in order to print smooth-edged images. This happy circumstance is one reason why Illustrator can make such good-looking artwork; most printers are designed specifically for printing path-based images.

Dot-matrix printers of the '80s gave way to laser printers and inkjets, and with them came a dramatic increase in speed (not to mention blessed quiet).

Which is faster — a square or a square?

For basic shapes, path-based artwork prints much faster than pixel-based artwork. For instance, a 5 x 5–inch, path-based square prints in a fraction of the time that it takes to print the same pixel-based square. Why? The printer needs only the four corner locations for the path-based square. For the pixel-based square, the printer needs to see each and every pixel that's on the way to the printer. (Imagine trying to count sand grains with tweezers, really fast.)

Printing paths: The evolution of Bézier curves

Printers create paths in much the same way that Illustrator does — by using points connected by lines. Think of a Connect-the-Dot game you did as a kid. Instead of processing each pixel, the Illustrator print code says, "Connect this point to that point, that point to this one over here, and so on." All it takes is another bit of code to say, "Now fill that shape with solid red" or some other color.

This approach works well for objects with (flat) sides, but curves are another matter entirely. You'd need to connect an infinite number of dots to make a perfect curve. Here's where Illustrator gets really clever. Instead of using straight lines between points, PostScript uses curves between points: *Bézier curves,* named after their creator, world-famous mathematician Pierre Bézier (pronounced *BEZ-zee-ay*).

The idea behind Bézier curves is that you need no more than four points to define any curved line: one point to say where the path begins, one point to say where the path ends, and two control points in between. Where you put each control point (relative to the end points) determines how much the line curves — and in what direction — on its way to meet the end point. Figure 2-9 shows a curved path with the handles showing.

Fortunately, Illustrator spares users the headache of having to work out the math; you have a little magnet-like handle onscreen (the *Bézier control point*) that changes the direction of the curve. Okay, actually using it might be far from intuitive, but it does give Illustrator the capability to generate complex shapes with curves.

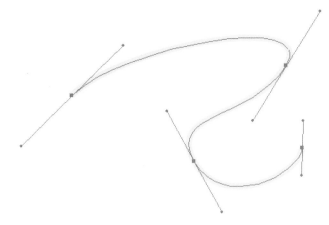

Figure 2-9: A curved path (the yellow one) is defined by a path, it's anchor points (on the line itself), and control points (the control points stick out from the line).

What's my vector, Victor?

You often hear the words *vector graphics* used to describe the kind of art created in Illustrator. In mathematics, a *vector* is a quantity — such as a force or velocity, having direction and magnitude — and a line representing such a quantity drawn from its point of origin to its final position. In artists's terms, a *vector* is a line of a specific size drawn in a specific place. Hmm, vector graphics are simply graphics made with lines! The basic building blocks of every Illustrator graphic are just a bunch of lines. Those lines may have other information attached to them (such as color and width). Still, no matter how fancy they get, they're still just lines underneath.

So why not call such graphics *line art?* Unfortunately, that term is already taken. Line art is a specific type of traditional graphic. I could call such illustrations *Illustrator illustrations,* but that term is a little alliterative (is there an echo in here?) and not quite accurate. So this book follows convention, using *vector graphics* to describe the kind of graphics you create in Illustrator. Pretty soon, you'll be doing the same!

Gray's Anatomy of a Path

Paths can be a thorn in your side while you're getting up to speed with Illustrator. At first, points might seem like a necessary evil (with *evil* being the key word here), but the more you know about how they're constructed, the easier it is for you to modify them. Eventually, you might even stop cursing at your poor, defenseless monitor.

In Illustrator, it's polite to point

Each path consists of a series of points. These are called *anchor points* because they anchor the path. Another type of point is a *direction point,* which is a point that determines the direction and distance of a curve. When most people refer to a point in Illustrator, though, they mean an anchor point, which appears only in a curved path. A path has at least two anchor points: to determine where it starts and where it ends. (Refer to Figure 2-9.)

You can handle the truth

For basic shapes with straight lines, points are all that paths need. As soon as you want curves on a path, though, you need *direction points* (also known as *handles* among Illustrator insiders). Direction points are connected to anchor points by *direction lines.* They control how a path curves. Figure 2-10 shows the same path but with direction points showing.

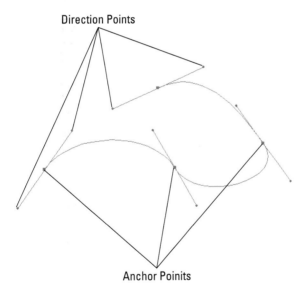

Direction Points

Anchor Poinits

Figure 2-10: A path with direction points and direction lines showing.

Direction points are invisible unless the curve is selected with the Direct Selection tool.

Handles work like magnets for the paths that extend from points. The farther you drag a handle away from the path, the more that path curves toward the handle. Figure 2-11 shows a few variations of a path between two points. In each of these variations, only the handle on the right has been moved.

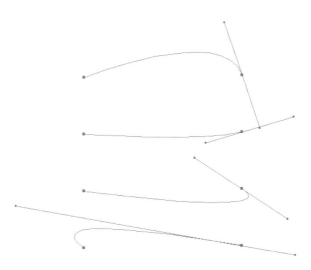

Figure 2-11: Variations of a path. The changes in the curve of the path occur as the handle on the left moves.

 You can move the handles of paths by using the Direct Selection tool (the hollow arrow at the top of the Tools panel).

1. Click the curve you want to adjust.

This selects the curve, making the direction points visible.

Direction points are invisible unless the curve is selected with the Direct Selection tool.

2. After the direction point is visible, click and drag the handle.

Figure 2-12 shows a circle with handles showing.

Even basic Illustrator shapes use handles to create curves.

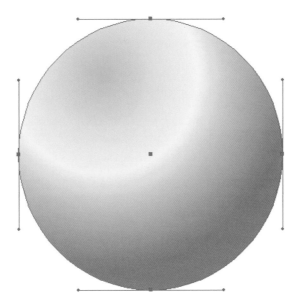

Figure 2-12: A circle with all the handles (direction points) showing.

Doing Everyday Things with Illustrator

The hard part for new users of Illustrator is figuring out what it does. The program is so vast and has many capabilities that aren't immediately obvious or self-explanatory. Even seasoned Illustrator veterans often discover that they use many convoluted steps to accomplish something they could do with a single hidden command. This chapter is a tell-all exposé of everything that you can do in Illustrator (at least as much as I can in a single chapter). You'd need an entire book to cover such a complex program (erm, um, which is why you're reading this). By the end of this chapter, you'll have a good overview of the features of Illustrator and know where to look to find the things you need to get the job done.

Picking Up Stuff and Moving It Around

Any time you want to do something to an Illustrator object, you must select it first. After you get the whole select-then-do thought lodged in your brain, many of Illustrator's functions come to you much more easily.

Illustrator offers a wide variety of ways to select things, including five tools, a bunch of keyboard commands, and several menu items. Fortunately, even if you know only one or two of these methods, you can be off and running with Illustrator selections in no time, just like a pro. Just remember that using a selection tool enables you to select virtually anything in your document.

In Chapter 6, I discuss selecting paths and objects in more depth. In this chapter, you discover the basics — all the ways of selecting, from tools and commands to menu items.

Comparing the selection tools

Illustrator has five selection tools. You choose a tool according to the type of object(s) that you want to select. The selection tools are as follows (I love a parade):

- **Selection tool:** This solid black arrow is the regular Selection tool. Use the Selection tool to select entire paths or groups by clicking them or dragging around them. If the object you click or drag around is part of a group, all the paths and objects in that group are selected as well. (Read more about paths and groups in this chapter.) The Selection tool, located at the top of the Tools panel, is plain but powerful.

 Direct Selection tool: Also known as the *hollow arrow or white arrow,* use the Direct Selection tool to select *portions* of paths — single points or segments — by clicking or dragging said points or segments. You can also use the Direct Selection tool to select other objects, such as placed images or text. Using the Direct Selection tool, located near the top of the Tools panel, selects only the portions of the path that you click or drag.

- **Group Selection tool:** This tool looks like the Direct Selection tool (a hollow arrow) but with a + symbol beside it. Use it to select "up" through paths and groups. The first click selects the entire path you click. Click the selected path again to select the group that the first path is in. If you keep clicking, you continue to select groups of groups, all containing the group that the first group is in. The Group Selection tool shares a toolslot with the Direct Selection tool. Just click and hold the Direct Selection tool to make the Group Selection spring out from behind it.

- **Lasso tool:** This tool looks like an anemic loop of string until you use it to select points and path segments within an area you designate by dragging the mouse pointer — at which time it still looks anemic. The Lasso tool is a go-anywhere version of the Direct Selection tool.

- **Magic Wand tool:** Photoshop users will recognize this much-beloved tool. Use the Magic Wand tool to select multiple objects with similar attributes — fills, strokes, transparency — within a specific tolerance range. For example, you can select all objects that have a stroke weight between five and ten points. The Magic Wand panel controls the various attributes and tolerance settings. For more on the Magic Wand, see Chapter 6.

Illustrator provides two primary ways of using the Selection, Direct Selection, and Group Selection tools:

- ✔ Click and release the object or group you want to select.

- ✔ Drag a marquee around the objects you want to select.

  Marquee is techno-speak for the dotted line that's created when you drag with these tools. (And all this time you thought it had to do with movie theater signage.)

Note: Consider which tool you use to make the selection. One key difference between the arrow-shaped selection tools and the Lasso and Magic Wand selection tools is that the arrow tools also move objects that are selected, but the Lasso and Magic Wand tools do not. For example, if you attempt to use an arrow tool to drag a marquee around an object but you click the object first, you *move* the object instead of *select* it. No marquee appears.

The Select menu also provides a handy way to make selections. All the Illustrator selection commands are centralized within this menu. (You can find more on the Select menu in Chapter 6.)

Here's how to tell when an object is selected in Illustrator: Any selected object shows its "guts" on-screen — the path used to create the object, as well as any points needed to create the path. Text and placed images also show points (and sometimes paths) when they're highlighted, even though they aren't made up of paths and points (weird, isn't it?). Figure 3-1 shows a pair of light bulb illustrations; the light bulb on the left is unselected, and the one on the right is selected. Note the points and paths (in blue) that appear on a selected object.

After you select an object, you can do any number of things to it, such as change its color, move it, transform it, or even delete it.

Moving and transforming objects

To move a selected object (or objects), just follow these steps:

1. **Select the object or objects you want to move by using one of the selection tools.**

2. **Using either the Selection tool or the Direct Selection tool, click and drag the selected object to where you want it.**

   Using the Selection or Direct Selection tools to click and drag an object that's already selected doesn't add to the selection or release the selection, but this action does enable you to move what's selected.

3. **Release the mouse button after the object is in position.**

   The object is all settled in at its new location.

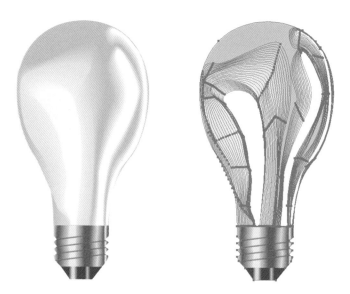

Figure 3-1: The left light bulb is unselected; the right light bulb is selected.

Instead of dragging with the mouse, you can use the keyboard arrow keys to nudge anything selected a little bit at a time. This trick works no matter what tool you selected in the Tools panel.

Illustrator power-users refer to call the other actions you can do to an object as *transforming* it. These actions include rotating, resizing, reflecting, and skewing objects. Illustrator puts all these transformation tools together in the middle of the Tools panel. Regardless of which transformation tool you use, the process, shown in Figure 3-2, is much the same as for moving objects. Just follow these steps:

1. **Select the object you want to transform, using one of the selection tools.**

2. **Choose the Rotate tool (or any transformation tool) from the Tools panel.**

3. **Click the selected object and drag.**

   While you drag, the outlines of the object show how the object will be transformed after you release the mouse button.

4. **Release the mouse button when the object's preview matches how you want the object to appear.**

   As soon as you release the mouse, the object is transformed.

Figure 3-2: The original object (left), rotating (middle), and after rotatation (right).

For more in-depth information on transforming objects, see Chapter 12.

Distorting paths

Moving and transforming paths make them look different, but you can tell that the moved or transformed path is pretty much the original path in a different position, at a different angle, or maybe at a different size. *Distorting* paths, however, can make them look drastically different from how they look originally. (If you're new to paths, read through Chapter 2.)

Illustrator provides a number of different ways that paths can be distorted, but the majority of these ways fall into the category of effect-based distortions. These distortions, found from the Effect⇨Distort menu (shown in Figure 3-3), can create all sorts of interesting (and some down-right ugly) effects.

Distortion effects have no "right" settings, but they do produce immediate and profound changes to your artwork. They also all have *previews,* so you can see what's going to happen to your artwork before you make any permanent change to its appearance.

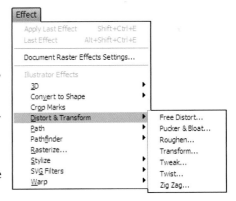

Figure 3-3: The options in the Distort Menu.

Figure 3-4 shows how an innocent path can become grossly distorted in a number of ways by using some of the different distortion effects.

Figure 3-4: The original path (left); then Pucker, Scribble, Zig-Zag, and Roughen.

To use a distortion effect, follow these steps:

1. **Select your artwork, using any selection tool.**

2. **Choose Effect⇨Distort⇨*any distortion effect* (for example, Pucker & Bloat).**

   A dialog box opens, showing the various options for a particular distortion effect. (Figure 3-5, for example, shows the options for the Pucker and Bloat effect.) Enable the Preview check box (mark it) so you can see the result of using this effect on your artwork.

3. **Use the slider (a little triangle under a straight line) to set the amount of the distortion.**

   Drag the slider to the left; watch what happens to the artwork (the value decreases, and the artwork changes). Drag it to the right (increasing the value) and look again — change yet again, but a different kind of change.

4. **When you get something you like, click OK.**

   If you don't like the result from using the effect, click Cancel to exit the effect without changing your artwork.

Figure 3-5: The Pucker & Bloat dialog box.

All effects change only the *appearance* of your artwork — not the artwork itself. At any time, you can select the original object and delete the effect within the Appearance panel. (See Chapter 11 for more details on effects and the Appearance panel.)

If you'd like to permanently change your artwork when distorting it, you can use the Liquefy set of tools, all accessible from the Warp tool on the Tools panel. The Warp tool and all the tools hidden under it can quickly modify paths in a number of flexible, mind-bending (and path-bending) ways.

Organizing objects

Illustrator provides many tools to help you organize your artwork. You can move objects above or behind each other, group objects, and distribute objects to layers for heavy-duty organization. (Read more about layers in this section as also in Chapter 13.)

To move an object behind all the other objects in a document, as shown in Figure 3-6, follow these steps. On the left, the green polar grid is in front of the meeple; on the right, it's moved behind the meeple.

Figure 3-6: Move an object behind another.

1. **Use any selection tool to select the object that you want to move behind another object.**

2. **Choose Object⇨Arrange⇨Send to Back.**

   The selected object moves behind all the other objects in the document.

Conversely, choosing Object⇨Arrange⇨Bring to Front moves the selected object in front of *all* the objects in the document. To move a selected object *just one level* to the back or front of a stack of three or more objects, use the Send Backward and Bring Forward options. The Send to Current Layer command moves the selected object to the active layer in the Layers panel.

These commands control the basic movement of objects back and forth in a document. You can also *group* a set of objects so that they always stay together (and are all selected at once, all the time). To group a series of objects, follow these steps:

1. **Select the objects that you want to group.**

   Drag a marquee around the objects or hold down the Shift key and click each object you want to include in the group.

2. **Choose Object⇨Group.**

   The objects are grouped. The next time you click any one of them with the regular Selection tool, all are selected.

You can group two or more groups to form a bigger group, and you can select objects along with a group (or several groups) and create a group out of them. Then you can group that group with more groups or objects. If you haven't turned into a full-fledged groupie by now, you can group that last group yet again with other groups or objects. And on and on until the men in white coats put you in a nice soft room.

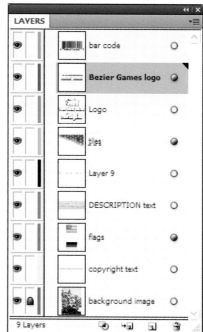

Figure 3-7: The Layers panel.

Another even more effective method of organizing your artwork is to put related objects on layers. Using layers is like placing your artwork onto separate sheets of clear plastic. Here are some handy things to know about layers:

- A single layer can have as many pieces of artwork on it as you want.

- You can select all the pieces of artwork in a layer at the same time.

- You can lock the layers to keep them from being selected while they still remain visible.

- You can hide a layer (and everything on it) to get rid of artwork as if you'd deleted it, but you still have the option of bringing it back whenever you want.

- You can apply appearances and styles directly to layers.

- Layers are created, selected, and hidden (and that's just for starters) by using the Layers panel. See the Layers panel in Figure 3-7.

You can do all sorts of amazing things by organizing your artwork into layers, so I devote a big section specifically to layers in Chapter 13.

Using the "Hard" Stuff

Have you ever looked at an illustration, and scratched your head and thought, "How did they do *that?*" Here's a secret: Chances are that it wasn't that hard. A slew of features in Illustrator let you do really cool things with little difficulty. The only catch is that you must walk before you can run. In Illustrator, this means being able to create simple shapes, color them, and move them in front of or behind one another (which I cover in Chapters 4, 5, and 6, respectively).

After you have those skills down, you're ready to move on to the fun stuff. You'll be amazed at the things you can do with a simple command or two.

Transparency

When you draw a shape in Illustrator that's filled with a solid color or a gradient, the shape covers up any objects beneath it. As I mention in the preceding section, you can move the object behind other objects in the document by selecting it with a Selection tool and choosing Object⇨Arrange⇨Send to Back. However, you can't see through that shape to the objects behind it.

Transparency breaks those rules by enabling you to fade away an object (from 0%/completely transparent to 100%/completely opaque, or any degree in between) to reveal the objects hidden beneath it. Figure 3-8 shows this basic transparency at work with a partially transparent logo appearing in front of a city image.

Figure 3-8: The Moolaville logo is set to be partially transparent.

Use transparency to see through one part of a shape more than another part, or to blend the colors of a shape with the colors beneath it in strange and interesting ways. Thumb through Chapter 10 for more on transparency.

Blends

In the 1990s, morphing was all the rage in movies and TV shows. *Morphing* combines (averages) two images together in a series of steps so that the first image appears to magically turn into the second. In Illustrator, you can use a similar technique — *blending* — to transform one object into another in as many steps as you want.

Blending lets objects change color, shape, and size, resulting in exciting effects. Illustrator's blends are "live," meaning you can blend between objects but still edit them after you create the blend. The objects in between change automatically to match the changes you make to the original objects, which allows you to tweak how the blend looks but without having to start over. Figure 3-9 shows a step blend occurring between a purple ellipse and a yellow star. Only the rightmost and leftmost objects were drawn. The other objects are an average of the two created by the Blend tool. I cover blends in more detail in Chapter 12.

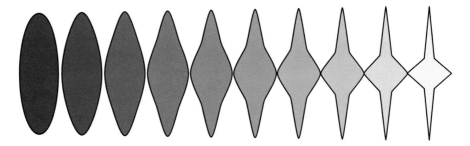

Figure 3-9: An example of a blend between two objects.

Clipping masks

An Illustrator *clipping* mask (commonly referred to as a *mask* by longtime Illustrator users) is a path used to hide objects outside itself. For instance, you can mask out everything in an Illustrator drawing except for the area inside the path so only the area shows — a vignette, if you will. Creating a clipping mask, as Figure 3-10 shows, is really quite simple. All you need to do is make your way through the following steps.

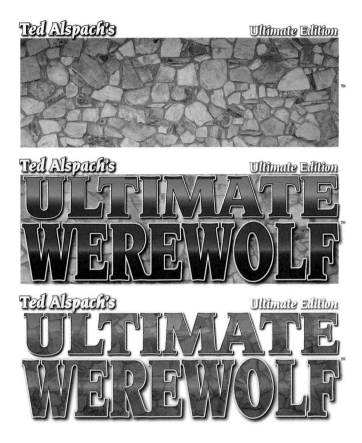

Figure 3-10: Mask an image with text.

1. **Create the original image or artwork that you would like to mask.**

2. **Create the art or type that you would like to use as a mask.**

   The art beneath the clipping mask can be as complex and have as many parts as you want. The top path masks all paths beneath it. You can use any tool to create this path (such as the Pen, Pencil, or Rectangle).

3. **Select the new masking object along with the art to be masked and then choose Object⊏⊃Clipping Mask⊏⊃Make.**

   Anything selected that's outside the masking path is hidden, and the masking path itself becomes invisible. Remember that nothing is deleted when you make a mask; it's just hidden. You can restore your artwork to its unmasked state by choosing Object⊏⊃Clipping Mask⊏⊃Release. (You can learn more about clipping masks in Chapter 10.)

Compound paths and shapes

Compound paths join two or more paths so that one path makes part of another invisible. Compound paths might sound complicated, but if you've ever typed anything in any computer program, you've been using them all along without knowing it. If you want to place art over something else and see things through the holes in the art, use compound paths, as shown in Figure 3-11.

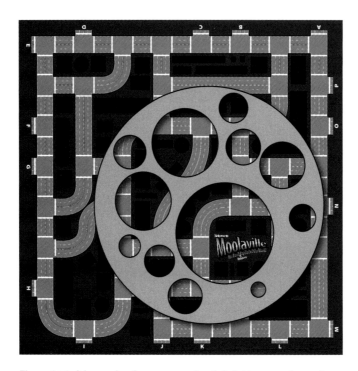

Figure 3-11: A large circular compound path is laid over a piece of background art (which is visible through several round holes).

A figure eight is a single compound path, made up of three paths. The two paths in the middle are *holes* — areas made transparent so you can see the background artwork through them.

As you might imagine, text characters have lots of holes in them, so they're all compound paths. For example, many letters are really compound paths; for example, any letter with a hole in it (such as *B* or *O*) is a compound path. A typical character, such as a lowercase *a,* is made up of two paths; the hole in the middle is one of those paths. To magically transform a bit of text into a graphic object made of paths

1. **Select the text with a selection tool.**

2. **Choose Type⇨Create Outlines.**

   The text changes from a text object to a series of compound paths (which you can then edit as you edit any other path).

You can make any number of overlapping paths into a compound path by selecting them and choosing Object⇨Compound Path⇨Make. Conversely, if you want to turn the compound path back into two (or more) individual paths, select the compound path and choose Object⇨Compound Path⇨Release. Figure 3-12 shows what happens when you release compound paths that were originally text objects. When you release the compound paths, the hollow part of the letter fills in because the purpose of the compound path in the letter is to make those hollow parts of the letter transparent.

Illustrator

Illustrator

Illustrator

Figure 3-12: Text as text (top), as compound paths (middle), and as compound paths after release (bottom).

Compound paths work best when you keep things simple. If you stack too many objects on top of each other and try to make a compound path, holes might appear where you didn't expect them. However, if you try to keep things to a minimum (use only a few objects, and try not to have more than two objects overlapping in any one place), you'll get splendid results with the Compound Paths command.

Illustrator has also gone one step better, providing you with an easy way to create better compound paths — by using compound shapes. Check them out in all their glory in Chapter 4.

Flares

Use the Flare tool to create effects, such as lens flares and reflections, that are photo-realistic yet totally vector-based (as shown in Figure 3-13). That is, the effects can be easily edited — moved and scaled — to produce just the right look.

Figure 3-13: A boring sun (left) gets transformed into a dazzling star of rays and rings.

To create your own lens flare, first create some interesting art and fill with the colors of your choice; then follow these steps:

1. **Select the Flare tool.**

   It shares a toolslot with the Rectangle tool.

2. **Double-click the Flare tool to bring up the Flare Tool Options dialog box (shown in Figure 3-14). Play with the various settings and then click OK.**

Flare Tool Options

Center		Halo	
Diameter:	100 pt	Growth:	20%
Opacity:	100%	Fuzziness:	50%
Brightness:	50%		

OK
Reset
☐ Preview

☑ Rays		☑ Rings	
Number:	15	Path:	100 pt
Longest:	300%	Number:	10
Fuzziness:	100%	Largest:	41%
		Direction:	42°

Figure 3-14: The Flare Tool Options dialog box.

These are the settings used for Figure 3-14:

Center	100% Opacity and 50% Brightness
Halo	20% Growth and 0% Fuzziness
Rays	Number 15, 300% Longest, and 100% Fuzziness
Rings	Path 100 pt, Number 10, 41% Largest, and 42% Direction

3. **Place your cursor over the place on your art where you want to establish your light source, then click and drag.**

   You should see the appearance of some funky lines and circles. These are the rays and the halo.

   Use your up or down arrow keys to interactively increase or decrease the number of rays.

4. **Place your cursor over the place on your art where you want to center your rings. Click and drag.**

   The distance you drag also determines the length of the flare.

   Circles of varying size and opacity magically appear on your image. Your sun should now be decked out with a bright and beautiful lens flare.

5. **Deselect the flare by clicking on an empty area of your document using any Selection tool and then admire the results. If you're not quite happy, select the flare you just drew, double-click the Flare tool, and enter some different settings.**

Entering the Wide World of the Web

Illustrator is a Web-happy application. Anything that you create in Illustrator can make an appearance on the Web in one form or another. Illustrator gives you mighty powers to create both vector-based and pixel-based images for use on the Web, like the images and logo shown on the Web page in Figure 3-15.

Figure 3-15: The logo, gradient bar at the top, and images were all created using Illustrator.

I devote an entire chapter (Chapter 17) to the Web. Illustrator does all sorts of Web-specific tasks, such as creating animations, optimizing pixel-based images, and providing a preview of how your artwork looks when viewed in a Web browser.

The following is a laundry list of Web-happy things you can do with Illustrator at no extra charge:

- **Create images without resolution headaches.** When you use a pixel-based graphics program, you must continually worry whether your graphics have enough resolution to display with the quality you want. In Illustrator, you can always create Web graphics with optimum quality because you decide on the resolution after you complete the image instead of when you start creating it.

- **Optimize artwork as pixel-based images.** You can save your art as JPEG, GIF, or PNG images, using the Save for Web command to preview how various color reductions and compressions affect the artwork.

- **Export artwork as Flash or SVG vector graphics.** Flash (SWF) and Scalable Vector Graphic format (SVG) are technologies that enable you to display vector (path-based) graphics on the Web. Before Flash and SVG, only pixel-based artwork could be displayed. Vector graphics on the Web are smaller and look better than their pixel-based counterparts.

- **Preview artwork as pixel-based graphics.** If you plan to save your artwork as GIF, JPEG, or PNG files, you can turn on the Pixel Preview mode while you create it. This makes Illustrator show you your artwork just like how it'll look after it's on the Web. With this mode turned off, the artwork displays as close as possible to how it'll look in print.

- **Apply object-based slicing.** Simply put, *slices* enable you to divide your image into pieces so that you can later apply separate loading or optimization settings or other HTML features, such as animation. However, rather than slicing an entire image based on a square grid, as in Photoshop or ImageReady, Illustrator enables you to apply slices to objects, groups of objects, or layers.

For more information on any of these topics, see Chapter 17.

Saving the World

Well, maybe saving the world is a little bit of an overstatement, but saving your work is arguably the most important thing you can do in Illustrator. And you may feel as if you have saved the world when your client mentions — 40 hours into the job — that she needs the graphics to work in AutoCAD, and you say, "Sure, no problem!" instead of breaking down in tears. Or when your graphics look every bit as good on the Web as they do in print. Or when your computer crashes, and you laugh it off because you didn't lose any work. The key to all these heroic scenarios is Illustrator's massive Save features, all found under the File menu: Save, Save As, Save a Copy, Save for Web, and Export.

Save

Choosing the Save command writes the document that you're working on to the hard drive, which is the fastest way to save a file. Illustrator documents are saved with the `.ai` extension.

Saving a file in Illustrator creates a not only file that Illustrator can read, but also creates a bona fide PDF file as well, so anyone with Acrobat or the Adobe Reader can read and print the file.

If you open an Illustrator file from an older version of Illustrator and click the Save button in Illustrator CS4, the file saves as an Illustrator CS4 file. To save the file to be compatible with a previous version of Illustrator, you need to use the Export command.

Save As

Use the Save As command to save the open document to a different location from where it was originally, or to save an SVG, an EPS, or a PDF version of the file. Using the Save As command also saves new documents that haven't been saved before. When you create artwork for print, Save As is the command to use 90 percent of the time; it allows you to save in the EPS (Encapsulated PostScript) format. The EPS format is supported by many other non-Adobe applications for both the PC and the Mac. When you save a file in this format, you're assured almost universal compatibility in the world of print.

You also have the option of saving your file as a PDF (Portable Document Format). PDF is great for exchanging files for review and approval processes because it only requires that the recipient have Adobe Reader (a free download from Adobe, `www.adobe.com`) installed. The recipients don't need Illustrator or any graphics program. They don't even need to have any fonts you may have used in the file. ***Note:*** If you save your file as a PDF, select the Preserve Illustrator Editing Capabilities option in the Adobe PDF Format Options dialog box. Then you can later open the file as an Illustrator file with access to edit the elements, fonts, colors, patterns, and type blocks.

The only differences between an Illustrator file saved as a PDF file (with Illustrator editing capabilities on) and one saved as a native Illustrator file are the extension following the filename, and also the appearance of the icon in Windows or the Finder (Mac). PDF creates .pdf files, and native Illustrator creates .ai files. Both can be read in either Illustrator or Adobe Reader/ Acrobat.

For more information on the Save As command and file formats, see Chapter 16.

Save a Copy

The Save a Copy command has all the features of the Save As command but adds a twist: You can also use it to save all the information in your current document as a different file on your hard drive — at a different location and sporting a different file format — without changing anything in the current file. You can save multiple versions of the same file (say, one for printing and one for the Web). Moreover, if you need to restore the file to the way it was the last time it was saved using Save or Save As, you have a handy way to do so: the File⇨Revert command. Revert breezes right past the Save a Copy command, allowing you to make a completely different series of changes.

Save for Web

The Save for Web and Devices command, as you probably guessed, enables you to save Illustrator graphics for display on the Web. Even better, you can use this command to save your files in any of the most commonly used Web graphics file formats: JPEG, GIF, PNG, Flash (SWF), or SVG. Best of all, the Save for Web dialog box (shown in Figure 3-16) provides a preview of what the file will look like after you save it, as well as what the file size and download time will be, so that you can manage the delicate balance between graphic quality and short download time. You can find a whole lot more information on the Save for Web and Devices command in Chapter 17.

Export

The Export command could be called "Save for Everything Else." Use it to save Illustrator files in an astonishing variety of formats — from the common-place (Photoshop) to the obscure (Pixar). Use the Export command when you need to save a graphic in a specific format that you can't find under the Save As or Save for Web command. Here's where to find every other file format you can use when you save an Illustrator file.

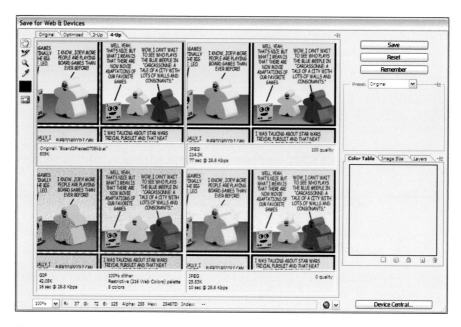

Figure 3-16: The Save for Web and Devices dialog box can show up to four different possible output results for your artwork.

To save artwork so that you can open it in a previous version of Illustrator, choose the Legacy Illustrator (.ai) option in the Save as Type drop-down menu in the Export dialog box.

The most commonly used formats found here are Legacy Illustrator (.ai), Flash (a format for displaying vector graphics on the Web), SVG, and Adobe Photoshop. Legacy Illustrator (.ai) allows users of older, lesser versions of Illustrator to open files you created and edited in Illustrator CS4. Flash (SWF) files can be opened and edited in Flash-savvy applications, such as Adobe Flash. The Photoshop format re-creates your Illustrator file as a Photoshop file, maintaining the features of the original file (such as Layers and Transparency) as closely as possible. Chapter 16 provides further information on using Illustrator with these formats.

Illustrator can save in a format optimized for Microsoft Office applications. Choose File➪Save for Microsoft Office to create a file that's guaranteed to work well in all your Office applications.

Using Illustrator for What It Does Best

Illustrator is a powerful tool, but it's limited to certain types of tasks. Knowing what Illustrator does best is key to getting the most out of the software.

Illustrator does anything having to do with path-based artwork extremely well and performs beyond the basics with pixel-based artwork. You can use Illustrator for page layout, but it really isn't designed for documents longer than a single page. You can also use Illustrator for some basic image adjustment, but that sort of thing is easier with Photoshop.

Any time you want to create art or graphics pieces that need to serve multiple purposes, use Illustrator. Illustrator's flexibility in transforming artwork is second to none. With equal ease, you can create artwork to appear on a business card, a bottle label, a poster, a billboard, television or film, or on the Web.

Illustrator isn't limited to portraying the way things are in the real world. You can use it to create things that may have no real-world equivalents. Give light bulbs spikes. Create a monster out of eyeballs. Whatever you imagine, Illustrator can help you create an image of it.

Part II

Drawing and Coloring Your Artwork

The 5th Wave   By Rich Tennant

"That's a lovely scanned image of your sister's portrait. Now take it off the body of that pit viper before she comes in the room."

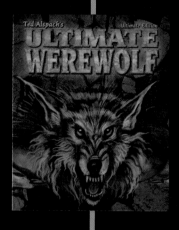

This is where you find out about the basic core of drawing and coloring inside Illustrator. Remember your first coloring book and that crazy huge box of 64 crayons your Aunt Shari got you for your first birthday? Remember the waxy taste of those crayons and the frustration you had at not knowing what Burnt Umber was? And remember the excitement when you first put crayon to paper and saw the great artist that you would one day be? Okay, you probably don't remember any of that. But you were probably just as excited as you are now, with the entire world of shapes and colors opened up to you. This time around, it's in digital form and tastes better (even if the color names are just as strange).

Shaping Up, Basically

In This Chapter

▶ Creating objects the easy way

▶ Customizing basic objects

▶ Combining objects to create other objects

▶ Spewing objects onto a page with the Symbolism tools

A regrettably large number of people avoid using Illustrator because they find the whole point/path thing so intimidating. This situation is unfortunate but not surprising. When most people look at artwork, they see it as complete shapes, not as the lines that form the shapes. Working with points and paths, though, forces you to see your artwork in a way that many people have never thought of before, which creates enough of a hurdle to scare people away from Illustrator.

Fortunately, Illustrator offers shape-creation tools as a way to get a running start to clear that hurdle. With these six tools, you can create basic shapes, such as rectangles, ellipses, stars, and polygons. You can even create graphics without ever having to think about points and paths! (Don't be fooled — the points and paths are still there, but the tools create them all for you with just a single click-and-drag. Ah, progress.)

In this chapter, you discover how to use the shape-creation tools, giving you a good foundation for understanding and using the more complex features of Illustrator. You also find out how to combine simple shapes. Although you use the shape-creation tools to create basic elements, they are by no means limited, especially when used in conjunction with the Pathfinder panel — an Illustrator feature that allows you to combine multiple shapes in a whole array of interesting ways. Some people discover that they can create such an astonishing variety of graphics with the shape-creation tools that they can bypass more complex tools altogether, such as the Pen and Pencil tools!

Creating Basic Shapes

Illustrator has six tools for creating shapes. Although you could create all those shapes with the Pen tool, you'd torment yourself if you did so. The specialized tools in Illustrator make creating shapes easy. The six tools are named for (and look like) the shapes they create, and are located in a single row that can be pulled from the Tools panel by dragging the Rectangle tool out to the side, as shown in Figure 4-1.

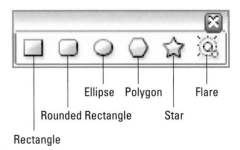

Figure 4-1: The six shape-creation tools.

- **Rectangle:** Use this tool to make rectangles and squares. Hold down the Shift key when using this tool to get a perfect square.

- **Rounded Rectangle:** As you might expect, you get rounded corners on your rectangles and squares when you use this tool. Of course, if you recall high school geometry, you know that a round rectangle is a contradiction in terms. By definition, a rectangle is a four-sided polygon, with each corner forming a 90° angle. Oh, well. So much for Euclid.

- **Ellipse:** Use this tool to make ellipses and circles. Hold down the Shift key when using this tool to get a perfect circle.

- **Polygon:** Use this tool to make objects with any number of sides — from 3 to 1,000, to be precise — with each side the same length *(equilateral)*. You can use this tool to create triangles, pentagons, hexagons, and so forth.

- **Star:** Use this tool to make stars with any number of points between 3 and 1,000.

- **Flare:** Use this tool to create lens flare and reflection effects that are photo realistic yet entirely vector-based. See Chapter 3 for the complete lowdown on this exciting tool.

Drawing rectangles and squares

Illustrator offers simple tools to choose from when drawing many types of rectangles and squares to draw. Just choose your shape, and use the best tool.

Rectangle

To draw a rectangle, select the Rectangle tool in the Tools panel, and then click and drag where you want the rectangle to go. After you release the mouse button, a rectangle appears.

Square

To draw a square, you follow a slightly different procedure, as I describe in the following steps:

1. **Choose the Rectangle tool from the Tools panel.**

2. **Click and drag with the tool. Don't release the mouse button yet.**

   This draws an initial rectangle.

3. **Press the Shift key.**

   The rectangle snaps into a square.

4. **Still holding the Shift key, release the mouse button.**

   Don't release the Shift key until after you release the mouse button. If you release the Shift key before you release the mouse button, the square snaps back into a rectangle.

   A square appears.

5. **Release the Shift key.**

Rounded-corner rectangle

Draw a rounded-corner rectangle by choosing the Rounded Rectangle tool (hidden in the toolslot with the Rectangle tool) and drawing with that instead of the regular Rectangle tool. You can make a rounded corner square by keeping the Shift key pressed while drawing with the Rounded Rectangle tool.

You can access any hidden tool by clicking and holding on the visible tool; after a second, the other tools in that toolslot appear.

Rectangle with exact dimensions

To create a rectangle with exact dimensions (for example, 28 points x 42 points), select the Rectangle tool and click and release your mouse, but don't drag. A dialog box appears, as shown in Figure 4-2.

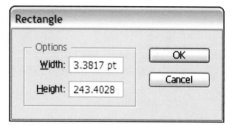

Figure 4-2: Set rectangle dimensions here.

Type in height and width, and then click OK. Illustrator draws a rectangle to those exact specifications. To create a square, just make sure the width and height are the same.

Note that, for any shape that you create, you can always move that shape by clicking on it and dragging with the regular (black) Selection tool.

Illustrator places the rectangle's upper-left corner at the spot where you click with the Rectangle tool. If you hold down the Option key (Mac)/Alt (Windows) at the same time, Illustrator places the rectangle's center at the spot where you click with the Rectangle tool.

Drawing ellipses and circles

Drawing an ellipse or a circle in Illustrator is a snap.

- ✏ **To draw an ellipse:** Choose the Ellipse tool and then click and drag in the document window. After you release the mouse button, an ellipse appears.

- ✏ **To draw a perfect circle:** Hold down the Shift key while you draw with the Ellipse tool.

If you hold down the Option key (Mac)/Alt (Windows) at the same time you click (but don't drag) with the Ellipse tool, Illustrator places the ellipse (or circle) from its center instead of from its upper-left edge relative to where you clicked.

Like with the Rectangle tool, click-ing (without dragging) causes the Ellipse dialog box to appear, as shown in Figure 4-3. Here you can type in an exact height and width for the ellipse. These values represent the distance across the ellipse at its widest and narrowest points. Typing in the same number for both values (as in Figure 4-3) results in creating a circle.

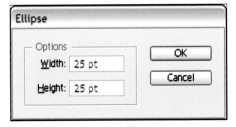

Figure 4-3: Set ellipse dimensions here.

Creating polygons and stars

Illustrator has tools designed specifically for creating polygons and stars. Like rectangles and ovals, you could draw these shapes with the Pen tool, but having a tool for creating them makes the process easier, faster, and more accurate. Using these tools is fairly straightforward. Like with the Rectangle and Ellipse tools, just click and drag and then release the mouse button when the shape is the size you want. Also, like with the Rectangle and Ellipse tools, just clicking (without dragging) with the Polygon or Star tool opens their respective dialog box, which you use to specify the shape's exact size (and other attributes).

Need to create stars at various sizes with a certain number of points? Or different sized polygons with the same number of sides? The dialog boxes for the Polygon and Star tools remember the number of sides and points you enter and use those settings for each subsequent shape you draw, even if you click and drag.

Pulling polygons

To create a polygon, simply click and drag with the Polygon tool. When the polygon is the size you want, release the mouse button. The new polygon appears. Because polygons are more complex than ellipses or rectangles, you can get all sorts of special capabilities by pressing certain keys while you draw. To customize the polygon while you create it, hold down any of the following keys while you drag:

- **Shift:** Constrains one side of the polygon so that it's parallel to the bottom of the page.

- **Up arrow/down arrow:** Adds or deletes, respectively, sides of the polygon while you draw it.

- **Spacebar:** Moves the polygon while you draw it (instead of changing the size of the polygon).

- **Tilde (~):** Creates multiple polygons while you draw. At times, you can have so many polygons that they look like one solid figure, but each is a separate entity that you can separate and move wherever you want. This feature can create quite astounding effects, as shown in Figure 4-4.

To use this feature, you must release the mouse button before you release the key, or all the duplicates disappear. This works when you draw any of the other shapes, too!

By the way, to get the swirly effect, move your mouse clockwise or counterclockwise while you draw.

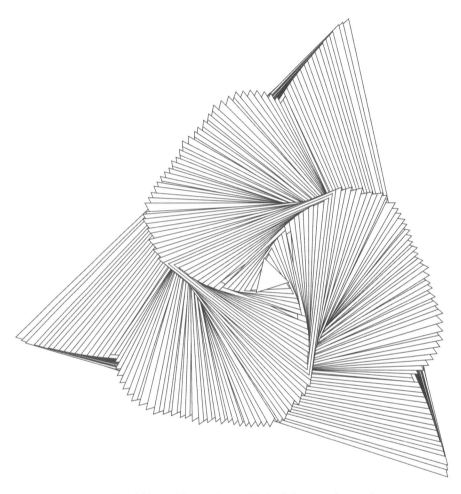

Figure 4-4: Press the tilde (~) key while you draw with the Polygon tool to produce a unique effect.

Clicking (without dragging) with the Polygon tool opens the Polygon dialog box, as shown in Figure 4-5. Polygons use a radius value instead of height and width. All sides of the polygon are the same distance from the center; this distance is the Radius value. To create a polygon of a specific width, type in half the width you want in the Radius field. You can type in any number of sides, from 3 to 1,000.

Figure 4-5: Set polygon dimensions here.

Seeing stars

To create a star, click and drag with the Star tool. After you release the mouse button, a star is born. Stars are even more complex than polygons. Fortunately, you also have more keys for customizing options. To customize a star, use the following keys as you drag:

- **Shift:** Constrains one side of the star so that the bottom two points of the star are parallel with the bottom of the page.
- **Up arrow/down arrow:** Adds/deletes points of the star while you draw it.
- **Command key (⌘; Mac)/Ctrl (Windows):** Constrains the middle points (the inner radius) of the star; the outer ones still move.
- **Spacebar:** Moves the star while you draw it (instead of changing the size of the star).
- **Tilde (~):** Creates multiple stars while you draw.

Clicking (without dragging) with the Star tool opens the Star dialog box, as shown in Figure 4-6. Stars have two radii that you can set here. The first radius determines how close the inner points of the star are to the center. The second radius determines how far the outer points are from the center. You can also set the number of points the star has. After you make your settings, click OK to create the star you specified.

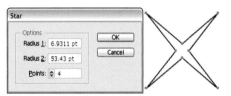

Figure 4-6: Choose quantity and length of star points.

After you create a star using the Star dialog box, each star you create by clicking and dragging uses the same specifications, more or less. Regardless of each star's size, it has the same number of points (unless you change them, using the up and down arrows), and the first and second radii maintain the same proportions, if not the same size. For example, if you enter 2 inches for the first radius and 1 inch for the second, the second radius is 50 percent smaller for every star you create after you establish the settings in the dialog box, regardless of the star's size.

Figure 4-7: The Rectangular Grid Tool Options dialog box.

Creating grids

 Use the Rectangular Grid tool, which shares a toolslot with the Line tool, to create grids of any size and configuration. Double-click the Rectangular Grid tool or simply click the tool on your Artboard (the area on which you draw) to access the Rectangular Grid Tool Options dialog box, shown in Figure 4-7.

Enter values for the size of the grid and the number of columns (Horizontal Dividers) and rows (Vertical Dividers). You can also enter a *skew* value that progressively increases or decreases the size of the rows and columns. When left unchecked, the Fill Grid option creates a grid without a fill; enabling the Use Outside Rectangle as Frame option surrounds the grid lines with a rectangle.

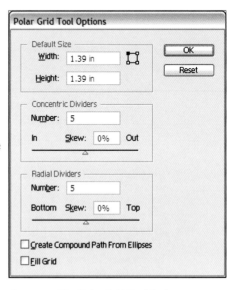

Figure 4-8: The Polar Grid Tool Options dialog box.

The Polar Grid tool, located in the Line toolslot next to the Rectangular Grid tool, operates in a similar manner as the Rectangular Grid tool. In the Polar Grid Tool Options dialog box, as shown in Figure 4-8, you find options for Size and the number of Concentric Dividers (smaller circles that appear within the largest outer circle) and Radial Dividers (the lines that radiate from the center of the smallest circle to the edge of the largest circle).

Using both radial and concentric dividers creates a spider web effect, as shown in Figure 4-9 (right). You also have the same Skew and Fill Grid options as for the Rectangular Grid tool. The Create Compound Paths from Ellipses option creates a polar grid where every other concentric circle is transparent. The effect creates a bull's-eye target, as shown in Figure 4-9 (left).

In addition to the grids created by the Rectangular Grid and Polar Grid tools, Illustrator can transform your background into electronic graph paper. Choose View➪Show Grid to show a grid behind all of your artwork. (Note that the grid itself won't print; it's just there for alignment and spacing purposes).

Figure 4-10 shows a document with a grid behind it.

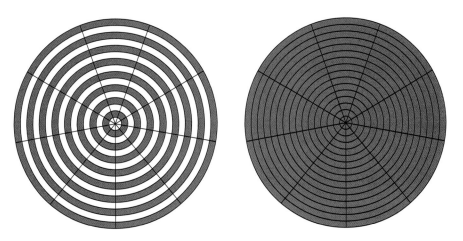

Figure 4-9: A polar grid with and without the compound paths option selected.

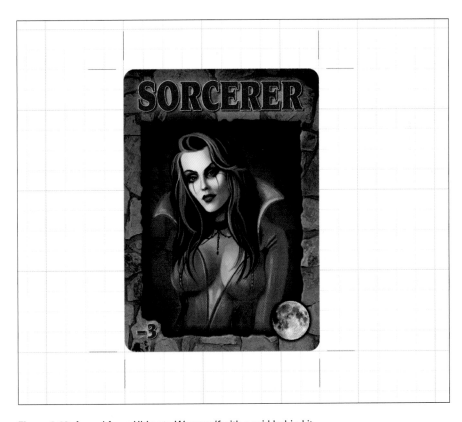

Figure 4-10: A card from *Ultimate Werewolf* with a grid behind it.

To change the settings for the grid, choose Edit⇨Preferences⇨Guides and Grid. The Guides and Grid Preferences dialog box holds options for changing the color, style, and increments of the grid. If you choose View⇨Snap to Grid, your objects snap to the grid corners whenever you move them or whenever you create new objects. When I say *snap,* I don't mean the objects automatically jump to the grid corners. What happens is a lot more subtle: When you drag an object by using any selection tool, it sort of sticks a little when an edge of the object is over a grid corner. If you don't want the object to reside at that point, you can keep dragging. The stickiness is just enough to help you align the object.

Putting Together Shapes

The basic shape-creation tools are great starting points for creating more complex illustrations because most complex shapes are simply many basic shapes put together. You might be astonished at what you can create simply by combining one basic shape with another. One of the quickest and easiest ways to do so in Illustrator is by using the Pathfinder panel.

The Pathfinder panel has a misleading name. All it really does is combine or separate two or more shapes in a variety of ways. You can use the Pathfinder panel to join two or more objects into one object, remove the shape of one object from another, cut apart two shapes where they overlap, or combine objects in many other ways.

To access the Pathfinder panel, choose Window⇨Pathfinder. The Pathfinder panel appears, as shown in Figure 4-11.

Using the Pathfinder panel is simplicity itself: Just overlap two or more objects, select them all by clicking them with any selection tool (to select multiple objects, hold down the Shift key while clicking each additional object), and click the button in the Pathfinder panel that does the operation that you desire.

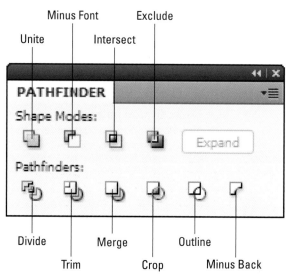

Figure 4-11: Use the Pathfinder panel to work with complex shapes in a variety of ways.

Knowing which button to click isn't always obvious, but don't worry about that. Simply keep in mind that when you want to combine or separate two or more objects, you're likely to find a button to help you in the Pathfinder panel. Click a button; if it doesn't give you what you want, choose Edit➪Undo and try a different button. And if you take the time to read the following sections, you'll actually have a fairly good idea of what each of the buttons will do.

The results of the Pathfinder panel depend heavily on which object is in front and which object is behind. To change the stacking order of objects, select a single object with the Selection tool and choose Object➪Arrange. In the Arrange submenu, you can send the object to the back, bring it forward, or move it backward and forward one level at a time. To help you get a better idea of how the Pathfinder

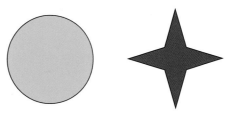

Figure 4-12: Start with these two basic shapes.

panel functions, follow along as I use it on two basic objects (in this case, the circle and the star in Figure 4-12). The next few sections show the magic you can do by putting a few simple shapes through the Pathfinder wringer.

Shape Modes

Not only does the Pathfinder panel enable you to create complex artwork from basic shapes, but all the artwork you create can remain fully editable if you press Option (Mac)/Alt (Windows) when you click the appropriate Pathfinder button. Overlap two or more objects by selecting one with the Selection tool and dragging it over another object, select them all, and click the button of the effect you want. The Shape Modes buttons along the top row of the Pathfinder panel consist of the following:

✔ **Unite:** Groups multiple objects so they're selectable as a unit but can also be selected individually with the Direct Selection or Group Selection tools. The resulting objects use the fill and stroke of the object that was on top before the objects were added together. By pressing Option (Mac)/Alt (Windows) when clicking the button, the shapes are formed into a *compound* shape — meaning they are treated as a single shape by most operations in Illustrator, but still exist as two shapes that can be separated in the future.

In all Shape Modes, the Expand Compound Shape command "flattens" the compound shape into a single path which cannot then be separated back into the original shapes.

Use the Direct Selection tool to edit any path or anchor point on the compound shape.

✔ **Minus Front:** Cuts away all selected objects in front of the backmost object, leaving a hole in the backmost object in the shape of whatever was in front of it. In Figure 4-13, Minus Front cuts away the star in front of the circle, creating four separate curved sections.

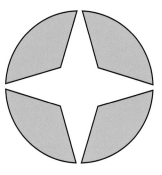

Figure 4-13: Using Minus Front.

✔ **Intersect:** Cuts away all parts of the objects that don't overlap, as shown in Figure 4-14. The resulting object uses the fill and stroke color of the object that was on top before the objects were intersected. Here, Intersect joins the circle and star, using the fill and stroke color of the star (which was on top before the objects were intersected). Intersect also works on more than two objects.

✔ **Exclude:** Removes all parts of the objects that overlap and unites what's left into a single object (the opposite of Intersect). The remaining object uses the fill and stroke of the object that was on top before the objects were united. In Figure 4-15, the Exclude command cuts away all parts of the circle and star that overlap, uniting what is left into a single object that uses the fill and stroke color of the star (which was on top before the objects were united).

Figure 4-14: Using Intersect.

Compound Shapes

All the Pathfinder effects I discuss here can be combined if applied as compound shapes, so knock yourself (and other paths) out. If you want to undo your compound shapes, choose the Release Compound Shape command from the Pathfinder panel pop-up menu. By clicking the Expand button (refer to Figure 4-11) or

Figure 4-15: Using Exclude.

selecting the Expand command from the Pathfinder panel pop-up menu, you can further clean up or simplify your paths by eliminating unnecessary anchor points. The compound shapes are flattened and condensed into a new simplified shape. But be warned: After you use the Expand Compound Shape command, you can no longer release your compound shape by using the Release Compound Shapes command. The Expand feature permanently fuses your effect — just as if you had clicked without the Option (Mac)/Alt (Windows) pressed — so there's no going back.

Pathfinders

The commands under the Pathfinders portion of the Pathfinder panel are a mixed bag of effects. The Divide and Minus Back commands achieve results by cutting away specific parts of the image. Figure 4-16 demonstrates the results of applying Minus Back, removing everything but the tips of the stars. (Now *that's* what I call minus!) The Trim, Merge, Crop, and Outline commands provide the means for tidying up your artwork before sending your creation out into the world. In Figure 4-17, this cleanup crew takes a bow.

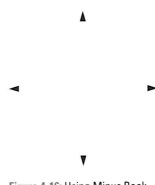

Figure 4-16: Using Minus Back.

Figure 4-17: Cleaning up and checking the circle and star, using (left to right) Trim, Merge, Crop, and Outline. In this case, Trim and Merge cause the same result.

Here's a quick rundown of the Pathfinder commands found under the Pathfinder panel:

- ✔ **Divide:** Breaks two overlapping objects into separate objects. This operation might look as though it hasn't done anything after you first apply it. However, after you divide an object, you can move or color each piece individually.

✔ **Trim:** Removes any parts of objects hidden by other objects and also removes any strokes. Like with Divide, this command might not produce visible results immediately: That is, you might not see anything until you start changing the position of the pie slices of the circle, where you'll suddenly notice that they can move as separate objects. (Refer to the first image in Figure 4-17.)

✔ **Merge:** Removes any parts of objects hidden by other objects, removes strokes, and merges overlapping objects that have the same fill colors. This command functions almost the same way as the Trim command does, with the key difference being that this commands merges objects of the same color into a single object, but Trim leaves them as separate objects. In the second image in Figure 4-17, the Merge command removes any parts of the circle hidden by the star, removes strokes, and merges overlapping objects that have the same fill colors (which the star and the circle do not).

✔ **Crop:** Divides two overlapping objects into separate objects where they overlap and then deletes everything outside the boundaries of the front most object. In the third image in Figure 4-17, the Crop command divides the star and circle into separate objects where they overlap and then deletes everything outside the boundaries of the star (the front most object).

✔ **Outline:** Breaks objects into separate line segments with no fill colors. The last image in Figure 4-17 shows the visible effects of the command.

✔ **Minus Back:** Cuts away from the front most object all selected objects that are behind the front most object. The remaining object uses the fill and stroke color of the front most object. Here, Minus Back cuts away the circle from the star and unites what's left (those four forlorn-looking points; refer to Figure 4-16) into a single object that uses the fill and stroke color of the star (which is the front most object).

If you stumble upon the Pathfinder commands under the Effects menu, don't confuse them with those found under the Pathfinder panel. The commands under the Effects menu change the appearance of an object without changing the underlying object itself. The Pathfinder commands found under the Effects menu are designed to be applied to groups of objects, layers, and type objects. They usually have no effect on a few overlapping shapes. For more on appearances and effects, see Chapter 11.

Creating Objects by Using the Pathfinder Panel

By combining basic shapes, you can create just about anything you can imagine. So, how do you actually use the Shape Modes and Pathfinders commands to create such complex shapes? (Details, details.) Consider a couple of examples — a crescent moon and a sunrise.

Crescent moon

A crescent moon seems fairly simple to draw, but trying to draw one accurately by hand is frustrating. The Pathfinder panel, however, makes drawing a crescent moon almost as easy as smiling and saying, "Green cheese." Just follow these steps:

1. **Choose the Ellipse tool to draw a perfect circle (click and drag the Ellipse tool while holding down the Shift key).**

   As I describe earlier in this chapter, let go of the mouse button before you let go of the Shift key.

2. **Repeat Step 1, creating a second circle that's just slightly smaller than the first one.**

3. **Using the Selection tool, click on the second circle and then drag it over the first, as shown in Figure 4-18.**

Figure 4-18: Creating a crescent moon.

4. **Select both circles.**

   Hold down the Shift key and click each circle with the Selection tool to select more than one object at a time.

5. **Click the Minus Back button in the Shape Modes portion of the Pathfinder panel.** *Presto!* A crescent moon appears!

Sunrise

What better way to follow a crescent moon than with a beautiful sunrise? Just follow these steps:

1. **Click and drag with the Rectangle tool to create a box.**

2. **Click and drag with the Star tool to create a star. As you drag with the Star tool, repeatedly press the up-arrow (↑) key.**

   A many-pointed star appears.

3. **Choose the Selection tool and use it to position the star over the rectangle so the two objects overlap, as shown in Figure 4-19.**

Figure 4-19: Creating a sunrise.

4. **Select both the star and the rectangle.**

   Hold down the Shift key and click each object with the Selection tool so both objects are selected.

5. **Click the Minus Back button in the Pathfinders portion of the Pathfinder panel.**

   Voilà! A beautiful sunrise! (Well, almost. Still needs colors and a caffeinated beverage.)

Legal Graffiti

The Symbol Sprayer (which has the honor of being the preeminent tool in the Tool panel's Symbolism toolslot; see Figure 4-20) is how Adobe makes your job of producing repeating graphics easier and quicker. Feel like a kid (okay, a bad kid) and spray onscreen repeating graphics all over the place to your heart's content. No clogged spray nozzles, no paint drips, no fumes. Who could possibly resist that intriguing spray can sitting there in the Tools panel just begging to be picked up?

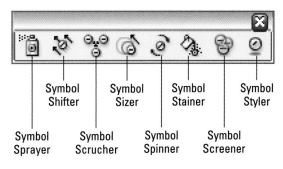

Figure 4-20: He who has the best toys wins: The Symbolism tools.

Symbols are reusable and repeatable elements that are used in animation. Although they can be graphics, buttons, movie clips, sound files, and even fonts, in Illustrator, they can be composed of any Illustrator object — vector- or pixel-based images or text. Each individual symbol is an *instance.* The beauty of symbols is that although you might have multiple instances of a symbol in your file, each instance references a single symbol in the Symbols panel, thereby keeping the file size extremely small.

Symbols provide a quick and easy way to create a large group of similar objects and an easy means to collectively edit these objects. Symbols can be used for most anything, but are especially handy in creating navigation buttons; borders; map icons; and masses of graphics, such as foliage, snowflakes, and stars.

Using the Symbol Sprayer

I like it when tools, such as the Symbol Sprayer, work the way I think they should (unlike the tedious Pen tool). Follow these steps to become the master of your personal digital spray can:

1. **Select the Symbol Sprayer.**

   Note that the sprayer icon is surrounded by a circle, which represents the diameter of your sprayer. (Read the upcoming section, "Setting the Symbolism options," to discover how to change that size.)

2. **Choose Window⇨Symbols.**

The Symbols panel, shown in Figure 4-21, appears with a default library of symbols to choose from.

3. **Select a symbol from the Symbols panel, click the Symbolism tool on the Artboard, and drag it around the page.**

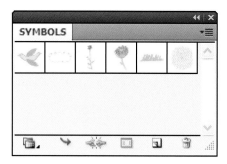

Figure 4-21: The Symbols panel.

A trail of symbols (of the one you chose) appears, mirroring the movement of your cursor while you drag it across your Artboard. (Check it out in Figure 4-22.) Unless you feel the need to edit your symbols or create your own custom symbol, you're done!

Figure 4-22: Pssst: Graffiti never had it so good (or legal).

Creating a custom symbol

If you're the creative type, create your own symbol. First create the artwork, which can include any Illustrator object — vector- or pixel-based images or text. You can even use a combination of objects, as shown in Figure 4-23. Next, select your artwork and do one of these three things:

- Click the New Symbol button (the little piece of paper at the bottom of the Symbols panel).

- Choose the New Symbol option from the Symbols panel pop-up menu (accessed from the little triangle at the upper right of the Symbols panel).

- Drag and drop the art onto the Symbols panel.

Voilà! A symbol is born.

Figure 4-23: Combine object types to create custom symbols.

Editing your symbols

The other Symbolism tools hiding behind the Symbol Sprayer enable you to tweak your symbols to graphic perfection. To edit your symbols, first select the symbols with the Selection tool. Note how you select the *bounding box* (a temporary border surrounding objects) of the symbols and not the individual instances. That's because symbols are a unique breed of graphic that require a unique kind of editing.

Symbols used in a document are tied to the original symbol chosen in the Symbols panel. If that original symbol changes, all the associated symbols in your document change. This ability can allow you to quickly make dozens or hundreds of changes to a document. For instance, if you were using little stop signs based on a symbol throughout a map you've drawn, you could change all the stop signs to traffic lights simply by replacing the original symbol in the Symbols panel.

After you select the symbols, click and drag with the Symbolism tool of your choice. Depending on where you click and how you drag, you will get different results. Each of the tools is described in more detail below:

- ✐ **Symbol Shifter:** Click and drag your mouse to shift the position of the symbols in relation to each other. The symbols move around the cursor while you drag, creating a sort of ripple effect.

- ✐ **Symbol Scruncher:** Click and hold down your mouse to move the symbols closer. Hold down the Option (Mac)/Alt (Windows) key while clicking and holding down your mouse to move the symbols apart.

- ✐ **Symbol Sizer:** Hold your mouse button down to size the symbols larger. Hold down the Option (Mac)/Alt (Windows) key while manipulating your mouse to reduce the size of the symbols.

  You can also use the regular Rotate and Scale tools to rotate and size symbols.

- ✐ **Symbol Spinner:** Click and drag your mouse in the desired direction to rotate the symbols.

- ✐ **Symbol Stainer:** Hold your mouse down to tint the symbols by using the current Fill color.

- ✐ **Symbol Screener:** Hold your mouse down to increase the transparency of the symbols.

- ✐ **Symbol Styler:** Applies a style from the Graphic Styles panel (found by choosing View➪Graphic Styles) onto the symbol. With the Symbol Styler, select and drag a style from the Styles panel onto a symbol instance.

Setting the Symbolism options

Double-click any of the Symbolism tools to bring up the Symbolism Tools Options dialog box, as shown in Figure 4-24. Here you adjust the behavior of each tool.

Select your tool icon from the row and then adjust its Diameter (1–999 points), the Intensity (1–10), and the Symbol Set Density (1–10). Most of the tools provide shortcut keys with which you adjust settings while you draw. I recommend keeping the Show Brush Size and Intensity option selected (checked) so that you get a good idea of your tool coverage.

Figure 4-24: Control the look of your symbols here.

In the Symbolism Tools Options dialog box (refer to Figure 4-24), choose the User Defined setting to apply the settings within your Illustrator application to the Symbolism tools. For example, if you choose User Defined for your Stain setting for the Symbol Sprayer, the symbols appear with your current Fill color, regardless of the original color of the symbol.

Here are some other handy tips to keep in mind when working with symbols:

✔ **If you export your file as a Flash (SWF) file,** your symbols are included in the symbol library of your Flash application. (See Bonus Chapter 1 on the Web site associated with this book for more info.)

✔ **To place a single instance of a symbol,** choose the Place Instance of Symbol option from the Symbols panel pop-up menu, or click the Place Symbol Instance button at the bottom of the panel.

✔ **To convert a symbol into a regular, Illustrator editable graphic (to use either as regular artwork elsewhere or to add/replace a symbol using that symbol's artwork),** select the symbol instance and click the Break Link to Symbol button at the bottom of the Symbols panel, or select the command from the Symbols panel pop-up menu. You can then modify the graphic, select it, and click the original symbol in the Symbols panel. Then, choose the Redefine Symbol option from the Symbols panel pop-up menu. Not only is the symbol revised, but any symbol instance on your Artboard is revised as well. Imagine having to change 1,000 little leaves on a tree if they were regular graphics and not symbols!

✔ **To take advantage of a pressure-sensitive tablet,** select the Use Pressure Pen option (only available if a pressure-sensitive tablet is hooked up to your computer) in the Symbolism Tools Options dialog box.

✔ **To name or rename your symbol,** double-click the symbol in the Symbols panel or choose Symbol Options from the Symbols panel pop-up menu.

✔ **To delete a symbol,** select it in the Symbols panel and click the Delete Symbol at the bottom of the Symbols panel, or choose the command from the Symbols panel pop-up menu.

✔ **To duplicate a symbol,** select it in the Symbols panel and choose Duplicate Symbol from the Symbols panel pop-up menu. Duplicating is handy for making variations of a symbol. (After duplicating, you can turn it into regular art on the artboard, modify that art and then replace the duplicated symbol with the modified artwork.)

5

Getting Your Fill of Fills and Strokes

In This Chapter

▶ Filling open paths

▶ Discovering how to use strokes

▶ Getting to know the Color and Swatches panels

▶ Using and creating patterns

▶ Applying textures to paths

▶ Working with gradients

Fills and strokes give life to your artwork. If Illustrator were a coloring book, the fills and strokes would be the biggest, best box of crayons ever (only better because these colors always stay inside the lines). Better still, they're magic colors. You're not limited to a single solid color within an area. You can have gradients and patterns as well. And not only can you color inside the lines, but you can color the lines themselves, make them thinner or thicker, or hide them altogether. Best of all, unlike crayons, these don't make a mess when your big sister grinds them into the carpet because you ran to show Mom your new artwork and forgot to clean up after yourself.

In this chapter, you discover the different boxes of crayons Illustrator has to offer, such as the Color and Swatches panels, and how to color your artwork with them by using the Fill and Stroke boxes. You find out how to create your own colors. Rounding things out, you get to know the special colors, gradients, and patterns in Illustrator, which stretch the meaning of what color really is.

Understanding Fill and Stroke

A *fill* is a color enclosed by a path. A *stroke* is a line of color that precisely follows a path. To run the coloring book metaphor into the ground (carpet?),

the stroke is the line, and the fill is the inside-the-line that you aren't supposed to color outside of (but you did anyway because you weren't about to
let your parents stifle your creativity!). *Color* is a loose term here: It can mean
a solid color, a pattern, or (in the case of fills) a gradient. In Figure 5-1, you
can see a variety of paths with different strokes and fills applied to them.

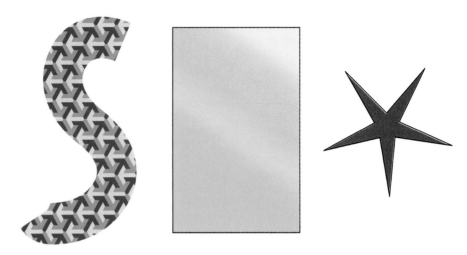

Figure 5-1: Paths with different fills and strokes applied to them.

Although a stroke can be any thickness, it always uses a path as its center.
And although you can stylize your strokes with solid colors or patterns,
you can't use a gradient. (*Patterns* and *gradients* are special combinations of
colors; read more about them in the upcoming section "All the colors in the
rainbow and then some.") Remember that a *path* surrounds the area where
you put the color. This area is the *fill* because, um, it's filled (with color).

Fills and strokes can obscure the boundaries of your paths, especially
when you have very thick strokes on your paths, such as the S-shaped
purple pattern in Figure 5-1. To temporarily hide all fills and strokes, choose
View⇨Outline. This shows your artwork as just the paths, with all strokes
and fills hidden. You can still edit the artwork as you would any other time.
The only difference is that you can't see fills and strokes. To show all the
colors again, choose View⇨Preview.

You have many ways to create and modify fill and stroke color in Illustrator, but
the quickest and easiest way to apply them is by using the Fill and Stroke boxes
in the Tools panel, which looks remarkably like what you see in Figure 5-2.

You can change a fill or a stroke, but not both at the same time. You decide
whether to change the fill or the stroke by selecting an object and then clicking the Fill (solid) box or the Stroke (bordered) box. The box you click comes
to the front; after that, every color change you make is applied to whichever
one you chose . . . until you choose the other one.

Some very useful features surround the Fill and Stroke boxes. Just to the upper right is a little curved line with arrows on both ends. Click this thingamajig (the Swap Fill and Stroke button) to swap fill and stroke colors. (Go figure.)

Press Shift+X on your keyboard to swap fill and stroke colors without having to click anywhere!

To the lower left of the Fill and Stroke boxes are miniature white (Fill) and black bordered (Stroke) boxes. Click this Default Fill and Stroke button to set the Fill and Stroke boxes to their default colors: white for Fill, and black for Stroke.

If you prefer fills and strokes in festive colors, here's the story: Beneath the Fill and Stroke boxes live three square buttons that handle colors. Click the first square (the Color button) to change the fill or stroke color to the last color that you used. Click the second square (the Gradient button) to change the color of the stroke or fill so that it matches the last-selected gradient you used. Click the third square (the None button) to use no fill or stroke color at all.

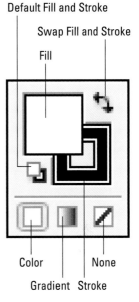

Figure 5-2: Fill and Stroke in the Tools panel.

Double-clicking the Stroke or Fill boxes summons the *Color* Picker, shown in Figure 5-3, from which you can specify colors in a variety of ways. You can choose a color from a spectrum, using the true color field and the color slider, or define a color numerically. You can also select colors from the Color and Swatches panels, as I describe later in this chapter.

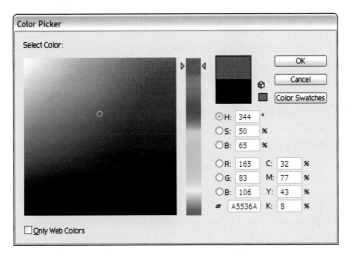

Figure 5-3: The Color Picker is a quick way to get to pretty much any color you want.

Filling and stroking paths with color

You can fill a path with one color and stroke it with another, as shown in Figure 5-4.

To fill a path with one color and stroke it with another, just follow these steps:

1. **With any of the selection tools, select the path that you want to color.**

2. **In the Tools panel, click the Fill box (the solid one).**

   Doing so tells Illustrator to apply the next color you choose to the fill (but not the stroke) of the selected path.

Figure 5-4: Filling and stroking a path with two different colors.

3. **Choose Window⇨Swatches.**

   The Swatches panel appears. The squares in this panel function in much the same way as the three squares beneath the Fill and Stroke boxes in the Tools panel. Click any square in the panel to apply that swatch to the selected stroke or fill. (For more information, see "The Swatches Panel" later in this chapter.)

4. **Click any solid-color swatch.**

   Well, okay, any swatch in the panel works. The ones that aren't solid colors are special colors, such as patterns and gradients — but sticking to solid colors is less confusing early on.

5. **Click the Stroke box (the thick-bordered one) in the Tools panel.**

   Illustrator is ready for you to pick a stroke color.

6. **In the Swatches panel, choose a solid color, just like you did for the fill color in Step 4.**

You can also drag and drop color onto your path. Simply drag a color swatch from the Swatches panel and drop it onto your path. Depending on whether the fill or stroke is selected in the Tools panel, either the fill or stroke is colored anew.

Making a bold stroke

When you follow the steps to color a stroke and don't see any change, you probably have too narrow of a stroke. Stroke widths can range anywhere from 0 points (pt) to 1,000 pt (18 inches, or about 46 centimeters), as shown in the examples in Figure 5-5. If the stroke is too narrow to be visible onscreen, you can change the stroke width by using the Stroke panel, as shown in Figure 5-6.

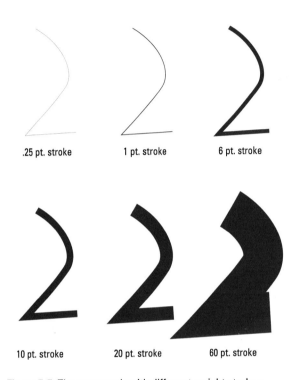

Figure 5-5: The same path with different weight strokes.

To give the path a different stroke width

1. **Select the path with any selection tool.**

2. **Choose Window⇨Stroke.**

   The Stroke panel appears.

3. **Enter a new value in the Weight field. Or, if you like, just choose one from the field's drop-down menu.**

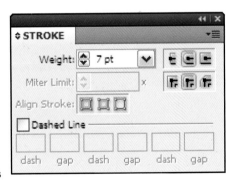

Figure 5-6: The Stroke panel.

You can make the stroke you've created dashed by putting numbers in the Dash and Gap fields at the bottom of the Stroke panel. Dash fields are solid chunks of stroke, while Gap fields are empty spaces. You can also change the end cap type to Butt (snicker), Rounded and Projected, as well as change the corner type to Miter, Round or Bevel.

Adding multiple strokes to a single path

This power-user tip will have your friends writhing in jealous agony: Choosing the Add New Stroke option from the Appearance panel pop-up menu places a second stroke on your path. You can make this stroke a different color or width, and even apply an effect directly to it. To avoid confusion, always check to see which stroke is highlighted in the Appearance panel (accessed by choosing Window➪Appearance); that's the one that will be changed when you fool around with settings in the Stroke or Color panel.

Filling crossed and open paths

Sometimes a path crosses itself. For instance, a path in the shape of a figure eight crosses itself once. If you fill this path, the two round areas of the eight end up full, as shown in Figure 5-7.

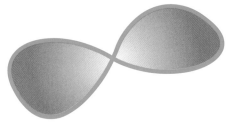

Figure 5-7: A filled path in a figure eight shape.

Open paths, which have separate starting and ending points, can also be filled, but the results are a little different from what you might expect. When you fill an open path, an *imaginary path* connects the first and last points of the original path. This imaginary path marks the limits of the fill area. If you apply a stroke to the figure, the stroke doesn't apply to the imaginary path. Figure 5-8 shows open paths with fills in them. The fill of the paths results from an imaginary line drawn between the two endpoints of the path. (If you look closely at Figure 5-8, you'll notice that the blue highlights marking a real path are missing from the imaginary path connecting the endpoints.)

Figure 5-8: Open paths with fills.

The Swatches Panel

Illustrator stores colors in the Swatches panel for quick and easy access — and no matter how fast you grab a color, you never have to worry about splattering paint. The Swatches panel comes with a whole set of colors that are ready to use just by clicking them in the panel.

Additionally, Illustrator comes with many *swatch libraries* — sets of colors created for special purposes — so if your first-grade crayon box never seemed to have enough colors, you're in luck. You can even create your own custom colors by using the Color panel (see the later section "The Color Panel") and adding them to the Swatches panel.

Using the Swatches panel (shown in Figure 5-9) is almost as easy as looking at it. Select an object with any selection tool, click the Stroke or Fill box in the Tools panel, choose Window⇨Swatches so that the Swatches panel appears, and then click any square in the Swatches panel to choose that color. The selected fill or stroke updates the instant you click the new color. No fuss, no muss, no melted crayons.

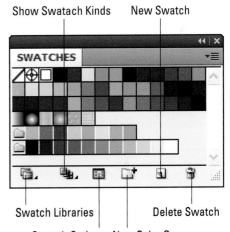

Figure 5-9: Choose colors from the Swatches panel.

All the colors in the rainbow and then some

The Swatches panel contains several different types of color swatches, each with its own range of purposes and uses. Such swatches are used primarily for two purposes: first, to quickly access commonly used colors, gradients and patterns; second, for setting "global" colors that you can apply in your illustration and then change later, affecting all the objects that have that color applied to them. You can even group colors together.

Here's the lineup:

 ✔ **Process color:** This is your run-of-the-mill, straight-up color with no added bells or whistles. You can make a color for use on-screen or for print by mixing varying amounts of red, green, and blue (RGB) or cyan, magenta, yellow, and black (CMYK). For more information on using RGB versus CMYK colors, see Chapter 1. These appear as solid color squares.

✏ **Spot color:** (Nope, not for creating polka dots or Dalmatians.) Spot colors are used exclusively in printing. The four-color CMYK printing process can create only a limited range of colors from its four basic color ingredients. To compensate, the process can also use spot colors of specified inks that come in a particular color. Many companies make spot colors, but most countries have one dominant company that sets the standards for spot-color printing in that country. (In the United States, it's Pantone; in Japan, it's TOYO.) The range of all colors that a company produces is its *library.* Illustrator includes swatch libraries from all the swatch-producing companies. Spot colors show up in the Swatches panel with little triangles in their lower-right corners; these triangles have a tiny spot in their corners.

✏ **Registration color:** Registration is a special Illustrator color that uses 100 percent of all inks. Although it looks like black on-screen, it's not for artwork. Registration (as a color, at least) exists for a very specific technical purpose: creating the Registration marks used by commercial printers to get things in proper alignment on press. If you aren't a commercial printer or haven't been specifically told to do so by a commercial printer, you should never use Registration. Registration looks like a crosshair in the Swatches panel.

If you use Registration to color your artwork, you get an unprintable sticky mess that will probably stink (chemically, at least), waste ink, and never dry.

✏ **None:** This color choice differs from White, which tells a printer to *put no ink in a particular space,* on the assumption that the paper itself supplies the white color. None, on the other hand, is the *complete absence* of color. In a picture, a white object is opaque — it blocks your view of any objects behind it. (You can't see the electric outlet behind a white refrigerator.) An object with a color of None, however, is transparent — invisible. If you want to use a stroke but also want other objects to show through the fill (or let the fill show through the objects), choose None for the specific on-screen area you want to see through. None appears in the Swatches panel as a white square with a diagonal red line through it.

✏ **Gradients:** *Gradients* combine two or more colors in a smooth transition that shades from one color into the other.

✏ **Patterns:** If you really love wallpaper, you can use one or more objects in a tiled pattern to fill other objects.

The icons at the bottom of your panel (refer to Figure 5-9) allow for different swatch-related functions. They are, from left to right:

✏ **Swatch Libraries:** This displays a list of all of the Swatch Libraries available. There are an awful lot of them available when you install Illustrator, and you can use any existing document as a swatch library by choosing Other Library from the list and browsing to an Illustrator document of your choice.

- ✔ **Show Swatch Kinds:** This allows you to filter the types of swatches shown; pick from All, Just Color, Just Gradients, Just Patterns or Just Color groups.

- ✔ **Swatch Options:** This displays the options for the currently-selected swatch (allowing you to name it and change other attributes of it).

- ✔ **New Color Group:** This creates a folder where you can organize related swatches.

- ✔ **New Swatch:** This creates a new swatch based on the current active color.

- ✔ **Delete Swatch:** This deletes selected swatches from the swatch panel.

Swatch options for super colors

Swatches are a quick way to retrieve colors, but they do more. Double-click any swatch in the panel to open the Swatch Options dialog box, shown in all its useful glory in Figure 5-10.

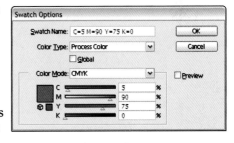

Figure 5-10: The Swatch Options dialog box.

The Swatch Options dialog box keeps you busy with choices and gives you creative possibilities. Here's the list:

- ✔ **Swatch Name:** Here, you can give the color a distinctive name (such as Maine Blueberry) or change its name.

- ✔ **Color Type:** You can change a spot color to its closest CMYK or RGB equivalent. This is a handy option when your client provides you with a logo rendered in spot colors ("Metallic puce? You're not kidding?"), and you have to produce an image in CMYK or RGB.

  Unfortunately, you can't go the other way around. Trying to change a process color into a spot color doesn't give you the closest spot color equivalent from the Pantone, TOYO, or any other color library. (For more about color libraries, see the following section, "Swatch libraries.")

- ✔ **Global:** After you select (check) this option, Illustrator remembers everything you color with a particular swatch. When you change the color of the swatch, everything with the old swatch's color updates to the new color. (Mercifully, Adobe didn't call this feature *The Old Swatcheroo.*) This feature's a great timesaver when you want to change a color scheme. You don't have to go back, reselect, and recolor everything — very handy, indeed.

✔ **Color Mode, gamut warnings, and color sliders:** These features are especially powerful when used with Global color. They all work just like the Color panel except that they apply your changes only to the selected swatch. See more on this panel in the upcoming section, "The Color Panel."

Swatch libraries

Illustrator comes loaded with color choices in the form of *swatch libraries* — sets of color swatches created for specific purposes. (Pantone, for example, has several libraries devoted just to spot colors.) The libraries you get with Illustrator draw from all the major spot-color sources in the world. A Web library provides tried-and-true colors that work best on the Internet. To peruse these libraries, choose Window⇨Swatch Libraries. If you turn up a color that you simply must have, go ahead and add it to your Swatches panel. To do that, open the specific library you need, find the color you want, click it and then choose Add to Swatches from the panel's drop-down menu. The color shows up in your Swatches panel.

Some libraries contain hundreds of swatches, which can make finding a particular color difficult. Fortunately, swatch libraries have a Find field at the very top of the window. For example, if a client wants a logo done on a report cover in Pantone 185, just open one of the Pantone libraries (by choosing Window⇨Swatch Libraries⇨Pantone Coated). When the swatch library appears, type **185** in its Find field (the empty white rectangle at the top of the panel) to highlight Pantone 185C (the C is for coated) automatically — you don't have to press any other key! Click Pantone 185C to add it to your Swatches panel, and you're good to go.

If you need to choose spot colors for a project that will be offset printed, make sure to select your color from a printed swatch book manufactured by your chosen ink company. Never select the colors based on your on-screen view of the swatches in the library. Because of many variables, your screen can give you only its best match of the printed color. It will never be exact and frequently will be quite different.

The Color Panel

The Color panel is as close as Illustrator gets to a real-world artist's palette. You use it to create new colors by blending. Instead of mixing splotches of pigment and linseed oil with a brush (and getting half of it on your jeans), you move sliders to adjust how much of each component color goes into your new color.

Dissecting the Color panel

The Color panel (see Figure 5-11) has several cool features, in addition to the color sliders, that make creating colors easier.

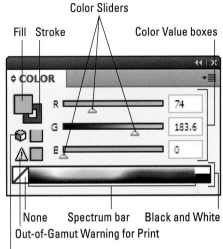

Figure 5-11: The Color panel is the closest you can get to a real artist's palette in Illustrator.

✐ **Fill** and **Stroke boxes:** These function identically to the Fill and Stroke boxes in the Tools panel. They're available here in the Color panel for your convenience.

✐ **Color sliders and Color Value boxes:** You can create a new color by dragging these sliders to the left or right. The color in the Fill or Stroke box (whichever is in front) updates to reflect the change, as does any selected artwork. To specify an exact amount of a particular color, type a number into the Color Value box to the right of each color slider.

✐ **None:** Click the None button to choose a Stroke or Fill value of None.

✐ **Black and White:** You guessed it! Click Black to make the color black, and White to make it white. (Wait a minute. Was that a trick question?)

✐ **Spectrum bar:** In this little rectangle are all the colors that you can possibly create. Click anywhere on the Spectrum bar to choose a color. Well, okay, the spectrum is tiny; almost nobody picks exactly the right color on the first click. Use the spectrum to get a color that's in the right ballpark, and then use the sliders to make the color precisely what you want.

✐ **Out-of-gamut color warnings:** When you create colors, tiny color boxes appear, warning you whether the color is outside the color gamut for print or the Web. (The *gamut* is the total range of colors that a method can create without having to alter any of the colors.) For the Web, the gamut is 216 colors; for print, it's several thousand. If you choose a color outside this range, that color can shift to another color. The Out-of-Web Color Warning is a square of color with a little cube beside it; the Out-of-Gamut Warning for Print is a square with an exclamation point inside a triangle beside it. Click the square to choose a color within the gamut that's closest to the color you chose. If you're creating for the Web, you can ignore the print gamut warning — and vice versa if you're creating for print.

To create a new color by using the Color panel, follow these steps:

1. **Choose Window➪Color.**

   The Color panel appears.

2. **From the Color panel pop-up menu, choose a color model.**

   See the upcoming section "Modes and models" for more information.

3. **Click the Fill or Stroke box in the panel.**

4. **Move the sliders of each component color to the left or to the right until the color you want appears in the Stroke or Fill box.**

Of course, if you actually want to use the colors that you create in the Color panel (what a concept), you can do so in a couple of ways:

- **Use the color while you use the panel.** Anything already selected when you create a new Fill or Stroke color is filled or stroked with that color. (For example, you can fill a selected pterodactyl with pteal or pturquoise.)

- **Save the new color for later.** After you create the new color, you can save it to use again later. Here's how:

   a. *Open the Swatches panel by choosing Window➪Swatches.*

      The Swatches panel appears.

   b. *Click the Fill or Stroke box (whichever you just created) in either the Tools panel or the Color panel.*

   c. *Drag the Fill or Stroke box onto the Swatches panel.*

      Don't worry, you won't damage the Color panel when you drag away the Fill or Stroke box. Instead, you get a ghostly outline of the box while you drag it away. Release that outline on top of the Swatches panel to add the Fill or Stroke to the panel.

   After you release the mouse, the color shows up in the Swatches panel for you to use again and again! (Pteal pterodactyls ptravel in flocks? Who knew?)

With the new color in the Swatches panel, you can double-click it to open the Swatch Options dialog box. Here you can give it a name, make it a global color, or use any of the options I describe in the earlier section, "Swatch options for super colors."

Modes and models

Mode and *model* are the Illustrator terms to define color. *Color mode* is the language of color your document speaks — either CMYK or RGB. *Color model* is a way of describing how to form the colors in the mode (color-language) your document uses.

All the colors used in the document (except spot colors) exist in one particular color mode, no matter what color model you use to create them. When you open a new document, you must decide whether to work in RGB or CMYK color. (See Chapter 1 for the tale of two color modes.) With that out of the way, you then get to choose a color model for your color mode from the Color panel pop-up menu (accessed by clicking the small horizontal bars in the upper-right of the panel); see Figure 5-12 for a mug shot.

Figure 5-12: Different color models within the Color panel pop-up menu.

Suppose, for example, that you want a shade of gray while you're working in RGB mode — the RGB color model of the RGB mode, to be more precise. Shades of gray are hard to create in the RGB color model, though, because you have to drag all three red, green, and blue sliders to get the color you want. To dodge that complexity, switch the color model to Grayscale in the Color panel pop-up menu. Then you have just one slider to deal with, and you can quickly create the exact shade of gray you want.

The Color panel is where you create the colors you need, using a variety of color models: Grayscale, RGB, HSB, CMYK, and Web Safe RGB. Each has a specific purpose, but really these different colors exist only to help you visualize the color that you're trying to create. The Color panel enables you to mix colors in any color model, but as soon as you apply them, they convert to the color mode you're using.

The following list describes these color models and the best ways to use each:

- **Grayscale:** Here, colors express everything as a shade of gray. This model is handy when you're creating a black-and-white printing or just want a quick way to specify a shade of gray. Grayscale is measured in terms of ink values, with black as 100 percent — the most ink possible.

- **RGB:** With this model, colors are based on the three colors (red, green, and blue) used by your monitor to generate all the colors that you see on-screen. These colors are designed for on-screen use, such as graphics for the Web or for video. The amounts that you see in the Color Value boxes range from 0–255. They correspond to the intensity of the light projected by your computer screen. Computer screens use tiny red, green, and blue phosphors that glow with different intensities to create the colors that you see. The higher the value, the brighter the glow. Specifying 255 for all colors gives you pure white; a 0 value for all colors gives you pitch black. These numbers, however, are less important than your practical results. Pay attention to the Fill or Stroke boxes when you drag the sliders and see the color that results.

- ✔ **HSB:** Here, colors are seen in terms of hue, saturation, and brightness. Think of an HSB color in terms of a crayon. Hue is the color of the crayon, such as red. Saturation is how red that crayon is, such as brick red versus cherry red. Brightness is equivalent to how hard you press down when you use that crayon. This way of thinking might seem weird, but many painters and traditional artists find it very intuitive.

- ✔ **CMYK:** In this model, colors are based on the four colors (cyan, magenta, yellow, and black) used in process printing. (Cyan is a light, bright blue; magenta is a bright purple color that's almost pink. You're on your own for yellow and black.) CMYK colors are designed to specify colors for print. *Process printing* enables people to achieve a wide variety of colors (including photographic-looking images) using only those four colors.

  CMYK colors work the opposite of how RGB colors work: The more of each individual color, the darker the total color becomes. For instance, 0 percent of cyan, magenta, yellow, and black results in white; 100 percent of cyan, magenta, yellow, and black results in black. But nobody who knows better would ever create black for print by using 100 percent of all four colors — that would put way too much ink on the paper, resulting in a sticky mess.

  Well, okay, in theory you could create black by using 100 percent of cyan, magenta, and yellow. However, printing inks (for the most part) are designed to be partially transparent, so they mix together better. The result would be a dark gray mess, not a crisp black. To create a black that really looks black, you have to add black to cyan, magenta, and yellow (fortunately, black ink is cheaper than those colors). Try using 100 percent black for black, adding just a little of the other three colors to make it look really black. (Such complications of even a basic concept may have driven some folks to make graphics only for the Web.)

- ✔ **Web Safe RGB:** Most folks are probably used to working with the 16.7 million colors that most computer monitors can display these days. Of those colors, however, only 216 of them display consistently on Windows, UNIX, and Macintosh computers. This reduced range of color is because of differences in operating systems, Web browsers, and color cards. Colors outside this range of 216 can dither when displayed on a system that can't really show them properly. *Dithering* is the computer's attempt to create the missing colors by using dots of two colors it can display, creating an optical illusion that the missing color is there. Dithering usually looks awful. (See Bonus Chapter 1 on the Web site associated with this book for more on dithering.)

  Use Web Safe RGB when you need colors that look their best on as many different computers and browsers as possible. (A corporate logo is a classic example.)

✔ **Hide Options, Invert,** and **Complement:** The remaining choices in the Color panel pop-up menu aren't color models at all.

Hide Options collapses the Color panel so that just the Spectrum, Black and White, and None options show.

The *Invert* command changes the selected color into its opposite, as if you had taken a color photograph of it and were looking at a negative.

To understand *Complement,* think back to art class and the color wheel: *Complementary colors* are the colors on opposite sides of the color wheel. (Orange, for example, is the complementary color to blue. Roughly, blue never looks bluer than when it's next to orange, and vice versa.) Put another way, choosing Complement chooses the one color that will contrast the most with the currently selected artwork. Figure 5-13 shows both inverse and complement colors of a single color.

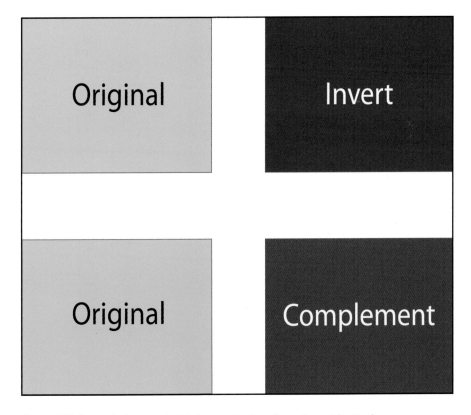

Figure 5-13: An original color with it's inverse (top) and complement (bottom).

Filling with Patterns and Textures

You can fill and stroke any path with a pattern. Patterns fill areas with repeating artwork.

Applying patterns to paths

To fill a path with a pattern, select the path, make sure the Fill box is active by clicking it in the Tools panel, and then click the pattern you want to use in the Swatches panel. The path fills with the pattern you selected. Figure 5-14 shows the same path filled with different patterns.

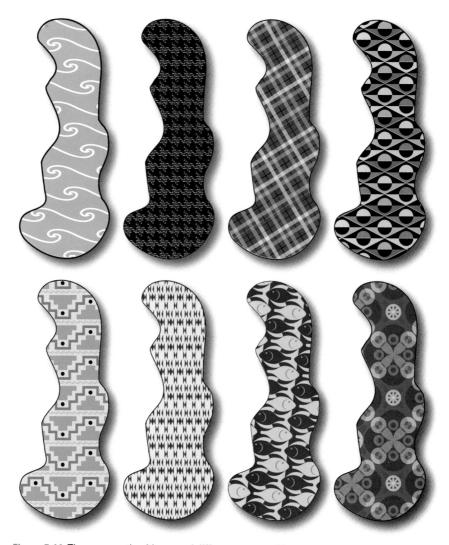

Figure 5-14: The same path with several different pattern fills.

You can apply a pattern to a stroke as well as to a fill. Applying a pattern is exactly like applying a solid color. (See the section, "The Swatches Panel," earlier in this chapter.) Click the object, click the Fill or Stroke box to put the pattern in the proper place, and then click the pattern swatch in the Swatches panel. When you apply a pattern to a stroke, you might need to make the stroke extra thick for the pattern to be visible. (See the section, "Making a bold stroke," earlier in this chapter.)

Making patterns

You can easily turn most path-based artwork into a pattern (which hotly pursues the steps required to create a pattern out of paths).

To create a pattern out of paths, just follow these steps:

1. **Create the artwork that you want to use for a pattern.**

   For this example, I use a US flag.

2. **Select the artwork by using any of the selection tools.**

3. **Drag the artwork from the Document window onto the Swatches panel and release the mouse button.**

   A new swatch appears in the Swatches panel containing a very tiny version of your artwork.

4. **To name the new swatch — a good idea if you want to identify it with relative ease later — double-click the swatch to open the Swatch Options dialog box.**

5. **Enter the name of the pattern into the Name field.**

6. **Click OK.**

   The custom pattern appears in the Swatches dialog box.

Figure 5-15: Creating a pattern from vector art of a flag.

7. **Apply your custom pattern to any path.**

   Check out how much I obviously love America in Figure 5-15.

Occasionally, you might want to space out your pattern artwork so that the repeated pieces of artwork are farther away from each other. You can easily trick Illustrator into doing this by drawing an invisible rectangle (a rectangle with a fill and stroke of None) over the artwork you're using as the basis for your pattern. The bigger the rectangle, the farther apart the repeated pieces are. Select the artwork and the rectangle before you make your pattern. Illustrator isn't quite smart enough to realize that the rectangle is invisible. The program sees only the paths that make the rectangle and repeats the artwork based on those edges.

Using the Gradient Fill

You can fill paths with *gradients,* which are colors that smoothly blend from one to another. Gradients can have any number of colors in them, with results that are nothing short of astonishing. Figure 5-16 shows three paths with gradient fills.

Figure 5-16: Path objects with gradient fills.

Filling a path with a gradient involves two steps: creating the gradient and then applying it to a path. However, you can do this in any order. Often, it's easier to create a gradient, apply it to a path, and then continue to tweak it by changing, adding, or removing colors or by modifying the position or angle of the gradient. You can see how the gradient looks on an object instead of just in a small box.

To fill a path with a gradient, select the path and then click a gradient in the Swatches panel. The object fills with a gradient that probably doesn't look a thing like what you want — but that's okay. By using the Gradient tool and the Gradient panel, you can tweak this gradient to your heart's content.

You can also load gradients from the Swatches panel. Illustrator comes with all sorts of Gradient swatch libraries with dozens of different swatches to get you started.

The Gradient tool

The Gradient tool (shown in the margin) doesn't actually create anything. Instead, it enables you to set a gradient's direction as well as its *duration —*

the distance across which the gradient makes its transition from the start color to the end color.

To use the Gradient tool, first use any selection tool to select an object that's filled with a gradient. Then click and drag across the gradient with the Gradient tool and release the mouse button when you get to the other side. The direction that you drag sets the direction of the blend. You see a bar showing the direction and angle of the gradient (and a circle if you're using a radial gradient). The place where you click gets 100 percent of the start color; the place where you release gets 100 percent of the end color. The gradient happens as a smooth blend between those two points (as you can see in Figure 5-17).

Figure 5-17: Left: The square shows a default gradient applied. Center: Clicking and dragging with the Gradient tool. Right: The result.

Modifying gradients

If you don't like the colors of your gradient, you don't have to settle for the gradients that come in the Swatches panel. You can either change, add, or remove colors; and/or change how the colors behave directly on the object with the Gradient tool or use the Gradient panel (by choosing Window⇨Gradient) to do the same actions. (See Figure 5-18.)

The Gradient panel looks simple compared with other panels, but don't be deceived. In spite of its humble appearance, this panel lets you create just about any gradient you could ever want. The Gradient panel works with the Color panel and the Swatches panel, so keep both those panels open whenever you edit a gradient.

Midpoint sliders

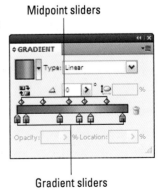

Gradient sliders

Figure 5-18: Control color from the Gradient panel.

The *gradient sliders* slide left and right. You use them to change how gradually (or not-so-gradually) your colors blend with each other. If you want the colors to blend without much nuance over a short distance, drag the sliders closer together. If you want the colors to blend more gradually across a longer distance, move the sliders farther apart.

Whenever you select a gradient slider, you can change its opacity in the Opacity field below the slider. In addition, you can specify the exact location of the slider in terms of left-to-right percentage in the Location field.

You can do most activities that the Gradient panel allows you to do directly on a selected object when the Gradient tool is selected. However, sometimes the angle or size of the object makes it difficult to use the tool for these purposes. As a rule, the smaller the object, the more you'll want to use the Gradient panel instead of editing the gradient directly on the object.

Gradient-mania: Color-tweaking made simple

When you change a gradient in the Gradient panel, selected objects that are filled with that gradient update to reflect that change. You can see what's going on with the gradient more easily if you make an object and fill it with the gradient before you start making changes in the panel.

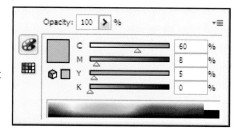

Figure 5-19: The mini Color panel that appears when you double-click a gradient slider.

To change gradient colors, here's the highly artistic approach (no smock needed):

1. **Double-click one of the gradient sliders beneath the gradient bar.**

   The color associated with the slider appears in a mini Color panel right next to the slider, as shown in Figure 5-19.

2. **Choose a different color in the mini Color panel.**

   The color updates in the Gradient panel automatically. Is that slick or what?

As an alternative, you can click any solid color in the Swatches panel and drag it to the Gradient slider in the Gradient panel. You can also press Option (Mac)/Alt (Windows) and simply click a solid color swatch in the Swatches panel. The gradient updates with the new color.

Adding colors to the gradient is a lot easier than going to the paint store. Just follow these steps:

1. **Click beneath the gradient bar where there isn't any gradient slider.**

   A new slider appears where you click.

2. **Change the color of the new slider in the Color panel, double click on it to access the mini color panel or press Option (Mac)/Alt (Windows) and then click a solid color in the Swatches panel.**

3. **(Optional) Adjust the position of your gradient sliders.**

To remove a color, click the gradient slider and drag it off the Gradient panel. To save the gradient, drag the gradient swatch from the Gradient panel (or from the Fill box in the Tools panel) to the Swatches panel. You can also simply click the New Swatch button (a dog-eared page icon) in the Swatches panel.

Between every pair of gradient sliders (on top of the gradient bar) is a mid-point slider. This sets the point at which the two colors blend at 50 percent of each color. You can also move this point by dragging it to the left or to the right. Figure 5-20 gives you a look at ways to change the gradient.

Radial: The secret gradient

If you click the gradient swatches in the Swatches panel, you might notice that some gradients look like spheres or sunbursts — radial gradients. No amount of clicking and dragging with the Gradient tool — and no amount of moving gradient sliders — can make a radial gradient from the default Linear style.

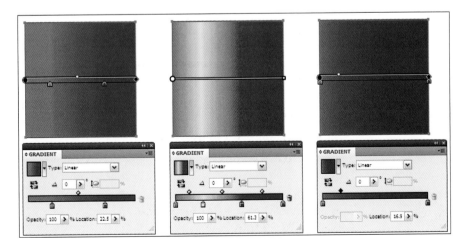

Figure 5-20: First, moving the sliders closer together. Second, adding new color sliders. Third, moving the gradient midpoint.

The trick is in a hidden option in the Gradient panel. Click the little triangle in the upper right of the Gradient panel. The Gradient panel pop-up menu, with only one item (Show Options), appears. Choose this option to make several more options appear in the panel. The one you want is the Type option, which reveals two choices: Linear and Radial. Choose Radial. The beginning color is the center color. When you click and drag, the spot where you click sets the center of the gradient. Figure 5-21 shows the same gradient from Figure 5-16 in radial gradient form.

Figure 5-21: Create a radial gradient.

6

Selecting and Editing Paths

In This Chapter

▶ Discovering different methods of selection

▶ Selecting objects, points, and groups

▶ Adding to and taking away from selections

▶ Using the Magic Wand tool

▶ Selecting without tools

▶ Understanding the Select menu

▶ Fine-tuning points

To change — *edit* — a path in Illustrator, you have to first select it. In fact, 99 percent of the time, you can't make any changes at all to a path unless it's selected. Some exceptions are when you change Document Color Mode (see Chapter 1) and when you use the Pen tool to continue on an existing path (see Chapter 7). Every other action, though, requires that you make a selection first.

As I talk about earlier, making a selection in Illustrator says, "From this moment forward, I want to change this part of the artwork and nothing else." You're targeting a point, a path, an object, or objects for change. And with Illustrator's wide variety of selection tools and commands, you can target everything from a single point to your entire document. Changes you make — size, rotation, fill or stroke colors, and so on — simultaneously affect everything that you select. (If the term path makes you visualize a narrow walkway through a forest instead of a line with little dots and squares on it, head back to Chapter 2 for a quick refresher.)

This chapter tells you what you can do with those paths, as in how to select them and how to make changes to them.

Selecting with the Illustrator Tools

Suppose you create a mondo-cool logo. With Illustrator, you can select

- The entire logo
- Any group of paths within the logo
- Any single path within the logo
- Any portion of any path or paths

All these possibilities might make selecting in Illustrator seem rather daunting. As if that weren't enough, Illustrator gives you five different selection tools: namely, Selection, Direct Selection, Group Selection, Lasso, and Magic Wand. (I also talk about these a bit in Chapter 3.) See Figure 6-1.

Figure 6-1: Illustrator has all sorts of selection tools.

Compared with Selection, the names of the other selection tools aren't quite as accurate in describing their functions, but hey — *Selection tool* was already taken. To keep the confusion to a minimum, I call the tools by their Adobe-given names. That way, you know what the cute label refers to when you pause the cursor over a tool in the Tools panel and see the name in the ToolTip.

The following sections describe these tools and what happens when you use them.

Two oddities of selecting in Illustrator

When selecting in Illustrator, here are a couple of oddities.

- **When you select just a point on a path,** the point is all that you've selected. It shows up solid, but the rest of the points on the path remain unselected and show up as hollow. Then things get weird. Even though only one point is selected, any change that you make to the fill or stroke affects the entire path. (For more information on fills and strokes, see Chapter 5.)

- **When you select a line segment,** Illustrator never shows you that the line segment is selected. If you click a segment, all the points on its path show as unselected (hollow). Nothing appears on-screen to indicate that only the segment is selected — but once again, changing the fill or stroke affects the entire path.

Natural selection

Of the five selection tools in Illustrator, the Selection tool is (more or less) the main selection tool. It simply selects whatever you click.

 You use the Selection tool to select objects or groups of objects. When you click a path, you select the entire path. If the path is part of a group, you automatically select that group as well. A *group* is two or more separate objects that are joined by choosing Object➪Group. You join objects into a group to get the advantage of selecting them all at once when you use the Selection tool to select them — and that saves all that tedious clicking. (The Object➪Group command is just one of the fiendishly clever ways you can organize things in Illustrator. Explore 'em all in Chapter 13.)

You can select onscreen items with the Selection tool in two ways:

- ✔ **Click the object that you want to select.** The object and any other object that's grouped with it are selected.

- ✔ **Click and drag with the Selection tool.** As you do, a dotted rectangle — a *marquee* — appears. Anything inside or touching the marquee is selected, enabling you to select more than one object or group at a time, as shown in Figure 6-2. You'll notice that a lot of blue points are highlighted that were originally outside the marquee that was drawn; that's because at least a tiny bit of the objects with those highlighted points were touched by the edge of the marquee, and therefore the entire object was selected.

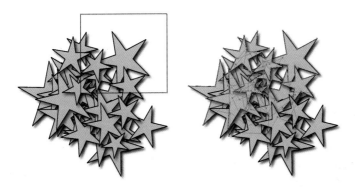

Figure 6-2: The Selection tool selects objects that are within (or touched by) the marquee.

 If you click another path when one path is already selected, the path that you click is selected, **and** the previously selected path is deselected. If you click an empty area, *everything* is deselected. If you press the Shift key when you click another path when one path is already selected, the new path is selected while the original one is still selected. In this way, the Shift key allows you to add to a selection (and if you Shift-click on a path that is already selected, you'll deselect just that path, letting you subtract from a selection as well). More details on adding and subtracting to selections below in the section "Selecting more or less of what you have."

Also, if you click inside a path that's filled with None, you can't select that path. To select a path that has no fill, click the path itself. Similarly, when you're in Outline view mode (a way of looking at your paths with all fill and stroke colors hidden, accessed by choosing View⇨Outline), you click your paths to select them. (See Chapter 5 for more info on fills and strokes.)

Direct Selection tool

The Selection tool selects entire paths or groups, while the Direct Selection tool selects exactly what you click on. Use the Direct Selection tool to select individual points, path segments, type objects, and placed images by clicking them one at a time. If you drag a marquee with the Direct Selection tool, everything that the marquee encloses gets selected — all placed images, type objects, and portions of paths. Figure 6-3 shows what's selected when you drag the Direct Selection marquee around several objects. (Note especially the star in the very center of the selected objects at the right of the figure: Some of its points are included in the selection; others aren't.) Since the Direct Selection tool allows points within objects to be selected, some points on some of the stars are selected (solid squares) while some are unselected, but visible (hollow squares).

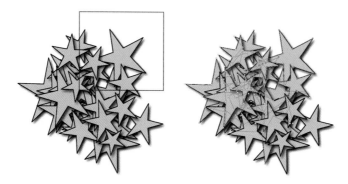

Figure 6-3: A selection in progress with the Direct Selection tool.

With the Direct Selection tool, if you select the interior of a path (if it's filled) rather than the edge or actual line of the path, you select the entire path rather than just the individual anchor point and path segments.

Group Selection tool

 Illustrator provides a special tool for selecting groups — Group Selection. (Go figure.) However, this tool selects groups a little differently. Whereas the plain ol' Selection tool selects everything that's grouped to the object that you select, the Group Selection tool selects only one subgroup at a time.

A *subgroup* is a group within a group. Remember Statistics 101? (Don't make that face. What if it froze like that?) Suppose you want to create a graphic of a pencil. You start with the easy part — the lead. Then you go on to create something harder: that conical bit of wood that flares out around the lead and eventually becomes the rest of the pencil. After you get those two pieces positioned together the way you like, you want to keep them that way — so you group them together. (That way, you have to click only one of them with the Selection tool, and they move together.) Next, you create the rest of the pencil separately. After you bring all the pieces together, you want to keep them that way — so you group the lead and the cone with the rest of the pencil. All three objects are now a group, and the lead and the cone are a subgroup of that group.

You can continue grouping things, having as many subgroups as you want. Illustrator remembers the order in which you group things from the first subgroup to the last big group. When you click multiple times with the Group Selection tool, the first click selects the pencil lead, the second selects both the lead and the wood, and the third click selects the lead, the wood, and the rest of the pencil.

The Group Selection tool selects only one subgroup at a time, such as an object within a group, a single group within multiple groups, or a set of groups within the artwork. To find out how the Group Selection tool works, follow these steps:

1. **Select the Group Selection tool from the Toolbox.**

2. **Click a path that's part of a group.**

   The path is selected entirely (all the points are solid; none are hollow), but the other objects in the group are not selected. (This result is an oddity of the tool. It first selects a single object, even though an object isn't really a group.)

3. **Click the same path again.**

   The next higher level of grouped objects is selected, as well as anything that's already been selected. Each time you click, you select the next higher level of grouping, until finally the all-encompassing group-of-all-groups is selected.

If you continue this crazed clicking, you wind up with groups of groups. For example, if you make several on-screen drawings of pencils, you can group them so that you can move them all at once, draw a pencil box, and then group the pencils with the box. The Group Selection tool lets you select "up" from a single object to the group that the object belongs to, and so on. Figure 6-4 applies this principle to the objects that form a pencil when grouped together.

Figure 6-4: The Group Selection tool selects first the path, then the group that the path is in, and then the group that the first group is in.

Selecting more or less of what you have

Suppose you want to select a path on the left side of your document, and you also want to select a placed image on the right side of your document, but lots of paths are in between. You can't drag a marquee because you get all those unwanted paths in the middle. So you select the path on the left and then click the object on the right — and the path on the left becomes deselected. Drat!

Use the Shift key to select more than one item at a time. If you hold down the Shift key and click a path with the Selection tool, you add that path to whatever is selected. If two paths are selected, pressing the Shift key and clicking another path results in all three paths being selected. You can also use the Shift key in conjunction with a selection marquee. The process is *Shift-clicking,* and you can also use it to select fewer paths. For example, if you Shift-click one of the three selected paths shown in Figure 6-5, you deselect that path, leaving only two selected paths.

Shift-clicking also works with the Direct Selection tool except that this action adds or subtracts single points instead of complete paths — unless you click the interior of a filled path, in which case you add or subtract complete paths.

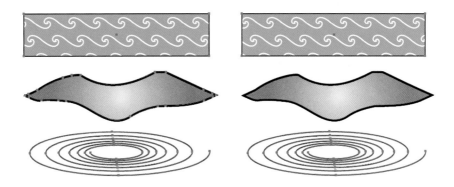

Figure 6-5: (Left) Three selected paths. (Right) Shift-clicking the middle path leaves only two paths selected.

Freeform selections: Lasso tool

The Lasso tool acts similarly to dragging a selection marquee except that this type of marquee can be any shape (not just rectangular). To use the tool, click and drag around the area that you want to select. When you release the mouse button, all points in that area are selected.

Pressing the Shift key with the Lasso tool allows you to add selections to anything that's already selected . . . but you probably guessed that already. What you haven't guessed (unless you're a bona fide psychic) is that you use Option (Mac)/Alt (Windows) to *subtract* from a selection. If you accidentally select something, you don't need to reselect. Just press Option (Mac)/Alt (Windows) and drag around the points you don't want selected.

Magic Wand tool

Use the Magic Wand tool to make selections based on similarities in various object attributes — exactly the same or based on a range of settings.

To use the tool, click the object, which can be either an open or a closed path (for example, a square or a line). Illustrator then goes out and selects all objects similar to the object you clicked. How similar do the objects have to be? Excellent question! Read on to get the scoop.

Choose Window⇨Magic Wand or simply double-click the Magic Wand tool to bring up the Magic Wand panel, as shown in Figure 6-6. Here you find settings for Fill Color, Stroke Color, Stroke Weight, Opacity, and Blending Mode attributes. Checking one or more of these attributes selects objects based on that particular attribute or attributes. The Tolerance setting establishes the range within which the attribute must fall to be selected.

For example, if you select a stroke weight with a Tolerance setting of 2 points (pt) and click an object with a stroke weight of 5 pt, all objects with a stroke weight between 3 and 7 pt will be selected (5 pt – 2pt, and 5pt + 2 pt). Similarly, if you select the Opacity option and set the Tolerance setting to 10 percent, all objects with an opacity between 40 percent and 60 percent are selected when you click an object with an opacity of 50 percent.

The Tolerance settings for Fill Color and Stroke Color range from 0–255, which equates to the number of brightness levels. Rather than go into the techno-geek definition of brightness levels, a lower Tolerance setting selects only colors that are very similar to the object you click, whereas a higher Tolerance setting selects a wider range of colors. The only attribute that must be exactly the same is Blending Mode. (For more on blending modes, see Chapter 10.)

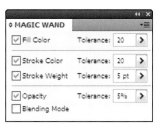

Figure 6-6: The Magic Wand panel offers Tolerance settings for object attributes.

Selecting without Tools: The Select Menu

Sometimes selecting objects in Illustrator without using tools is easier or more convenient than selecting with tools. Because selecting is so important, Illustrator provides a menu entirely devoted to selection commands.

Select menu options

Here are the options you can find on the Select menu, as shown in Figure 6-7:

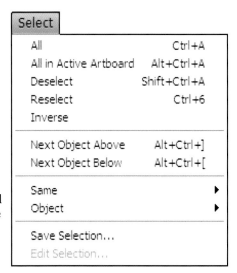

- ✓ **All:** By far, the most common selection method in Illustrator is the keyboard command ⌘+A (Mac)/Ctrl+A (Windows), which is the stalwart command for Select All. You can also choose Select➪All, but the keyboard command is so useful that you'll probably memorize it in no time at all.

Figure 6-7: The Select menu.

✔ **All in Active Artboard:** This command selects all the objects within whichever artboard is currently active. Objects that straddle multiple artboards will also be selected if a portion of that object is within the active artboard.

✔ **Deselect:** The opposite of All is the Deselect command, which deselects anything selected in the document (but you knew that). You don't have to select everything to use the command. If you have just one thing selected from 100 objects, Deselect deselects it. The keyboard command is easy to remember: ⌘+Shift+A (Mac)/Ctrl+Shift+A (Windows).

✔ **Reselect:** Using the Reselect command reselects whatever was last selected via the Selection menu. The keyboard command is ⌘+6 (Mac)/Crtl+6 (Windows).

✔ **Inverse:** Using the Inverse command selects the opposite of what's selected. In other words, everything that's selected becomes unselected, and everything else becomes selected. For example, if you select one of four squares, using the Inverse command selects the remaining three squares and deselects the original square. *Hint:* Inverse works only with entire paths. (The same goes for Reselect.) Using the same example, if you have only a single anchor point selected on the first square, using the Inverse command still selects the other three squares and ignores the unselected three anchor points on the first square.

✔ **Next Object Above** and **Next Object Below:** Using these commands selects objects based on their *stacking order*— how objects are placed in front of other objects. For example, say you draw a square, a circle, and then a polygon. If you then select the square and choose Select⇨Next Object Below, Illustrator selects the circle. If you choose the command again, Illustrator selects the polygon, and so forth.

Same and **Object:** Using the Select⇨Object⇨Same commands selects everything that is the same as the currently selected object. Using the Select⇨Object⇨All on Same Layers command selects everything that resides on the active layer (the one that's highlighted in the Layers panel).

The Same and Object commands are described in more detail below.

✔ **Save Selection:** Using the Save Selection command allows you to save selections. Select an object (or objects) and then choose Select⇨Save Selection. In the Save Selection dialog box, name the selection and then click OK. The saved selection now appears at the bottom of the Select menu, just begging to be chosen. You can delete the saved selection or modify its name by choosing Select⇨Edit Selection and making the necessary changes in the Edit Selection dialog box.

Specialized selection functions for important occasions

The Select menu contains a lot of other selection functions besides those mentioned in the preceding section. Located under the Same and Object submenus, these functions are designed to select objects that are similar in some way (such as style or fill color) to the object(s) already selected. Figure 6-8 shows what would happen if you went for the Same submenu.

Figure 6-8: The Same sub-menu provides a whole slew of selection goodies.

These commands can be vastly helpful in streamlining the editing process. For instance, if your client loves everything about the image except for that certain shade of blue, you can select one object that has that blue color in it, and then choose Select⇨Same⇨Stroke Color or Fill Color. With everything in that color selected, you can edit them all at once! If you're having trouble printing lines of a certain stroke weight, choose Select⇨Same⇨Stroke Weight and increase the stroke weight of all the lines. (See Chapter 5 for more information on fills and strokes.) Other commands select items that have a history of problems printing on certain printers, such as stray points, brushstrokes, and masks. Selecting such items lets you modify them before printing. (See Chapter 15 for more about printing.)

The four options that fall under the Object submenu are a bit less obvious:

- **Brush Strokes:** Selects all paths in the document that have brush strokes assigned to them.

- **Clipping Masks:** Selects paths used as masks in the document.

- **Direction Handles:** Selects the direction handles of the Bézier curves of selected objects. (For more on direction handles, see the next section on editing and adjusting points.)

- **Stray Points:** Selects paths in your document that contain only a single point.

Editing and Adjusting Points

After you go through the trouble of selecting specific points, what do you do with them? Well, you can move them and change the kinds of points they are. You can also adjust their handles to change the shape of a curve.

A relocation bonus for points

You can move any selected point to any location. Because points (and not entire paths) are what you're moving, use the Direct Selection tool. Click any point with the Direct Selection tool and then drag the point to move it. You can do this in one step (click and drag at once) or in two separate steps (click and release and then drag the point). Figure 6-9 shows a path with a point in its original location after it was moved with the Direct Selection tool.

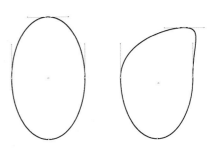

Figure 6-9: (Left) Original path. (Right) Path after you move the selected point with Direct Selection.

To move points just a tiny little bit at a time — yet with precision — use the arrow keys to nudge selected points in the direction of the arrow. One keystroke moves the point by an exact, smidgen-sized unit of measurement ($^1/_{72}$ of an inch, or .3528 millimeters) — a unit of measure known in the design and publishing trades as a *point*.

Fine-tuning curves with direction points

If a point has *direction points* (those little gearshift-like line segments) sticking out of it, you can use the Direct Selection tool to adjust the direction points, which adjusts the curves that shoot out from the points where the direction points connect to the curves.

Incidentally, the line that joins the direction point to the curve is called the *direction line.* Don't worry: Only you can see the direction lines. They don't print or show up in the graphic when it's on the Web. Their only purpose is to show which anchor point is currently under the control of the direction point. The combination of the direction line and direction point is also commonly referred to as *direction handles* or just plain *handles.*

You probably noticed already that sometimes you see those gearshift-like direction lines and direction points sticking out of points and sometimes you don't. When you click a point or a segment with the Direct Selection tool, you see the handles associated with that point or segment. However, if you Shift+click additional points, you lose those handles. Figure 6-10 shows what

Figure 6-10: A selected curve reveals its direction points and direction lines.

happens when you use the Direct Selection tool to click (or enclose in a mar-quee) a variety of different areas.

When you can see the handles that you want to move, click and drag them. Note that missing a handle is very easy if you aren't really careful. (And making crude remarks when you do miss them is still considered bad form, even if no one else is around.) Figure 6-11 shows the path from Figure 6-10 with the direction points moved to different positions.

You can change the size of those handles by choosing Edit⇨Preferences⇨Selection & Anchor Display. Just click on the appropriate picture showing the different handle and anchor point sizes, click OK, and you'll have an easier (or harder if that's your thing) time of clicking those anchor points.

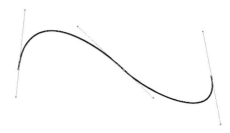

Figure 6-11: The curve from Figure 6-10 after the direction points are moved.

Converting anchor points

Illustrator has four types of anchor points: corner points; smooth points; and two types of direction-changing points. Every path has at least one of these types, and in many situations, you'll find that you need to change one type of anchor point into another, instead of going through the trouble of redrawing a path.

- ✔ *Straight-corner anchor points* are in the corners of squares or triangles. Two path segments join in a corner point when neither of the connect-ing ends has a direction point associated with it.

- ✔ *Smooth anchor points* are used when two path segments continue smoothly, as in a circle or in a curving path. Both path segments have direction points linked so that when you move one point, the other point moves in an equal and opposite direction, preserving the smooth curve.

- ✔ A *curved-corner anchor point* has two direction points that move in differ-ent directions, enabling you to impose abrupt changes in direction.

- ✔ A *combination-corner anchor point* has one direction point, allowing a straight line to join a curved line at an abrupt angle. (For more on anchor point types, see Chapter 7.)

Use the Illustrator Convert Anchor Point tool (which looks like an acute angle, and is located in the same slot as the Pen tool) to change a point from one type into another. (For more about the types of anchor points and their usual behaviors, see Chapters 2 and 7.) To use the Convert Anchor Point tool, put it on a point and click. What you do next determines the resulting point type:

✔ **To get a straight-corner anchor point:** Click an anchor point and release to change it into a straight corner point with no direction points.

This is a *quick-retract* method of point conversion.

✔ **To get a smooth anchor point:** Click an anchor point and drag it to change it into a smooth point with two linked direction points.

✔ **To get a curved-corner anchor point:** Click a direction point and drag. It moves independently of the opposite direction point.

✔ **To create a combination-corner anchor point from a smooth point or a curved-corner anchor point:** Click one of the direction points and drag it into the anchor point (leaving one direction point for the curved side of the point).

You can also quickly toggle back and forth between corner and smooth points by clicking the appropriate button in the upper left of the Control panel docked at the top of the work area. Click the corner-looking one to change the selected point(s) to a corner point, and click the curved-looking one to change the selected points(s) to a smooth point.

Adding and subtracting points (path math)

Illustrator has two tools that are used specifically for adding points to a path or for removing them. The Add Anchor Point tool adds points, and the Delete Anchor Point tool removes points. Both tools are located in the same slot as the Pen tool.

When you add an anchor point (or even several anchor points) with the Add Anchor Point tool, the path doesn't change shape (as shown in Figure 6-12), but you can then move the point or points with the Direct Selection tool or convert them to other types of points by using the Convert Anchor Point tool.

When you remove a point with the Delete Anchor Point tool, the path can change shape — slightly or dramatically, depending on the shape. Figure 6-13 shows what happens in two different circumstances.

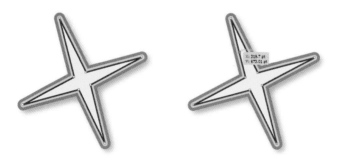

Figure 6-12: (Left) Original path. (Right) Unchanged shape with new anchor points added to three of the star's arms.

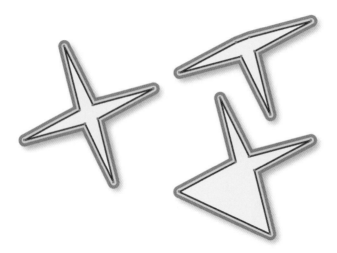

Figure 6-13: (Left) Original path. (Right) Removing two anchor points to create two different shapes.

Okay, have a squint at Figure 6-13 for a moment. (Ow, that's gotta hurt. Not that hard.) You can probably tell immediately which anchor points were zapped with the Delete Anchor Point tool to change the image on the left into the upper- and lower-right images. In each case, only one point was removed. Powerful creatures, those anchor points.

Wielding the Mighty Pen Tool

*B*ack in medieval times (circa 1982), straight and smooth-curved lines were drawn with elegant handheld implements, such as a Rapidograph pen (an unwieldy, blotch-making tool), a ruler, and a French Curve. If you never had to use these torturous instruments, consider yourself lucky. With a Rapidograph pen, you got bumpy globs of ink and huge splotches that goosh onto the page each time you paused or changed direction.

Today, if you need a straight line or a curved one — or even if you want the appearance of bumpy globs of ink — use the Illustrator Pen tool. This tool is a bit intimidating at first, but after you grasp a few concepts, you'll be drawing floor plans, customizing logos, and feeling really sorry for people who don't have Illustrator.

Unlike its handheld, inky counterpart, the Pen tool is not intuitive. You can't just pick it up and doodle; its functionality is far from obvious. This tool is unlike any drawing instrument in the world. But locked within the Pen tool are secrets and powers beyond those of mere physical ink. The Pen tool is a metaphysical doorway to the heavens of artistic exaltation; after you master the path of the Pen tool, all the riches of Illustrator can be yours. (You might even be unfazed by such hokey metaphors.)

Performing with the Pen, the Path, and the Anchor Points

No, this section isn't a retro look at obscure rock bands; it's about telling Illustrator where to go — that is, by creating the paths Illustrator relies on to create shapes and objects. *Paths* are instructions that tell your computer how to arrange straight- and curved-line segments onscreen. Each path is made up of *anchor points* (dots that appear on-screen). Between every two anchor points is the portion of the path called a *line segment.*

The Pen tool is probably as close as you ever get to calling up paths with the PostScript language — unless you're an Adobe programming geek (in which case, the thought that you might need this book is frightening). For sanity's sake, I assume otherwise and get right to the point. Make that *points.* Understanding the anchor points that make up paths is critical to using the Pen tool. Anchor points have the following traits:

- **At least two anchor points are required for every path.** "One point maketh not a path," saith the sage.

- **Any number of anchor points can appear on a path.** You can have dozens, even hundreds, as long as that number is *not* one or zero. "Zero points make not a path, either, O wiseacre," grouseth the sage.

- **If an anchor point has a direction point (a blue box you can grab and move with the mouse), the line segment extending from the anchor point is curved.**

- **If an anchor point has no direction point, the line segment extending from the anchor point is straight.**

- **You can use the Pen tool to create four types of anchor points** (smooth, straight-corner, curved-corner, and combination-corner) to tell the computer how to get from one line segment to another. Care for a closer look? Coming right up.

Smooth anchor points

Smooth anchor points create a smoothly curved transition from one line segment to another. When you want a line that reminds you of the letter *S* (or some S-words, such as *sinuous* and *snaky*), use smooth anchor points. Figure 7-1 shows two direction points creating a smooth anchor point on a path. The curve bends to follow the two direction points.

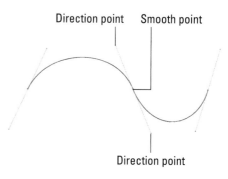

Figure 7-1: Smooth anchor points keep this path curving smoothly.

If you want to create circles or free-form shapes — such as puddles, or shapes like those nonslip flower stickers for your bathtub — smooth anchor points are the way to go. To create a smooth anchor point, click and drag with the mouse while using the Pen tool. While you drag, direction points (connected to the anchor point by direction lines) appear on either side of the anchor point (one at the tip of the Pen, and the other on the opposite side of the anchor point). Think of those wacky direction points as magnets pulling the line segment toward them. The line segment bends to follow the direction point — just that easy, just that simple. (So far.)

Straight-corner anchor points

Straight-corner anchor points function as their name suggests and have both the following characteristics:

- **One or two straight lines sticking out of them:** In Figure 7-2, for example, all the anchor points are Straight-corner anchor points.

- **No direction points sticking out of them.** (Remember, direction points make curves.)

Think of this type of anchor point as the corner of an angle that you draw with a pencil and a protractor. To create straight-corner anchor points with the Pen tool, click and release; *do not drag.* Promptly release the mouse button the second you hear it click.

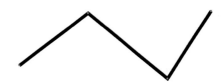

Figure 7-2: Use straight-corner anchor points when you need straight paths.

Use straight-corner anchor points to draw objects with hard angles — think rectangles and triangles (note the whole "angle" theme here) — anything that consists entirely of straight lines and *no* curves. Snakes, clouds, and country roads are entirely out of the question.

Curved-corner anchor points

Think of the *curved-corner* anchor point (also referred to as a *cusp point*) as the *m-curve* anchor point, or the point where the two bumps on a lowercase *m* are joined. If you look at this nice lowercase *m* through a magnifying glass, you can see a corner, between the two bumps, with curves coming out from it. The curved-corner anchor point might also remind you of a double fishhook turned upside down. You need these points to create not just lowercase *m*'s, but also hearts (the Valentine variety, as shown in Figure 7-3).

Consider the possibilities — clovers, moons (old-fashioned crescents-with-little-noses), and other shapes you might see in a cereal bowl. (Okay, not the blue diamonds — those you draw with straight-corner anchor points.) Beware, though, that curved-corner anchor points are a little weird. To create one, you have to modify an existing anchor point by following these steps:

1. **Create a smooth anchor point while you're creating a path.**

   This works best after you draw at least one line segment.

2. **Press Option (Mac)/ Alt (Windows) and then click and drag the smooth anchor point.**

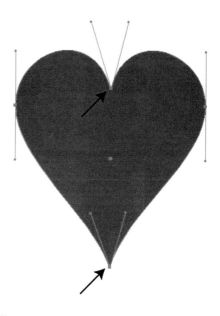

Figure 7-3: This heart shows two curved-corner anchor points.

A direction point appears — totally independent of the anchor point — on the oppo-site side of the point. This new handle controls where the double-fishhook corner goes. You can drag the new handle nearer to the first direction point (the one for the original smooth anchor point) — or anywhere else — without affecting that first direction point.

Combination-corner anchor points

If you want to use the Pen tool to draw rounded-corner rectangles — such as what you see on classic TV screens, archways, cylinders, and your friendly neighborhood iPhone screen — you need *combination-corner* anchor points. The combination blends smooth and straight-corner anchor points. You can identify a combination-corner anchor point by what you find sticking out of it: two line segments but only one direction point. This handle curves one of the line segments while leaving the other segment straight. If you keep in mind that the handle is controlling the *curved* segment, not the *straight* seg-ment, you'll have less trouble getting these points to work for you.

Like with curved-corner anchor points (mutant versions of their straight-corner cousins), you can't just say, "I want one of *those*" and *poof!* have one appear on-screen. To create the exotic combination-corner anchor point, modify an existing smooth or straight-corner anchor point. Which type you modify depends on where you want the curve to go:

- ✐ **If you want the curve *before* the anchor point** (the existing line segment is curved), you modify a smooth anchor point.

- ✐ **If you want the curve *after* the anchor point** (the existing line segment is straight), you modify a straight-corner anchor point.

Figure 7-4 shows a combination-corner anchor point in the middle of a path.

Figure 7-4: A combination-corner anchor point.

Starting with a smooth path

To create a combination-corner anchor point from a smooth one (so that the curve precedes the anchor point), follow these steps, shown in Figure 7-5:

1. **Click and drag the Pen tool.**

   Start in the upper-left quarter of a blank Illustrator document. When you're there, click and drag up and to the right for your first drag.

2. **Click and drag the Pen tool at another location to create a curved line.**

   Start your second drag at a place roughly parallel to your original starting point and about an inch to the right, dragging down and to the right.

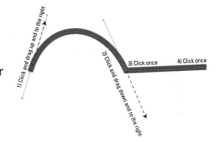

Figure 7-5: Steps for creating the path shown in Figure 7-4 when starting with a smooth path.

   To see what you're doing, you have to draw at least one line segment before you change the anchor point. That's the rule!

   When you complete Step 2, the most recent line segment ends in a smooth anchor point.

3. **Click (don't drag!) the smooth anchor point that appeared after you clicked and dragged in Step 2.**

   The direction point (handle) that extended out from the anchor point disappears.

4. **Move the mouse pointer to a place about an inch to the right of the most recent anchor point and click.**

   A straight path segment (straight because it's free from the influence of the direction point) appears. After you click, the two direction points (handles) disappear from the curved line that you drew in Step 2. The anchor point from which you drew your new straight segment is a combination-corner anchor point.

Starting with a straight path

To create a combination-corner anchor point from a straight-corner anchor point (so the curve comes after the anchor point), follow these steps, as shown in Figure 7-6:

1. **Using the Pen tool, click once and (without dragging) click again in a nearby location in the document.**

   To get a path that resembles the straight path on the right side of Figure 7-4, start in the upper-right quarter of a blank Illustrator document, and click once.

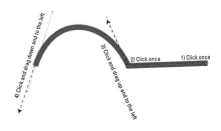

Figure 7-6: Steps for starting with a straight path to draw the path from Figure 7-4.

2. **Move the mouse pointer to the left and click (again without dragging).**

   A straight path segment appears. You need this line segment so that you can see the difference in the path as you change the straight-corner anchor point to a combination-corner anchor point.

3. **Click the straight-corner anchor point you just created; hold down the mouse button and drag.**

   To get an image that resembles the one in Figure 7-4, drag up and slightly to the left.

   A new, single direction point (handle) extends from the anchor point.

4. **Click in another location and drag away from the anchor point.**

   Click a spot to the left of the previous anchor point, and then drag down and slightly to the left.

   A curved path segment appears. The anchor point between the straight and curved line segments is now a combination-corner anchor point.

Creating Straight Lines with the Pen Tool

Using logic as valid as any followed by Holmes and Watson (not to mention Spock), you can deduce that you use straight-corner anchor points to draw straight lines with the Pen tool. Elementary. . . .

Harrumph. Elementary or not, you should jolly well see this marvel in action. To draw a triangle with the Pen tool using straight-corner anchor points (see Figure 7-7), just follow these steps:

1. **With the Pen tool, click (do not drag) in the Document window.**

   An anchor point appears after you release the mouse button. (Cute, isn't it? But lonely; it needs friends.)

2. **Click (don't drag) somewhere below and a little to the right of the first anchor point.**

   After you release the mouse button, a line appears between the first and second anchor points. They're joined, open, and ready to rock. You created a fine-looking path.

Figure 7-7: Draw a triangle with the Pen tool.

3. **Click (don't drag!) somewhere a bit to the left of the second anchor point.**

   A stunning-looking angle appears. Maybe it's a skateboard ramp. Maybe it's a less-than sign flopped over, worn out from all those equations.

4. **Put your cursor on the first anchor point and click that puppy.**

   You created a triangle! Congratulations! Euclid would be proud.

Well, okay, you've heard this tune before, but once more with feeling: *Do not drag* if you want straight lines. If you drag, you're going to get curves. In fact, *not* dragging to get straight lines is probably harder than dragging to get curves. (If you want to take a break and go drag something, be my guest; you've earned it.)

You can create right angles and 45° angles with the Pen tool by holding down the Shift key when you click each point with the Pen tool. If you're close to 45° away from the last click, you'll get a 45° angle. If you're closer to 90° from the last click, you'll get a 90° angle.

Open and Closed Paths

Paths in Illustrator are open or closed — one or the other, with nothing in between. Open and closed paths differ in the following ways:

- **Open:** An *open path* has endpoints. It starts in one place and ends in another place — clearly a line segment, and not a polygon.

- **Closed:** A *closed path* has no starting point and no endpoint. Like that psychotic bunny in the battery commercial, it just keeps going and going in the same place — clearly the boundary of a solid shape. (Think of complete circles, Möbius strips, and so forth.)

Creating artwork with the Pen tool is much easier if you set your fill color to None, regardless of the final color you're going to fill your artwork with. (To set the fill color to None, click the Fill square in either the Tools panel or the Color panel and then click the box with a red slash in it.) When you use the Pen tool with a fill color selected, Illustrator treats every line you make as though it were a completed object by drawing a temporary, invisible line straight from the first anchor point in the path to the last anchor point, and then fills the enclosed area with the selected fill color. This is confusing at best because it hides parts of the path that you are creating and creates an object that appears to change shape completely with every click of the mouse. To avoid this mess, set your fill color to None while you create your path and change the fill color when the path is complete.

Creating Super-Precise Curves with the Pen Tool

The Illustrator Pen tool is a model of precision and accuracy. With it, you can draw virtually anything (or draw anything virtually). That is, of course, after you master drawing curves.

The Pen isn't designed to be maddening (as far as I know), but using it to draw successful curves *does* seem to require a psychological breakthrough. Illustrator users who struggle to figure out the Pen tool by themselves, without the handy guide you hold in your hands, might slog through months (or even years) of frustration before the breakthrough occurs. They happen upon shapes and curves that work for them — and then they finally "get it."

Therefore, I vow to spare you the pain of all that trial and error. The following sections begin this noble quest, in which you find the knight. . . .

Taming the draggin'

(Sorry about the bad pun.) Where do you want your curve to go? Just drag in that direction. I know, I know, I told you *not* to drag. But in that situation, you were making straight lines. What's even less helpful, dragging is perhaps the most anti-intuitive action imaginable for creating curves. Regardless, I charge into the fray.

If you click and drag with the intent to create a curve, you get what looks like a straight line, as shown in Figure 7-8. (Weird, isn't it?) Oddly enough, the "line" you get is twice as long as the distance you drag, extending in two directions from the spot where you initially click. After you release the mouse button, this "line" is *still* a straight line and still no curve in sight.

At this stage, what do you suppose is the most natural thing in the world to do? Sure — it's to drag in another direction (typically at a 90° angle) from where you last released the mouse. And what are the most natural results? An ugly, curvy bump; a new "straight" line extending in both directions from the second anchor point; and a sudden yearning to direct a few choice expletives at Illustrator.

Figure 7-8: When creating a curve, drag out a straight line; the arrow shows the direction of the drag.

The problem is the second anchor point. Instead of clicking and dragging at a spot near where you first released the mouse button (a *big* no-no), you always click and drag (you don't *have* to drag, but I get to that later) *away* from where you released the mouse button which will get you a nice smooth curve like the one shown in Figure 7-9. You understood correctly — *away*. Weird, isn't it?

Figure 7-9: A nice smooth flowing curve, generated by the Pen tool.

To create a lovely, flowing curve for your own purposes, just follow these steps:

1. **Click and drag with the Pen tool.**

   A line extends from the anchor point where you clicked. That's okay; it's supposed to happen that way.

The line you see is actually a set of two direction points (connected to the curve by direction lines), cleverly disguised as lines with little control-handle boxes at each end. Whether you call them direction points or control handles, lines, or boxes, they don't print out. They're just tools for controlling the direction of the line segment that you're drawing.

2. **Without clicking, place your cursor *away* from both the anchor point *and* the direction points. Then click and drag in the direction *opposite* the direction you dragged to create the first anchor point.**

   At this stage, the best approach is to place that second click perpendicular to the direction lines. Note that as you drag, you can actually see the curve between the two anchor points take shape and change. If you drag the same distance that you dragged for the first anchor point, you create an even-looking curve.

3. **Finally, place your cursor away from the second point, still moving away from the first anchor point, and click and drag back in the same direction you dragged for the first anchor point.**

   After you release the mouse button, you see an *S* shape (or a backward S, depending on which way you first dragged). Rejoice! If you don't see the S or reverse-S shape, breathe deeply, count to 10, and try again, exercising superhuman patience and care. Think Clark Kent.

Remember that whole song and dance about pressing the Shift key so that new anchor points appear angled at 45° relative to the last anchor point? Well, you can also use the Shift key to *constrain* the angle of control-handle lines to 45°, if you prefer. This action lets you make much more accurate curves than by drawing freestyle. Just don't press and hold the Shift key until *after* you begin dragging with the Pen tool. If you press the Shift key before you drag — and release the key while you're dragging — you get the 45° anchor point. If you continue to hold down the Shift key, you get the whole shebang: 45° control-handle lines as well as the anchor point.

Following the one-third rule

The optimal distance to drag a direction point from an anchor point is about one-third the distance you expect that line segment to be. So, for instance, if you plan to draw a curve that's about three inches long, drag the direction point out about one inch from the anchor point.

The one-third rule is perfect for creating the most natural, organic-looking curves possible. Breaking the rule can have the following dismal results:

- **If you drag too little,** you get curves that are too shallow around the middle of the line segment and too sharp at the anchor points.

- **If you drag too much,** you get curves that are quite sharp (like Dead Man's Curve) around the middle of the line segment and too straight around the anchor points (like that curve on the right in Figure 7-10).

Fortunately, on the left, Figure 7-10 shows a "perfect" curve created with the proper use of direction point lines set to one-third the length of the path. Because you can use the Direct Selection tool (the hollow arrow) to adjust the position of the direction points after they're drawn, try to follow the one-third rule whenever possible. Doing so might keep you out of trouble (and your vocabulary fit for sensitive listeners).

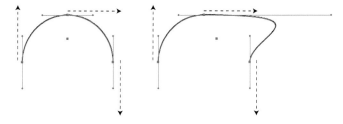

Figure 7-10: (Left) Anchor points with direction point lines one-third the distance along the path. (Right) Dragging too much.

Following rules for the other two-thirds

The one-third rule is the most important rule when you're using the Pen tool to draw curves. Of course, you still have to deal with the *other* two-thirds of the line segment; that's where a few humble rules can serve you well. Even if you don't plan to follow them right away — because you're still at that awkward, rebellious age — you at least want to be familiar with these rules:

✓ **Drag in the direction of the path.** Dragging back toward the line segment you just drew results in hard-to-control curves and awkward-appearing line segments between the previous anchor point and the anchor point you're working with. If you need to go back toward the line segment, place an anchor point closer to the previous anchor point you created. Figure 7-11 shows what happens to a path when you drag the wrong way . . . back towards the last point.

Figure 7-11: The 2nd point (on the right) was created by dragging to the left, resulting in this odd path.

✐ **Focus on the upcoming segment as well as the current one.** You might notice that the line segment between the prior anchor point and the current anchor point can distract you because it changes while you drag. If you concentrate only on this line segment, the direction point you're dragging out for the *next* line segment probably won't be the right length or angle. You must master the past, present, and future when you use the Pen tool. (Aside from that, it isn't hard at all.)

✐ **Don't overcompensate for a misdrawn curve.** If you mess up on that last outgoing direction point, don't try to "fix" the line segment with the anchor point you're currently dragging. Instead, focus on the *next* segment; try to ignore the goof-up for now. You can always use the Direct Selection tool to fix the poor thing *after* you finish the path. Chapter 6 has the lowdown on how you can adjust your path after you draw it.

✐ **Use different lengths for each direction point, as necessary.** This rule is the exception to the previous two rules. (You knew there had to be an exception.) If you click and drag and get a segment just right — only to realize that the next segment requires a longer or shorter control-handle line but the same angle — *release the mouse button when the segment is just right.*

Then click the same anchor point again and drag in the same direction as you previously dragged. Note that as you change the angle of the direction point on the "other" side (where the previous segment is), you aren't changing the length of that direction point line. And you can match the angle pretty easily because you can see both "before" and "after" versions of the previous line segment.

✐ **Place anchor points at curve transitions.** A *curve transition* is a place where the curve changes. Maybe it changes direction (going from clockwise to counterclockwise or vice versa). Maybe the curve gets smaller or larger. Figure 7-12 shows a nice curvy path with anchor points placed properly at the transitions.

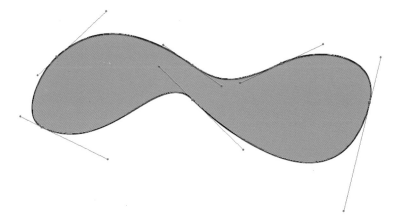

Figure 7-12: This path has points placed at the "correct" locations for the best possible curve.

✔ **Be environmentally conscious in your anchor point usage.** Don't place anchor points where they're not needed. This rule goes for all types of anchor points. The fewer you have makes editing sections of the path easier (keeping in mind the previous rule, of course). Fewer anchor points also allow for quicker and trouble-free printing.

Holding down the ⌘ key (Ctrl for Windows) changes the selected tool into whatever selection tool you used last. This is very handy when you're drawing with the Pen tool because it enables you to move points while keeping the Pen tool selected. Click the Direct Selection tool *before* you choose the Pen tool. If you click, start to drag, and then realize that you clicked in a spot that just isn't going to work, just press ⌘/Ctrl. This temporarily changes the Pen tool into the Direct Selection tool. Move your anchor point to a new location. Release ⌘/Ctrl, and your anchor point moves to the new location, just like that, and your cursor changes back to the Pen tool automatically!

Drawing the tricky anchor points with the Pen tool

A bit of practice with curves and smooth anchor points might get you used to smooth transitions from one line segment to another. Those anchor points are fairly easy to create. Just click and drag a new point, and *whammo!* You have a smooth anchor point. Both the curved-corner anchor point and the combination-corner anchor point are a little trickier, though: They always require two steps. Still, they can't scare a veteran of the draggin' wars. Not a bit.

Curved-corner anchor points revisited

Because curved-corner anchor points have two curves sticking out of them (one on each side), they need two direction points (one for each curve). But because these points are anchoring independent curves, you have to make those direction points independent of each other. Here's the move: While you're dragging out a smooth anchor point, you can quickly change it into a curved-corner anchor point by pressing and releasing the Option key (Alt for Windows). Doing so "breaks" the control-handle lines into independent lines.

Be sure to make your original line segment the proper length and angle before you press Option/Alt. After you press the key, the only way to edit the line is to stop drawing and modify it with the Direct Selection tool. See Chapter 6 for all sorts of great tips on how to get the most out of point adjustment by using the Direct Selection tool.

Combination-corner anchor points revisited

Using a similarly fancy move, you can create combination-corner points from smooth or straight-corner anchor points — while you're drawing. Here's how:

✔ **To go from a straight line into a curved line,** while you're drawing a smooth anchor point, press Option/Alt after you click *but before* you release the mouse button. This action lets you drag the direction point for the next line segment without affecting the previous segment, as Illustrator normally does. To create the curve, drag the direction point to wherever you need it.

✔ **To go from one curved line into another** (with a curved-corner point instead of a smooth point), click and drag as though you were creating a smooth point. After you have the first curve how you want it, *but before* you release the mouse button, press Option/Alt. As soon as you press Option/Alt, the second direction point moves independently of the first. Use this keyboard technique to move the direction point to wherever you need it.

These two techniques take a little practice because so much depends on the timing of when you press Option/Alt. Don't worry, though. If you don't get it right the first time, you always have the Convert Anchor Point tool to fall back on.

Drawing Shapes with the Pen Tool

This section walks you through drawing some other basic shapes. Knowing the best ways to do that can make the more complex shapes much easier to draw. Take, for example, a garden-variety circle — shapes don't get any simpler than that . . . or do they? When you draw one in Illustrator, you can get widely differing results with the Pen tool.

Drawing a sad, lumpy circle with the Pen tool

You're probably saying to yourself, "Why would anyone be foolish enough to draw a circle by using the Pen tool when you can draw a perfect circle in a single step by using the Ellipse tool?" (which I cover in Chapter 4). A couple of reasons are

✔ **Practice makes perfect.** A circle is an object made entirely of smooth anchor points. Master the circle, and you're the master of smooth curves!

✔ **The Ellipse tool makes perfect circles *every time*.** Sometimes you might want to be a little more creative than that, and drawing the imperfect circle you want with the Pen tool can be a lot faster than modifying a perfect circle created with the Ellipse tool.

So, without further ado, follow these steps, as shown in Figure 7-13:

1. **Hold down the Shift key, and click and drag to the right with the Pen tool; extend the direction point line about ¹/₄ inch.**

2. **Still pressing the Shift key, click about ¹/₂ inch above and to the right of the first anchor point, and drag up about ¹/₄ inch.**

   You've drawn an eye-pleasing arc — kind of a skateboard-ramp sorta thing.

3. **Keep pressing the Shift key, click about ¹/₂ inch above the second anchor point (directly above the first anchor point), and drag left about ¹/₄ inch.**

   You've drawn a lovely half circle. You're actually more than halfway there.

4. **With your left hand developing a cramp from holding down the Shift key, click about ¹/₂ inch to the left of the first anchor point and directly opposite the second anchor point, and then drag down about ¹/₄ inch.**

   You can probably guess where I'm going with this last click.

5. **Click the first anchor point, drag to the right about ¹/₄ inch, and then (finally) release the Shift key.**

   Your creation is a perfectly _lumpy_ circle! If your circle isn't as round as you want, select the Direct Selection tool (the hollow arrow) and tweak the points and direction points until the circle looks less lumpy.

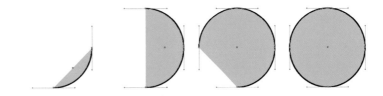

Figure 7-13: Drawing a circle (sort of) by using the Pen tool.

Congratulations — you just drew a circle! Try drawing a second circle by using the same steps. And another. You'll find that not only does each circle get easier and better, but you'll have much more control whenever you create a smooth curve anywhere.

Drawing a heart

Ah, a _real_ challenge. None of this "circle" stuff for you! Still, similarities to the circle abound. You do need four anchor points — two of them smooth points. And most of the anchor points need to be in similar positions to the anchor points you drew for the circle. Hmmm. Figure 7-14 shows the procedure in all its glory. Just complete the following steps:

1. **Click and drag up and to the right about ¹/₄ inch.**

2. **Move your cursor about ³/₄ inch above and ¹/₂ inch to the right of the first anchor point, and then click and drag up about ¹/₄ inch. Use the Shift key to constrain the angle of the direction point.**

3. **Move your cursor about ¹/₂ inch to the left and above the first anchor point, and then click and drag down and to the left about ¹/₄ inch.**

   This procedure is almost too easy, isn't it? Well, take heart (so to speak). The next step tests your mettle.

Figure 7-14: Drawing a heart with the Pen tool.

4. **Press Option/Alt, click the direction point you just created (that was extending from the anchor point), and drag *up* about ¹/₂ inch.**

   This action breaks the two control-handle lines and sets you up for a nice, curved-corner point at the top of the heart.

5. **Move your cursor about ¹/₂ inch to the left of the last anchor point, and then click and drag straight down about ¹/₄ inch.**

   Again, you can press the Shift key to make sure you're dragging a perfectly vertical line.

6. **Move your cursor onto the first point, press Option/Alt, and then click and drag down and to the right about ¹/₄ inch.**

   This completes the heart.

Creating Straight and Curved Lines without the Pen Tool

In This Chapter

▷ Discovering why the world loves to draw with the Pencil tool

▷ Generating paths with the Pencil tool

▷ Editing existing paths

▷ Using the Pencil tool preferences settings

▷ Smoothing out bumpy paths easily

▷ Deciding when to use the Pen or Pencil tool

▷ Using the Line Segment tool

▷ Creating and editing an arc

▷ Drawing amazing spirals

*I*n the beginning, there was the Pen tool. And users said that the Pen tool was good. But the users also said that the Pen tool was too hard. And too frustrating. And inefficient for quickly creating paths. And the users griped. And behold! Adobe gave them the Pencil tool — the wondrous, magical Pencil tool that makes creating paths as easy as drawing with a, well, *pencil*. And there was great rejoicing. But Adobe wasn't content to stop there, blessing users with three other tools: the Line Segment, Arc, and Spiral tools.

In this chapter, you find out all about the Pencil tool and its buddies, theSmooth, Path Eraser, Line Segment, Arc, and Spiral tools. You discover how to create and modify paths as well as customize these tools to match your personal drawing style. And then you can join in the rejoicing!

Using the Pencil Tool as a Pencil

 Computer mice (mouses?) have never been good drawing tools; you need a steady hand and more patience than the guy at the mall in the Santa suit. That was then. These days, the Illustrator Pencil tool makes even the most hopped-up-on-caffeine, impatient Picasso-wannabe into a computer artist. (Just looking at it makes you feel better about drawing, doesn't it?)

Minimal effort and hefty stress reduction

The whole idea behind the Pencil tool is to let you draw exactly what you want — as quickly or slowly as you want. Regardless of the speed at which you draw, the resulting path appears the same (a nice thought for those of us on a deadline).

The Pencil tool can create smooth lines even when you're jittering around. (Unless you don't want it to — in which case it makes funky, jittery lines.) The Pencil tool is also intuitive. Not only does looks like a pencil, but when you click and drag with it, it creates a line that more or less follows where you dragged, pretty much like using a real pencil. (For contrast, look at the Pen tool. It looks like a pen, and yet it does nothing even remotely penlike!) And it allows you to fix your mistakes without ever having to push or pull a point or a handle.

The following steps (deftly illustrated in Figure 8-1) show you how to use the Pencil tool:

1. **Choose the Pencil tool from its slot in the Tools panel.**

   Your cursor changes into (surprise!) a pencil.

2. **Click and drag in the Document window. As you drag, a dotted line appears.**

   Think of these dots as breadcrumbs that show you where you've been.

3. **Release the mouse button after you amass a nice little trail of breadcrumbs (dots).**

   A path forms where the breadcrumbs were. (If Hansel and Gretel had used the Pencil tool, that poor witch would be alive today.)

Figure 8-1: Drawing with the Pencil tool.

If you stop drawing with the Pencil tool, you can just start up where you left off simply by clicking at the end of the path and continuing. Be careful, though. If you don't click close enough to the end of the path, you start a whole new path. Fortunately, the Pencil tool tells you when you're in the right place. When you're creating a new path, a little X appears to the right of the tip of the Pencil (shown at the bottom in the margin). When you're close enough to a selected path to add to it, the X disappears (shown at the top in the margin).

A few unexpected exceptions to all this bliss

You're right. Using the Pencil tool *does* sound too easy. Although the Pencil tool is undeniably wonderful, it can cause frustration (or at least uncertainty) in the unwary. Here are instances to watch out for (and avoid if possible):

- ✐ **You can't continue your path.** You need to select a path in order to add to it. For example, if you stop drawing, do something that deselects the path, and then return to drawing your path, you create a *second* path instead of extending the first one. To continue the path you were originally working on, you must select it *before* you start drawing again with the Pencil tool. Press the ⌘ key (Mac)/Ctrl (Windows) to access the Selection tool, then click the path, let go of the ⌘ key (Mac)/Ctrl (Windows) and then start drawing, starting at either end of the newly selected path.

  To get to the selection cursor right away, hold down ⌘/Ctrl.

- ✐ **You accidentally edit an existing path.** If you start a new Pencil path near a *selected* path, you can edit the selected path instead of creating a new one. In fact, you can do so with any path that was created with the Pen, Pencil, Line Segment, Arc, Spiral, Star, or any other tool in Illustrator. You can edit any of them with the Pencil tool. (So is the Pencil versatile or overzealous? Your call.)

- ✐ **You create a path that's too lumpy or too smooth.** You can set up the Pencil tool to be very smooth *or* very accurate. (In this case, *accurate* really means that it follows all the skittles and bumps you make as you draw). If someone you love changes the Pencil tool preferences (which you can access by double-clicking the Pencil tool), the Pencil retains those settings. Pencil tool preferences are loyal to the most recent user; they never return to their original settings unless you manually change them.

- ✐ **You get a wacky fill or stroke while you draw.** This situation really isn't the Pencil tool's fault, but it's not exactly unknown to habitual Pencil tool users. If, before you start to draw, a nameless *somebody* sets the fill or stroke to something a little odd, *boom!* you get a mess. Fortunately, you can change the fill or stroke back to the default settings by pressing D. Before you know it, you're back to normal. (Well, at least the *path* is. . . .)

✔ **You can't close a path.** Often when you use the Pencil tool in an attempt to create a closed path (by ending the path where you started), you wind up with two points that are very close to one another without actually being joined. For some reason, the Pencil tool has a hard time making a closed path if you draw the entire path with one continuous stroke. When you near the end of the path, hold down the Option key (Mac)/Alt (Windows) and then release the mouse with Option/Alt still pressed when the end of the line you're drawing is near the beginning. The two ends of your path will be joined.

✔ **You can't draw a straight line.** In Illustrator, pressing the Shift key doesn't keep the Pencil tool on a horizontal or vertical plane. Just about every other tool in Illustrator draws or moves in straight lines at 45° angles. In fact, just about every other tool in every Adobe product moves or draws in straight lines when you hold down Shift! But the Pencil tool can't even *think* straight! Fortunately, you can switch over to the Pen tool to draw straight lines and then switch back to the Pencil tool to create the rest of the drawing.

Cherishing the Multipurpose Pencil Tool

If you ever had one of those pocketknives with enough blades to do or fix anything, you can appreciate how much more the Pencil tool does than a mere pencil! Use the amazing Pencil tool to edit existing paths, create new paths, append one path to another, and close existing paths.

But wait, there's more! You can tweak Pencil tool preferences to reflect how you want to draw. You can also use the Smooth tool and the Eraser tool (hidden in the Pencil toolslot), which are both handy variations on the Pencil tool. Use the Smooth tool (a striped pencil) to make paths less bumpy, with nary a smear. Use the Eraser tool (an upside-down pencil) to zap away portions of paths, leaving no rubber crumbs to get into your keyboard.

Making the Pencil tool work just for you

Set preferences for the Pencil tool by double-clicking the Pencil tool in the Tools panel; this opens the Pencil Tool Options dialog box, as shown in Figure 8-2. Straight out of the box, the Pencil tool works pretty well. To be honest, although it's really set up to work reasonably well for everyone, it might not be set up to work as well as it possibly can for you.

Hi-fi and lo-fi paths

The first slider under Tolerances (at the top of the dialog box; refer to Figure 8-2) is Fidelity. Nope, nothing to do with divorce courts. This kind of fidelity affects how closely the path follows where you drag the Pencil tool. A high setting (slider toward the left) means that the path matches precisely what you drew with the Pencil, adding as many points and corners as necessary. A low setting (slider toward the right) means that the path loosely follows what you drew, making a smoother line with fewer points. Paths created with the Fidelity slider all the way to the left appear more natural and bumpy; paths drawn with the slider all the way to the right appear smoother but more computer-like.

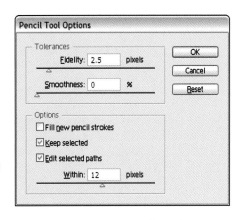

Figure 8-2: Set Pencil tool attributes here.

Compare the images shown in Figure 8-3. The path on the left was drawn with a Fidelity setting of .5 pixel; the path on the right was drawn with a Fidelity setting of 20 pixels. This Fidelity setting isn't just an arbitrary special effect; it's a way to make the Pencil tool match your personal drawing style.

Figure 8-3: (Left) High Fidelity. (Right) Low Fidelity.

Fidelity is measured in pixels. A pixel can mean many things as a unit of measurement. In this case, a *pixel* refers to a distance on your screen. (For more information, see the sidebar "Just how big IS a pixel?")

Drawing with a mouse is about as easy as drawing with a brick; the lines you make tend to be pretty shaky. The Fidelity slider determines how shaky your hand can be and still produce a smooth line. When you use the Pencil tool, you create a breadcrumb trail (a dotted line). After you release the mouse button, your computer pauses for a split second to create an imaginary line that's the average of all the movement you just made with the mouse. Then Illustrator compares that imaginary line with your breadcrumb trail and creates the actual path based on the Fidelity slider's setting.

Suppose that your Fidelity setting is 20 pixels — the highest Fidelity setting possible. As you draw your naturally shaky line, you move away from the imaginary average line. With a setting of 20 pixels, Illustrator assumes that everything less than 20 pixels away from that imaginary line is unintentional shaking, induced by the unwieldy nature of the mouse (or by too much caffeine), so Illustrator just ignores that stuff when it creates the path. Everything more than 20 pixels away is considered intentional, which prompts Illustrator to put in a curve or a corner point.

All this is just an extended way of saying that if you're at one with yourself and the Universe and are a Zen master of mouse movement, you want to keep your Fidelity settings high. That way, you move the mouse only to exactly where you want the path, and you don't have Illustrator second-guessing what you *really* intended. However, if you have really shaky hands (as most of us do when we get too much caffeine and not enough sleep), you probably want to use a low Fidelity setting. More than likely, you fall somewhere between these two extremes. So just double-click the Pencil tool and set the Fidelity slider to match your style!

Now, that is smooth!

The second slider of the Pencil Tool Options dialog box (refer to Figure 8-2) is a little harder for most people to figure out. After all, it's named *Smoothness* — but didn't the first slider (Fidelity) smooth out the image?

Just how big IS a pixel?

That question has no easy answer, my friend. In the olden days, a pixel was $\frac{1}{72}$ of an inch because computer screens used a fixed grid of 72 pixels x 72 pixels for every inch of screen. Nowadays, multisync monitors allow us to change the number of pixels on the screen. How big is a pixel? Take the current resolution of your monitor, divide by its size, and then. . . . Better yet, forget all that and just pay attention to how the Pencil tool works with different Fidelity settings. Choose the one that works best for you, and don't worry about the numbers!

Here's the difference. Because drawing with the mouse can be pretty shaky, this setting helps compensate for the shakiness in a slightly different way from the Fidelity setting. The Fidelity setting helps Illustrator determine whether you drew the path because you meant to or because you had a shaky mouse. Comparatively, the Smoothness setting helps Illustrator figure out what kind of corner you meant to create when you deliberately changed the direction of the path.

When you change the direction of a path, you can make a sharp corner point or a smooth, curving point. When Illustrator converts your breadcrumb trail into a path, it must determine which of these points you truly intended to use. A low Smoothness setting (say, 0%) makes the Pencil tool use a corner point almost everywhere that the path changes direction. A high Smoothness setting (say, 100%) makes the Pencil tool use a smooth point in all but the most extreme path direction changes.

The setting that works best for you is a matter of your personal style. If your lines are as shaky as a balloon vendor at a porcupine convention, set your Smoothness setting to 100%. If your hands are as steady as a gunslinger in a Western movie, leave it set to 0%. Experiment until you find the right setting for you. Figure 8-4 shows the same image created with different Smoothness settings. Note how the settings change the way the drawings look.

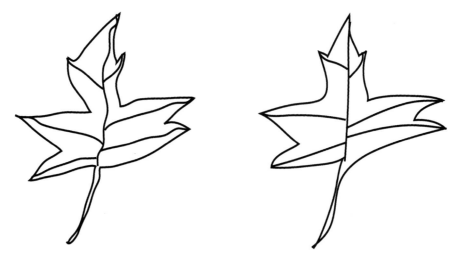

Figure 8-4: At left, a Smoothness setting of 0%; at right, a Smoothness setting of 100%.

At first glance, the differences between the drawings on the right in Figures 8-3 (low Fidelity) and 8-4 (high Smoothness) appear minimal. However, looks can be deceiving. The Smoothness and Fidelity settings are actually two distinct approaches to making a path: A low Fidelity setting creates a simplified curve by following the path you draw more loosely and using fewer points; a high Smoothness setting creates a smoother curve by using *different types* of points (smooth points as opposed to corner points) to create the path. Which is better? It really depends on your drawing style — and some experimenting!

Tweaking the Pencil tool: It's your option

Under the Options section of the Pencil Tool Options dialog box, you find three options: Fill New Pencil Strokes, Keep Selected and Edit Selected Paths. These settings determine what happens to the path after you draw it and how the Pencil tool interacts with that path (or with other selected paths).

- **With Fill New Pencil Strokes checked:** You end up with the fill color specified in the Tools panel as a fill for any path you draw with the Pencil tool. Uncheck this and your Pencil-drawn paths will have a fill of None.

- **With Keep Selected checked:** The path you just created with the Pencil tool stays selected after you finish drawing and release the mouse button.

- **With Keep Selected unchecked:** The path you just created doesn't stay selected. (But you knew that.)

The Keep Selected option also determines how the Pencil tool affects selected paths, as follows:

- **Edit Selected Paths:** When you use the Pencil tool near any selected path (with the Keep Selected option checked), the path you just drew with the Pencil tool replaces the previous path. You can even adjust how close you need to be to that path to edit it; just tweak the Within setting, located just beneath the Edit Selected Paths option.

  When the Edit Selected Paths option is not checked, the Pencil tool works the same regardless of whether Keep Selected is checked or unchecked. When the Edit Selected Paths option is checked, it changes the way the Pencil tool works. Instead of moving on to create a new path when you draw near a selected path, you linger over the old one to modify it.

- **With Keep Selected checked:** You can start drawing a path, stop, and then continue where you left off. If you decide to replace the path, you can place the Pencil tool near the path you just drew and start drawing a new one. (*Poof.* The old one disappears.) But beware: You have forbidden the Pencil tool to draw multiple paths that are close together.

- **With Keep Selected *and* Edit Selected Paths checked:** Every stroke you make that's close to another selected stroke replaces the old stroke with the new stroke.

✓ **With Keep Selected unchecked:** The Pencil tool can change only the paths you tell it to change (by first using a selection tool). By removing the check mark from Keep Selected, you enable the Pencil to draw hair or grass (for instance) with utter abandon. With Keep Selected unchecked you can also *edit* hair or grass, but don't forget to select the part you want to edit (by first using a selection tool).

Changing the path not penciled

A really amazing attribute of the Pencil tool is that you can use it to edit any path, and not just the paths created with it. For example, you can edit a circle, star, or path drawn with the Pen tool. You can replace any portion of any path with the Pencil tool, provided that the path is selected and the Edit Selected Path option is checked in the Pencil Tool Preferences dialog box. (See "Making the Pencil tool work just for you" earlier in this chapter.) Just make sure that the path is selected, and then click and drag near the path to reshape it. The following steps walk you through the process of editing an existing path:

1. **Using any selection tool, select the path you want to modify.**

   The path need not have been created with the Pencil tool.

2. **Select the Pencil tool.**

3. **Click near the part of the path you want to modify.**

   When the little X at the bottom right of the Pencil tool disappears, you know that you're close enough to click.

4. **Click and drag a new shape for the part of the path.**

   You can create any shape you want, but it must start and end near the existing path; otherwise, the new path won't reconnect with the old path.

5. **Release the mouse button.**

   The path reshapes itself into the new path you just drew.

Working with the all-natural "Smoothie" tool

Use the Illustrator Smooth tool (found in the Pencil toolslot) to make your paths, well, smoother. (Not that you need me to tell you that, huh?) Use the Smooth tool to change how a path looks after it's drawn, in the same way that the Pencil tool lets you change the way a path looks while it's being drawn.

Drag the Smooth tool over any selected path to smooth it. You aren't limited to smoothing paths drawn with the Pencil tool; you can smooth any path in

Illustrator. Your results, however, depend on the path that you're smoothing (for example, if you try smoothing a path that's already smooth, you aren't going to see much difference) and on the Smooth tool preferences.

You access the Smooth tool preferences by double-clicking the Smooth tool. The only two settings are Fidelity and Smoothness. These settings function identically to the settings in the Pencil Tool Options dialog box. (See the earlier section, "Making the Pencil tool work just for you.") The only difference is that you apply these settings to lines that are already drawn. Just sweep over them with the Smooth tool, and the result is as if you drew those paths by using different Pencil tool preferences settings.

As you may expect, using the Smooth tool is pretty smooth. Here's the drill (or is it a sander?), as shown in Figure 8-5:

1. **Using any selection tool, select the path that you want to smooth.**

2. **Drag the Smooth tool on or near the path that you want to smooth.**

   Et voilá! The path is smooth.

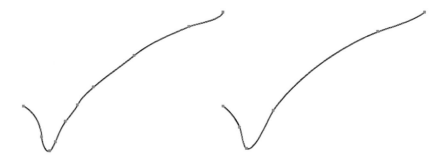

Figure 8-5: The Smooth tool in action.

The Path Eraser tool (also found in the Pencil toolslot) is so basic that it doesn't even warrant its own section. To use the tool, simply click and drag the tool over the portion of the path you want to remove. It might take a couple of swipes to eliminate what you want, so be patient. The Path Eraser tool also works with any path — not just those created with the Pencil tool. Also, with the Path Eraser tool, you don't have to set preferences.

In addition to the Path Eraser tool, there is also a regular Eraser tool in Illustrator. It's easy to get them confused, but they do quite different things. The Eraser tool works more like a real eraser, erasing away portions of your artwork regardless of the paths below it. The Path Eraser tool just erases paths.

Using the Pen with the Pencil

The Pen and Pencil tools are the primary tools for drawing in Illustrator, and they work really well together. As you gain a knack for knowing which tool to use when, your work flows more smoothly, and your illustrations look more and more how you want.

Swapping one tool for another

A common technique that's useful for combining the Pen and Pencil tools is to switch between them while drawing. You could click each tool whenever you decide to change from one to the other, but the really zippy way to do this is to press the key that corresponds to each tool. Just press the P key (on your keyboard) to switch to the Pen tool, and press N to switch to the Pencil tool.

As your drawing changes from free-flowing curves to precise straight lines and back, you want to change between the two tools: Just click the endpoint of the path you were previously drawing with the other tool and then continue drawing.

Watch those icons! Working with the Pen and Pencil tools together is much easier if you pay attention to what the icons are doing. When the Pen tool is over an endpoint, a little slash (/) appears to the lower right of the pen icon. When you're about to close a path, a hollow circle appears beside the tool. When you have the Pencil tool in position to edit a path, its icon doesn't have anything beside it. Both tools, however, get Xs beside them when they're about to create a new path.

Precision versus speed: You make the call

Keep in mind the types of shapes and paths that are best drawn with each tool. Here's a breakdown of the shapes and paths each tool draws best.

Shapes and paths best drawn with the Pen tool

To draw anything with straight lines, choose the Pen tool because the Pencil tool really can't draw a straight line. To create a path or shape that has a smooth curve, you choose the Pen tool because the line the Pencil tool creates is just an average of the total strokes you make, which means absolute precision is impossible. Finally, to trace a logo or other scanned art that requires precision and accuracy, you're better off choosing the Pen tool because it offers you precision down to the thousandth of a millimeter.

Shapes and paths best drawn with the Pencil tool

When speed is more important than accuracy in your drawing — when you need to put a lot of hairs onto your lovely kiwi-fruit illustration, for example, and the precise length and position of each and every hair doesn't matter — choose the Pencil tool. For quick sketching, such as doodling an insulting picture of your favorite co-worker, choose the Pencil tool because you don't have to worry about each and every point and handle the way you do with the Pen tool. The Pencil tool lets you focus on creating the lines where they should be — and lets Illustrator do the rest of the work for you. (Ah, progress.)

Lines Made Quick and Easy

If you've read this chapter to this point, you know you can't draw a straight line with the Pencil tool, and you've seen how tedious using the Pen tool can be. So, you're probably thinking that drawing a line would be easier with that gloppy rapidograph pen and a metal ruler. Don't fret! The powers-that-be at Adobe have bestowed yet another tool for pen-phobic users: the Line Segment tool. With the Line Segment tool, you can make lines quickly and easily.

Working with the Line Segment tool

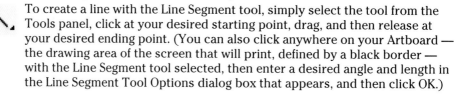

To create a line with the Line Segment tool, simply select the tool from the Tools panel, click at your desired starting point, drag, and then release at your desired ending point. (You can also click anywhere on your Artboard — the drawing area of the screen that will print, defined by a black border — with the Line Segment tool selected, then enter a desired angle and length in the Line Segment Tool Options dialog box that appears, and then click OK.)

Like most things that are super easy, the using Line Segment tool has its drawbacks. For example, you're limited to creating a single line, as shown in Figure 8-6. You can't create connecting lines like you can with the Pen or Pencil tools. You can, however, create lines that are perfectly vertical, horizontal, or at 45° angles. Just press the Shift key while you draw. You'll discover that when you drag your cursor, your line constrains to a 45° angle. After you create your line, you can edit it by selecting and moving either endpoint with the Direct Selection tool.

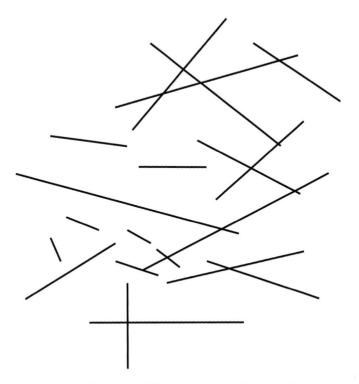

Figure 8-6: Line Segment tool lines are easy, but limited to single strokes.

Setting the tool options

Double-clicking the Line Segment tool in the Tools panel brings up the Line Segment Tool Options dialog box, shown in Figure 8-7. Not exactly one of the feature-rich dialog boxes out there, the Line Segment Tool Options dialog box offers only three options: Length, Angle, and Fill Line. When you deselect the Fill Line option, the line appears with only a stroke, regardless of whether you have a fill selected in the Tools panel or the Color panel. After you complete the drawing of your line, the Fill swatch in both the Tools panel and the Color panel automatically reverts to None.

Figure 8-7: The Line Segment Tool Options dialog box.

Curvy with the Arc Tool

In Chapter 7, I tell you how to create a curve with the Pen tool — a sometimes painful two-step click-and-drag process. With the Arc tool (found in the Line Segment toolslot), all you do is just click and drag. The longer you drag, the larger the arc. The angle you drag affects the angle of the arc. That's it. If only everything in life were so simple. To edit your arc, treat it is as you would any other curve. Use the Direct Selection tool to select and move either of the anchor points or direction points on the curve. See Chapter 6 for the complete editing lowdown.

Getting the arc you want

Maybe you're the finicky type and not completely satisfied with the arc created by using the default settings. Fortunately, the options in the Arc Segment Tool Options dialog box are numerous. Double-click the Arc tool to bring up the dialog box shown in Figure 8-8. The best thing about this dialog box is that it gives you a preview of the settings as you adjust them.

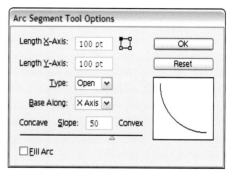

Figure 8-8: Design your arc here.

The preview thumbnail gives a nice visual representation of what happens to the arc as you change the lengths of the X (horizontal) and Y (vertical) axes. You have the choice of the type of arc — open (like a rainbow) or closed (think a slice of pizza). You can also choose where the base of your arc is anchored — either the X or Y axis. The slope slider allows you to adjust how *concave* (pushed in) or *convex* (pushed out) your curve appears. Figure 8-9 shows examples of both concave and convex closed arcs. Deselect the Fill Arc option to create arcs with no fill, regardless of whether a fill is selected. The small square to the left of the OK button is a proxy box, which allows you to specify the point of origin for the arc.

Figure 8-9: Two types of closed arcs.

When you select the Arc tool and click your Artboard, the Arc Segment Tool Options dialog box appears (just like it did when you double-clicked the Arc tool). When you click OK, an arc is drawn with the settings you established in the dialog box . . . no dragging required!

Spiraling out of control

Spirals are notoriously hard to draw — that is, without using the Spiral tool. With the Pen tool, you have to set up a complex grid and align points and direction points until the cows came home, had a good night's rest, went to work for the day, and then came home yet again. It's really, really hard. But the Spiral tool (found in the Line Segment toolslot) allows you to quickly create all sorts of snazzy-looking spirals from a loose-looking galaxy or whirl-pool to the super-tight grooves on a 45 rpm record (ask your grandparents, kids). Figure 8-10 shows some spirally artwork created primarily with the Spiral tool.

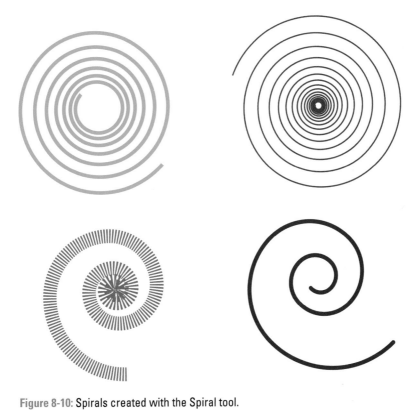

Figure 8-10: Spirals created with the Spiral tool.

To customize a spiral, hold down one of the following keys while you drag:

- **Up/Down Arrow:** Adds or deletes the winds of the spiral as you're drawing it.

- **⌘ (Mac)/Ctrl (Windows):** Winds or unwinds the spiral (the outside moves, but the center stays where it is, making the spiral tighter or looser), which changes the number of winds.

✓ **Spacebar:** Allows you to move the spiral around with the mouse while you draw it.

✓ **Tilde (~):** Creates multiple spirals while you draw.

Click the Artboard with the Spiral tool selected (instead of clicking and dragging) to open the Spiral dialog box, as shown in Figure 8-11. Here are the options:

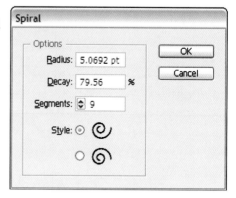

Figure 8-11: Use options in the Spiral dialog box to set the spiral's tightness.

✓ **Radius:** This option sets the distance from the center of the spiral to its outermost point.

✓ **Decay:** This option determines how much larger or smaller each coil of the spiral is from the previous coil. Values close to 100% result in a tight spiral, and 100% results in a perfect circle. Figure 8-12 shows a spiral with a decay of 75% and one with 95%, with the exact some radius and segments.

✓ **Segments:** This option determines how many coils make up the spiral. Each wind of the spiral is made of four segments; thus, if you want five coils in your spiral, type **20** in the Segments field.

✓ **Style:** The Style options control whether the spiral is clockwise or counterclockwise.

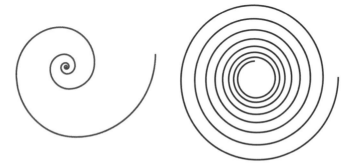

Figure 8-12: The green spiral on the left has a decay of 75%, while the purple spiral on the right has a decay of 95%.

Creating Magnificent Brushstrokes

Hardcore users of Illustrator would never call it a *painting* program. So what if you can mix colors and use a paintbrush tool? To hardcore users, painting programs are what you'd call 1980's pixel-based, crudlike SuperPaint and MacPaint. Only drawing and illustration programs are vector based. Regardless of what the hardcore users think, Illustrator has some of the most powerful painting capabilities of any graphics program, vector- or pixel-based.

What, for example, would you call this tool in the margin? In Illustrator, its name is the Paintbrush tool, but it's also at least one-third magic wand (the kind magicians use, not the Illustrator Magic Wand tool). In this chapter, you discover the magic of the Paintbrush tool and the wonders of vector-based brush strokes. You get to push the definitions of "brush" by creating brushstrokes of every conceivable size and shape, from brushes that make simple cal-ligraphic strokes to brushes that make strokes using other Illustrator artwork.

Brushing Where No Stroke Has Gone Before

Brushes are wildly creative strokes that you can apply to paths. If you think of them this way, brushes become much easier to get a handle on (especially if they make you, er, bristle with frustration).

Brushes come in four types: Art, Scatter, Calligraphic, or Pattern brushes. Figure 9-1 shows (left to right) examples of painting with an Art brush, a Scatter brush, a Calligraphic brush, and a Pattern brush.

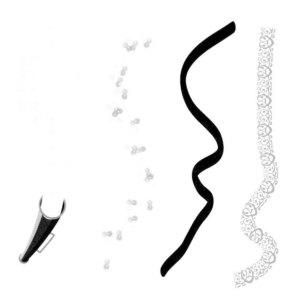

Figure 9-1: Art, Scatter, Calligraphic, and Pattern brush painting examples.

- **Art brushes:** Stretch a single piece of artwork along an entire path.
- **Scatter brushes:** Scatter artwork around a path. The artwork is repeated, scaled, and rotated randomly. The Scatter brush is oddly similar to the Symbol Sprayer, but you find distinct differences, which I point out later in this chapter.
- **Calligraphic brushes:** Emulate drawing or writing with a calligraphy pen.
- **Pattern brushes:** Repeat artwork along a path that you draw with the Paintbrush tool. Unlike the random Scatter brush, the Pattern brush repeats the artwork in a precise pattern.

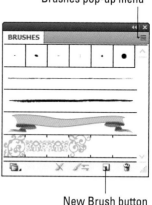

Brushes pop-up menu

New Brush button

Figure 9-2: The default Brushes panel shows examples of the brush types.

The Illustrator Brushes panel, shown in Figure 9-2, contains samples of each of the four brush types. (Choose Window⇨Brushes to display the Brushes panel.) In addition, see the "Creating a New Brush" section later in this chapter for help on taking virtually anything that you create in Illustrator and turning it into a brush.

There's also another brush, which isn't a brush but still is called a brush, precisely to confuse you. It's a Blob brush, which I discuss at the end of this chapter. Until then, forget I even mentioned it.

Embracing your inner artist

Regardless of your artistic background or intentions, you can make astounding artwork when using the Paintbrush tool with different brush types. Of course, someone with an utter vacuum of talent (or more than the legally allowed measure of bad taste) might face an uphill battle to create something that looks good. Even so, you can quickly whip up some snazzy images, like the one in Figure 9-3, by using the Paintbrush — even if you're new to computer graphics. (Your secret is safe with me.) Just follow these steps:

1. **Choose the Paintbrush tool from the Tools panel.**

   Your cursor changes into a little paintbrush.

2. **Choose Window⇨Brush Libraries⇨Artistic⇨Artistic Watercolor.**

   After you release the mouse button, the Artistic Watercolor brush panel appears quicker than you can say Wassily Kandinsky. (Um, he was a famous Russian artist who used watercolors. Really.)

3. **Click the topmost brush, "Light wash – thick."**

4. **Click and drag with the Paintbrush tool to draw a path where you want your new stroke to be.**

5. **Release the mouse button.**

   The path becomes the stroke of the brush that you chose. In this case, the Watercolor Art brush's gray, watery stroke stretches along the entire length of the path. Change the stroke color and draw some more strokes. Because of the partial transparency of the Watercolor strokes, the effect is mesmerizing.

Figure 9-3: Create some wild and wacky strokes.

Because brushes reside on paths, you can change the position and dimensions of any brushstroke just like you modify any path. You can use the Pencil tool to reshape an existing path. Or, if you're really brave, you can use the Direct Selection tool to push and pull points and handles around until the brushstroke looks how you want.

The Paintbrush tool options

The Paintbrush tool offers several options that you can use to customize how it draws. All these options are found in the Paintbrush Tool Preferences dialog box, shown in Figure 9-4, which appears after you double-click the Paintbrush tool. These preferences function almost identically to the Pencil tool preferences, with one exception: the Fill New Brush Strokes option. When you leave the check box for this option unchecked (which I recommend), Illustrator automatically sets the Fill color option to None. For a more exhaustive and exhausting explanation of the other settings, refer to Chapter 8 where I discuss the Pencil tool preferences. The options are exactly the same in both name and function.

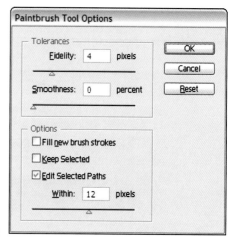

Figure 9-4: The Paintbrush Tool Preferences dialog box.

Why set the Fill color option to None? The path you make with the Paintbrush tool can contain a fill color, but brushstrokes can also be randomly placed pieces of artwork or have unique shapes. The stroke can appear partly inside and partly outside the fill color, which makes the fill seem random and unrelated to your stroke. Brushes work better when you don't use a fill color with them.

Creating a New Brush

Although Illustrator ships with several hundred brushes, obsessively creative folks can't stand to be limited to so few. To create your own brushes, go right ahead by using darn near any set of paths in Illustrator. (I'm using the art I created from Figure 9-3 as a new brush because I think it'll be really nifty.) Furthermore, you can use the process to create a new Art, Pattern, or Scatter brush — just not a Calligraphic brush, which doesn't require external artwork.

1. **Create (or open a document with) artwork that you want to use as a brush.**

2. **Select all the paths in the document by choosing Select⇨Select All.**

3. **Click the New Brush button or choose New Brush from the Brushes panel pop-up menu.**

   This button, located at the bottom of the Brushes panel, looks like a piece of paper. Refer to Figure 9-2.

   The New Brush dialog box (as shown in Figure 9-5) appears and asks what type of brush you want to create.

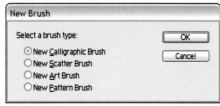

Figure 9-5: The New Brush dialog box.

4. **Select New Art Brush, New Scatter Brush, or New Pattern Brush; then click OK.**

   For this example, I select the New Art Brush option.

   The Art Brush Options dialog box appears, as shown in Figure 9-6.

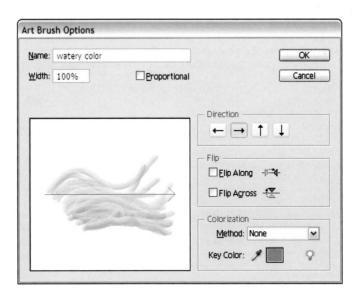

Figure 9-6: Create a new brush here.

5. **Click OK to accept the default settings.**

   If you'd like, you can name the brush first, but I find that doing so gets you emotionally attached to the brush in ways that classically trained artists tend to frown upon.

If you're concerned about accepting the default settings in the Art Brush Options dialog box, you can always make changes to the Art Brush options by double-clicking the Art brush itself in the Brushes panel. I talk about all those different options in the upcoming section, "Working with the Different Brush Types." These options have the same effect whether you're creating a new brush or modifying an existing one.

The new Art brush appears in the Brushes panel, ready for you to use.

You can create all sorts of interesting effects by using text as Art brushes. Because brushes can contain only paths (not text objects), you must first change the text into paths before you can make it into a brush. Select the text object with a selection tool and then choose Type⇨Create Outlines to effect the transformation from text to path.

Working with the Different Brush Types

This section looks at the four brush types and examines some of the options you can use when painting with them.

Art brushes for times when you're a bit wacky

Art brushes take any Illustrator paths and stretch them along a (different) path. Figure 9-7 shows the Art Brush I created in Figure 9-6 after I applied it along multiple paths.

You can use several Art Brush options to make Art brushes look exactly how you want. Figure 9-8 shows the Art Brush Options dialog box, accessed by double-clicking any Art brush in the Brushes panel.

In the Art Brush Options dialog box, you can find a variety of options to affect how the brush makes a stroke. The following list describes how to use some of those options:

- **Name:** Give the brush a descriptive name here. This name appears when you choose View by Name from the Brushes panel pop-up menu.

- **Preview:** Select the Preview option to see any stroke in your artwork that uses the brush stroke you're changing. What you see is what you get: that is, the stroke as it will look if you apply the new changes. This doesn't alter your actual artwork. This feature is extremely handy because you don't have to remember what all the different settings do — just watch what happens after you change them!

Figure 9-7: An Art Brush made from Art Brushes painted several times.

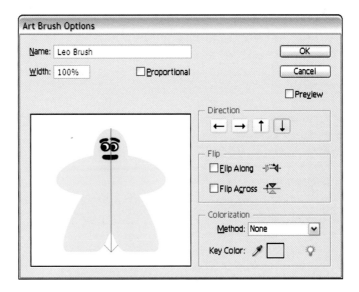

Figure 9-8: The Art Brush Options dialog box.

- ✔ **Width:** Enter a scaling percentage in the Width box, if that fits your needs.

- ✔ **Proportional:** When you select this check box, the artwork grows wider as the path gets longer. Keep the check box clear, and the artwork stretches as the path gets longer.

- ✔ **Direction:** These options determine whether the graphic rotates clockwise or counterclockwise (relative to the path) as you stretch it.

- ✔ **Flip:** These options resemble the Direction options except that they invert the artwork instead of rotating it.

- ✔ **Colorization:** Brushes have fill and stroke colors of their own. They are ordinary Illustrator artwork endowed with the power to be brushes, meaning that distinct fill and stroke values are part of the deal. The Colorization setting determines whether the brush keeps the colors of the original artwork or replaces them with Fill and Stroke colors from the Tools panel. A Method setting of None preserves the original artwork's colors. Other settings blend the fill and stroke colors with the artwork. How they perform this miracle depends on the colors in the original artwork for the brush and on the specific options you choose. As for the Key Color option, it lets you select a color from within the brush to base all colorization changes on.

  Click the Tips button (the little light bulb in the corner) for a visual illustration of the various colorization settings.

Figure 9-9 shows an Art Brush applied to a bunch of different paths.

Figure 9-9: The same brush applied to different paths produces variations like these.

Scatter brushes for times when you're a bit wacky

Scatter brushes are similar to Art brushes in that they are also made up of Illustrator paths. However, the similarities end there. Instead of stretching art along a path, Scatter brushes toss, fling, and, well, *scatter* art along a path. Figure 9-10 shows the result of using a Scatter brush.

Figure 9-10: This artwork is actually a single path used as a Scatter brush.

Scatter brushes have even more options than Art brushes, but Scatter brushes *need* more options. Imagine a brush of randomly scattered ladybugs becoming a brush of organized ladybugs that follow the path you create with the brush. To access the options of a Scatter brush, double-click any existing Scatter brush to view the Scatter Brush options dialog box. (You see the same options when you create a new Scatter brush.)

The Scatter brushes repeat and randomize artwork based on four variables: Size, Spacing, Scatter, and Rotation. You set the specific amounts for these options by dragging their respective sliders to the left or right. How the brush uses each of these values is determined by the method (Fixed, Random, or Pressure) that you select in the drop-down list boxes to the right of each slider. The following list describes how each method works:

- **Fixed:** This method uses the exact value in the associated text box, which you specify by using the slider.

- **Random:** This method gives you two sliders with which you can specify Minimum and Maximum amounts of variance in the associated option. For example, after you set the Size to a Minimum value of 50% and a Maximum value to 200%, the Scatter brush varies the artwork randomly between half its original size and twice its original size.

- **Pressure:** Like with Random, Pressure uses Minimum and Maximum amounts of variance in the associated option. This method works only when you have a pressure-sensitive tablet hooked to your computer. This feature is so cool that you might want to run out and buy one of these tablets, which is sort of using a mouse except that you draw with a pen-like stylus. Instead of just painting or not painting (your only options with a mouse), the stylus recognizes just how hard you press. The Minimum and Maximum settings correspond to the amount of pressure. The lightest pressure uses the Minimum value; the hardest pressure uses the Maximum value. The values you get vary according to just how hard you press.

Two versions of the Scatter Brush Options dialog box appear in Figure 9-11. Next to each version is a brushstroke created with the option settings shown in the dialog box.

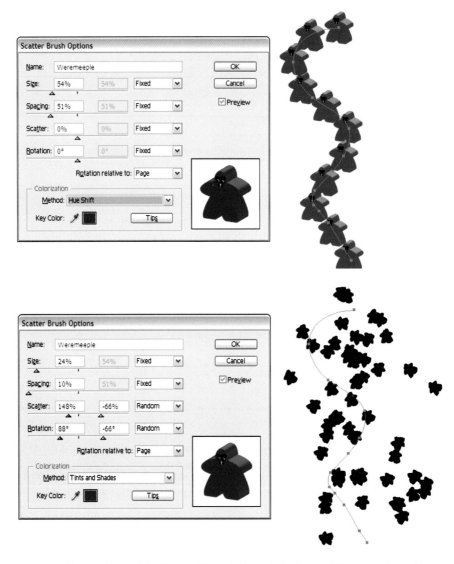

Figure 9-11: Two versions of the Scatter Brush Options dialog box and the artwork resulting from those options.

After you determine which method to use, set the sliders on the left of the dialog box to specify how you want the artwork repeated along the path. Here are the options:

- **Size:** This option controls the size of the scattered objects relative to the original.

- **Spacing:** This option controls the amount of space that appears between the scattered objects.

- **Scatter:** This option controls how far away objects can scatter on either side of the path.

- **Rotation:** This option controls how the objects are rotated and whether they're rotated in relation to the path or to the document. Figure 9-12 shows the difference between a Scatter brush rotation based on the path (left) and one based on the page (right). The Scatter brush on the left is set to rotate at 90° relative to the path; the one on the right is set to rotate at 90° relative to the page.

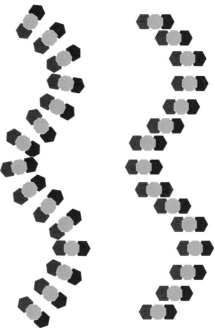

Figure 9-12: Set how objects are rotated when using the Scatter brush.

There are glaring similarities between using the Symbol Sprayer (discussed in detail in Chapter 4) and Scatter brushes. The results are often visually identical, and the process of making Scatter brushes is much like creating a symbol. Table 9-1 lists the differences between the two.

Table 9-1	Differences between Scatter Brushes and the Symbol Sprayer	
	Symbolism Tools	*Scatter Brushes*
Components	Paths, type, pixel-based images	Paths
Editability	Via Symbolism tools	Via Pencil or Direct Selection tools
Control	Nonexact manipulation	Precision changes via Options dialog box
Examples	Leaves on a tree, grass blades, hair, wisps of smoke	Footprints, marching ants
Good for	Fills	Strokes

Pattern brushes — too cool and utterly wacko

Pattern brushes (see Figure 9-13) are too cool for words, so I can just move on. Okay, no weaseling. For openers, you can use five different pieces of art for Pattern brushes rather than just one! Of course, that fact can also make them difficult to create. You need a graphic for straight lines and curves, one for inside corners, one for outside corners, one for the start of a line, and one for the end of a line. However, the results are worth the time and effort to make sure that these five graphics work together.

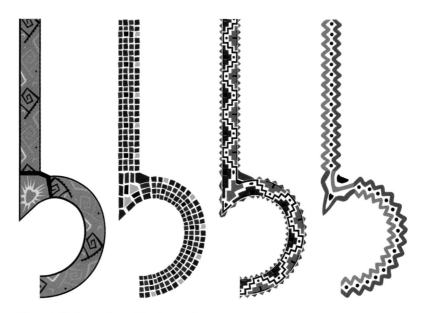

Figure 9-13: A sampling of the Pattern brushes.

Well, okay, if making five pieces of art is too time-intensive, you can get away with using just one. The Side tile is the key pattern. If you don't create five different graphics, the Pattern brush just repeats the Side tile for any missing pattern. But come on, now, that's cheating. If you want eye-popping results, make those five graphics and take full advantage of what this wonderful brush can do.

Making the artwork for a Pattern brush

If you find creating a Pattern brush tricky and counterintuitive, you're not alone; a lot of trial and error is par for the course, especially at first. The first step in building a Pattern brush is to create the five pieces of artwork. Before you can do that, however, you need to know just what these pieces of artwork are for. Double-click a pattern brush in the Brushes panel to open the Pattern Brush Options dialog box for a peek at the possibilities. Figure 9-14 shows the Pattern Brush Options dialog box, in which you tell Illustrator just where to put the artwork on a path. Pattern brushes are *context sensitive:* They know what the specific part of the path they are on is supposed to look like, so they use the graphic that corresponds to that part of the path.

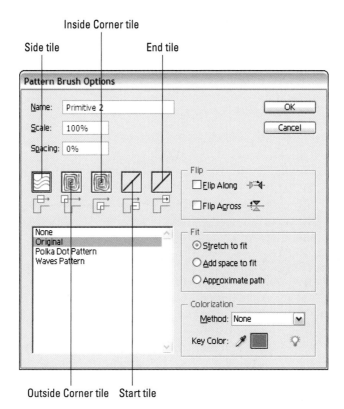

Figure 9-14: Each Pattern brush tile knows where it is on a path and uses the corresponding artwork.

Check out existing Pattern brushes. The Tile Options list in the Pattern Brush Options dialog box offers a sampling.

Setting Pattern Brush options

The Pattern Brush Options dialog box looks more complicated than it really is. Double-click any Pattern brush in the Brushes panel, and the Pattern Brush Options dialog box appears, displaying the following features:

✔ **Name:** Okay, you caught me. Naming your brush isn't really a feature. But you can name it if you'd like. Again, doing so may cause you to become emotionally attached to it. Which is why I still tear up when anyone mentions the name Hildegard, as that was a beautiful Pattern brush that I used back in the 90's . . . .

✔ **Tiles:** These squares are thumbnail representations of each piece of artwork. Beneath each tile, a graphic shows the artwork's position on the path. Click a thumbnail to modify it by using the Tile Options list.

✔ **Tile Options:** Click these options to change your pattern tiles. Click None to remove the selected tile's graphic. (The Original option is already selected if you added your own graphics.) The remaining options correspond to the Pattern swatches in the Swatches panel. This arrangement enables you to use Pattern swatches as an alternative to creating your own tiles.

✔ **Colorization and Flip:** See the earlier section "Art brushes for times when you're a bit wacky" for details on these options.

✔ **Scale:** Use the Scale option to enlarge or shrink the tiles as they run along the path.

✔ **Spacing:** If your tiles get too big and start to crowd one another, use the Spacing option to increase the distance between tiles.

✔ **Fit:** This option determines how the tiles get distorted to fit around spaces that don't quite match the five different Tile types. The Stretch to Fit option distorts artwork the most, mashing it into whatever shape it needs to be to fit the path. The Add Space to Fit option adds space between tiles to distort them as little as possible. The Approximate Path option works only when the path is rectangular.

Positioning the artwork in the Pattern brush

After you create your graphics, think about what position each graphic is going to play. You might find it helpful to create a single guide that actually contains all five positions, as shown in Figure 9-15. (I created this by just drawing a dotted line in Illustrator — using the Stroke dash feature — and then placing different pattern pieces in the appropriate places.) Use this graphic as a way of visualizing how each graphic element is going to work at the different points.

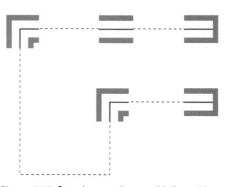

Figure 9-15: Start by creating a guideline with all five pattern positions.

Using the guideline, create five pieces of artwork to correspond to the positions on the path. Knowing exactly how each piece of the artwork needs to change in response to its position takes practice. Some differences can be subtle (such as between the starting art and ending art) or obvious (such as between the side piece and corner pieces), as shown in Figure 9-16.

Figure 9-16: Left to right: Start, side, outside corner, inside corner, and end pieces.

After you have all the artwork, you're ready to create the Pattern brush. Forward, intrepid artist! Just follow these steps:

1. **Select the artwork you want to use as your Side tile and click the New Brush button (it looks like a little piece of paper) in the Brushes panel.**

   The New Brush dialog box appears.

2. **Click the New Pattern Brush option and then click OK.**

   The Pattern Brush Options dialog box appears, with the Side tile in the proper position. (For a refresher on how that looks, refer to Figure 9-14.)

3. **In the dialog box, give the new brush a name (type it in the Name field) and click OK.**

   The new Pattern brush shows up in the Brushes panel; see Figure 9-17. (Don't worry about the other options right now. I come back to those!)

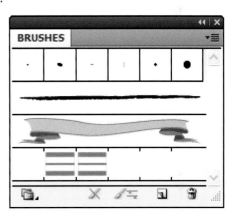

Figure 9-17: The new Pattern brush, awaiting the four remaining pieces.

Technically, the new brush is ready to use right now. (The Side artwork fills in the other positions.) But true artists (no slackers here!) want to add the rest of the artwork to the brush. Naturally, this part of the process gets tricky. Notice that the brush, as it currently appears in Figure 9-17, has six slots, two of which are filled by the Side artwork. The remaining four slots are for the remaining four pieces. The next set of steps creates them.

Here's how true artists (the aesthetically dedicated) add the rest of the artwork to the brush, one piece at a time:

1. **Select the next piece of artwork in line and press and hold down the Option key Mac)/Alt (Windows).**

2. **Drag the artwork onto the Pattern brush, over the appropriate slot, and then release the mouse button.**

You can tell that you're over a slot when a bold, dark line appears around the slot. Ah, but how do you know what the appropriate slot is? The brush has no label to tell you what's what. The Pattern Brush Options dialog box obligingly labels the slots, but tragically, the order of the Pattern bushes in that dialog box does not correspond to the order in the Brushes panel. The only way to add a new brush to the Pattern brush is to hold down Option/Alt and drag it (kicking and screaming) onto the slot in the Brushes panel. But you're in luck! I labeled the slots in the brush for you in Figure 9-18. So feel free to use the figure as a map.

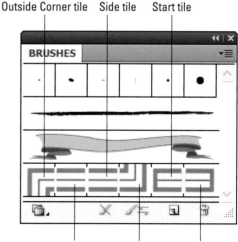

Figure 9-18: The Pattern Brush with its slots complete.

Nothing stops you from putting a corner piece into the straight section or vice versa — nothing but your concern for your artistic reputation, that is. Pay careful attention to where you drop your artwork when creating a pattern brush, or you can get some nasty-looking art as a result!

3. **The Pattern Brush Options dialog box appears, displaying the artwork in its appropriate place. Click OK.**

   Don't worry about the other options for now.

4. **Drag all the remaining graphics to their appointed places.**

   Each time you add a graphic, the Pattern Brush Options dialog box appears again. Just click OK and keep going.

Testing your new Pattern brush

When you finally have all your graphics in place, you can test the new brush by applying it to open and closed paths: After making sure that the new brush is selected in the Brushes panel, create two simple graphics. Anything you create when a brush is selected uses that brush as its stroke, even when you aren't using the Paintbrush tool. Any path will work, but because the Pattern brush uses different artwork at corners, testing the shape on an object that has corners (such as a rectangle) is helpful. In this example, I use the Rectangle tool to create a square. With the new brush still selected, I choose the Pen tool and create a basic shape. This procedure shows how the corner and side tiles look on straight lines. Testing this way (as I did in Figure 9-19) gives you a good idea of whether all your artwork is working well in the new brush.

If any of your tiles aren't working, tweak the original artwork, select it, and drag it back to the appropriate slot.

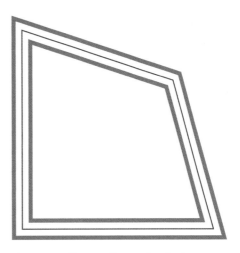

Figure 9-19: The new Pattern brush shown on a path.

Calligraphic brushes for formal occasions

Calligraphic brushes create strokes that emulate the kinds of strokes you make with real calligraphic pens; the strokes they make vary in width depending on the direction of the stroke. As the only brushes that aren't created by paths that you can drag into the Brushes panel, Calligraphic brushes are the nonconformist brushes in Illustrator. You set them up by using controls in the Calligraphic Brush Options dialog box (accessed by either creating a

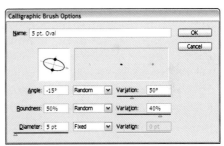

Figure 9-20: The Calligraphic Brush Options dialog box.

new brush or by double-clicking on an existing Calligraphic brush), as shown in Figure 9-20.

Although calligraphic brushes are deceptively simple, don't let the name fool you. You can use them to create any type of artwork — not just calligraphy — and they're especially good for emulating traditional pen and ink–type drawings.

Yep, the Calligraphic Brush tool seems a lot more like a real pen than the powerful-but-weird Pen tool. It may help to think of it this way: Calligraphy is an art practiced with brushes.

To create a Calligraphic brush, just follow these steps:

1. **Click the New Brush icon (it looks like a tiny piece of paper) in the Brushes panel.**

   The New Brush dialog box appears.

2. **In the New Brush dialog box, select the New Calligraphic Brush option and then click OK.**

   The Calligraphic Brush Options dialog box appears; refer to Figure 9-20. Although it might look intimidating, you have only the following three options to set (after you name the brush):

   - *Angle:* If you were using a real-world brush (or pen, as the case may be), this setting would be the angle at which you'd be tilting the brush.

   - *Roundness:* This setting enables you to change just how round the brush is — from a narrow ellipse to a circle.

   - *Diameter:* This setting determines how large the brush is.

   The boxes in the middle column determine how (and by how much) those first three options may vary, if at all. Select one of three options in these drop-down list boxes to determine whether the preceding three options may vary not at all (Fixed), randomly (Random), or according to the amount of pressure you apply by using a pressure-sensitive stylus (Pressure).

   The boxes in the third column enable you to set the amount by which those first three options may vary (if the method by which they may vary is either Random or Pressure). The higher the numbers, the greater the range of sizes the brush will produce. Figure 9-21 shows the same pattern using different calligraphic brushes.

3. **After you set your options, click OK.**

   The new Calligraphic brush appears in the Brushes panel for you to use.

As you begin creating artwork with brushes, you discover that it's just like painting with real paintbrushes — the best artwork requires a combination of several different brushes. Fortunately, you have an astonishing variety of brushes to choose from! The most well-stocked art supply store pales in comparison to the Brushes panel. Best of all, you don't have to pay extra whenever you need a new brush. You can just build your own!

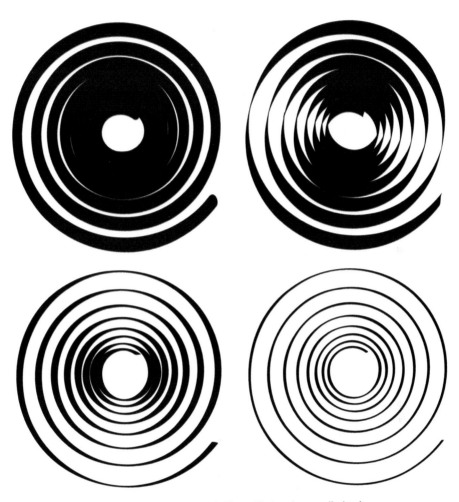

Figure 9-21: The same spiral with different Calligraphic brushes applied to it.

Extreme Fills and Strokes

In This Chapter

▷ Creating tone and shading using the Mesh tool

▷ Making artwork partially transparent

▷ Blending artwork

▷ Stroking your way to victory over drab art

▷ Creating custom strokes

▷ Using masks to hide objects with other objects

To say that in Illustrator, you can create just about anything you can imagine isn't an overstatement. The trick is to know which buttons to push to make your artistic vision become an Illustrator document. This chapter pushes fills and strokes to their limits, showing you how you too can create cool stuff. You know — the stuff that makes you scratch your head and say, "How did they do that?" And then you wonder whether you'll ever be able to create anything as artistic.

Well, it isn't so hard. You just need to use some of the more arcane Illustrator tools (the Mesh tool, for example) and a few cantankerous menu commands that don't want to do anything unless you apply them just right. This chapter shows you how to use them to get good results with the tools and commands that take center stage. Like temperamental sports cars, they're a little tricky to use — but worth the effort!

Messing Around with Meshes

Illustrator is really great at filling areas with solid colors, continuous patterns, or gradients. Illustrator gets testy, though, when you try to create a continuous tone — such as the many skin tones that define a human face, or how colors fade into one another in a piece of folded fabric. However, you can use the Illustrator Mesh tool, even if it is a bit of a crotchety magician. Just talk nicely to it, and it can help you bend the rules a bit. With the Mesh tool, you can create amazing shading and tonal effects.

And gradient meshes overcome the limitations of gradients (the other Illustrator feature that enables you to blend colors; for more, see Chapter 5). Simple gradients fill areas with linear and radial color blends. Period. Comparatively, gradient Meshes have no such limitation. You can use them to assign colors to the specific points and paths that make up an object. Where the mesh lines cross, you can assign a different color to every line and every point. These colors blend with the colors of the other points. Take a look at Figure 10-1 for a sample of what you can do with a gradient mesh.

Figure 10-1: The artwork that made up the Illustrator Venus was colored entirely with the Mesh tool.

Figure 10-1 might seem complex, but the difficulty lies much more in the artistry than in the technical aspects. The Mesh tool might seem daunting at first, but you can tackle it if you begin by adding a highlight to a simple shape, as shown in Figure 10-2. Do that, and you're well on your way to gradient mesh mastery, as spelled out in the next section.

Figure 10-2: Use the Mesh tool to create a highlight in a path.

Adding a gradient mesh manually

To add a gradient mesh to a simple shape, just follow these steps:

1. **Create a shape by clicking and dragging with any of the basic object tools (see Chapter 4 for more on basic objects) and fill the shape with a dark color.**

   You can use any shape. For this example, I created a circle and colored it black.

2. **Deselect the path (choose Select⇨Deselect).**

   Deselecting the path enables you to pick a different color for the Mesh tool. If you choose a different color with the path selected, you change the color of the object.

3. **Set the fill color to any light color.**

   Choose Window⇨Color to open the Color panel. Click the Fill box and choose a light color to use as a highlight. (Gradient meshes use only fill colors and ignore stroke colors.)

4. **Choose the Mesh tool from the Tools panel and click the object to which you want to add a highlight.**

   As if by magic, two intersecting paths appear on the object, crossing at the spot where you clicked. (You can see this intersection back in Figure 10-2 where all the blue lines are converging in the red middle of the star.) This intersection is the mesh point. These paths are the gradient mesh. The highlight appears where the paths intersect.

5. **Click other areas within the path to add more highlights — as many as you want.**

The paths that make up the gradient mesh can be edited the same as any other path. Click the mesh points in the path with the Direct Selection tool and move them to create different effects. Mesh points also have direction points, just like curved paths. (See Chapter 6 for more on paths.) These direction points can be moved to change the shape of the gradient mesh. You can also change the color of any point or path segment by clicking it and choosing a different color in the Color or Swatches panels. Figure 10-3 shows different effects made by mashing the gradient mesh around.

That's really all there is to this tool! I moved those points by using the Direct Selection tool and then tweaked the colors by selecting a point or a path and choosing a new color in the Color or Swatches panels (accessible by choosing Window⇨Color and Window⇨Swatches, respectively).

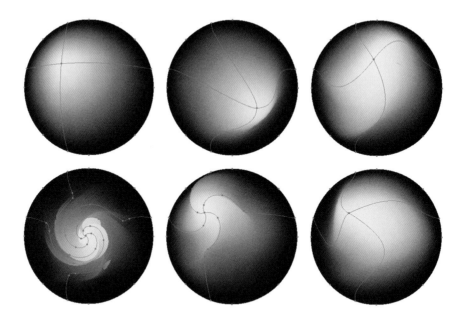

Figure 10-3: Same gradient mesh with mesh points moved.

Letting gradient mesh do the work for you

You can automate the process by clicking the object you want and choosing Object➪Create Gradient Mesh. This method adds a gradient mesh to the object automatically. Illustrator does its best to estimate where the mesh paths should go by looking at the shape of the object and figuring out where the mesh paths should go to shade the object so that it looks three dimensional. You can even have the gradient mesh create the shading for you.

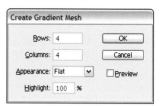

Figure 10-4: Set your Gradient Mesh here.

After you select the Create Gradient Mesh command, the Create Gradient Mesh dialog box opens (shown in Figure 10-4). Set your options, click OK, and the command does the mesh-y work for you. Here's the all-star lineup of options:

  ✓ **Rows and Columns:** These options set the number of mesh paths that the command creates. The higher the number, the more control you have over the colors in your object (but the more complicated the graphic is to work with).

✔ **Appearance:** Select one of three Appearance options. Figure 10-5 shows the differences between the three options.

- *To Center:* Lightens colors to place a highlight in the center of the object, creating the appearance that the graphic is being pulled outward

- *To Edge:* Places a highlight at the edges of the object, creating the appearance that the graphic is being pulled inward

- *Flat:* Doesn't change any colors but still creates the mesh, so you can change colors on your own

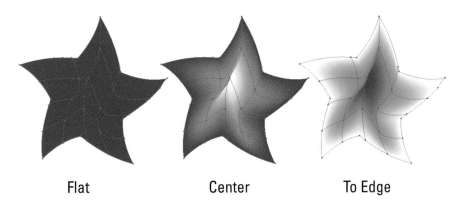

| Flat | Center | To Edge |

Figure 10-5: The same gradient mesh: Flat, To Center, and To Edge.

✔ **Highlight**: When you select an Appearance option of To Edge or To Center, the Highlight setting determines the maximum amount that the colors lighten to create the 3-D effect.

In Figure 10-5, the two examples on the right show objects with a highlight applied to them using the Illustrator automatic highlighting process.

Creating soft bevels with Gradient Mesh

You can use the Mesh tool to create a soft-beveled object. The following steps illustrate a very basic, yet quite handy, method for creating bevels:

1. **Create a square by choosing the Rectangle tool and then clicking the Artboard and dragging. Fill the square with a nice strong solid color, such as grass green or fire engine red.**

   Other shapes work with this, but a square is the simplest.

2. **Choose the Mesh tool, click just inside the upper-left corner, and then click again just inside the lower-right corner.**

This creates a total of nine mesh patches on the square, as shown in Figure 10-6.

3. **Using the Direct Selection tool, drag a marquee around the four points along the top edge of the square. Then press Shift and drag a marquee around the unselected three points on the left edge of the square.**

   You have seven points selected now, around the top-left corner, all on the outside edge of the square.

4. **Choose Window⇨Color.**

   The Color panel appears, as shown in Figure 10-7.

5. **Holding down the Shift key, drag one of the right-most triangles to the left about half-way. (In the example using the red color from Figure 10-7, you could choose either the Magenta or Yellow triangle.)**

   The Shift key "tints" whatever color you selected in Step 1 when you drag a slider in the Color panel.

6. **Again using the Direct Selection tool, drag a marquee around the three rightmost points along the bottom edge of the square. Then press Shift and drag a marquee around the middle two points on the right edge of the square.**

   With the lower-right points selected, you're now ready to darken this corner of the square.

7. **Drag the K slider on the Color panel to the right until you darken the lower-right edge to your liking.**

   The result looks something like Figure 10-8.

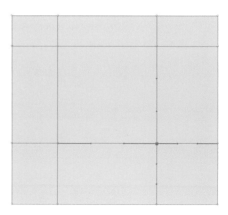

Figure 10-6: A square after two clicks with the Mesh tool.

Figure 10-7: The Color panel.

Figure 10-8: The resulting beveled square.

Making Objects Partially Transparent and Blending Colors

By default, Illustrator creates objects that hide whatever is behind them. However, the Transparency panel enables you to change this situation. With the Opacity option, you can fade objects so that the underlying objects show through them. You can also blend the colors in the top graphics with the underlying graphics (in an astonishing variety of ways) by using blend modes.

One of the powerful features of the Transparency panel is that everything you do in it is live, meaning that your paths suffer no permanent changes after you make them transparent. You can change opacity again and again — or remove it altogether if you want — without changing your path data. This capability gives you tremendous room to play and experiment with different opacities.

Fade away with opacity

In Figure 10-9, a red "no" symbol is faded-out to 50% opacity to partly reveal details behind it.

Figure 10-9: Original opacity (left) and faded to 50% (right).

To make something partially transparent, follow these steps:

1. **Select the object (or objects) that you want to fade.**

   When you select multiple objects, they all get the same opacity setting.

2. **Choose Window⇨Transparency.**

   The Transparency panel appears, as shown in Figure 10-10.

Figure 10-10: The Transparency panel.

3. **In the Transparency panel, drag the Opacity slider until it shows the percentage of opacity you want to give to the selected object(s).**

   After you release the mouse button, the selected objects become partially transparent.

By default, transparency applies evenly to both the fill and stroke. To assign the fill and the stroke independent Opacity values, use the Appearance panel. See Chapter 11 for details.

Big fun with math! Blending graphics with blend modes

Pssst! Listen very, very carefully while I tell you what's really going on with blend modes. Here's the scoop: Forget the math and pay attention to what the resulting artwork looks like.

Illustrator defines every color mathematically. You see that math when you drag sliders in the Color panel. A bright red color may be defined as R:216, G:20, and B:7 (in RGB) or C:20%, M:95%, Y:95%, and K:5% (in CMYK). Each of these numbers reflects a different amount of a component color; every different color has its own color value.

Blend modes take the colors in an object and mix them with the colors in underlying objects, performing a mathematical calculation using numbers that identify the colors of the objects. Therefore, if the top object is red, the underlying object is blue, and you have the blend mode set to Multiply, red's number gets multiplied by blue's number. The resulting color is what you see. Other modes do more complex calculations. What does that mean? What's blue times red? What's the difference between yellow and mauve? What's the sound of one hand clapping?

In short, it doesn't matter. What the result looks like is what matters! Try this approach for yourself: Select the top object and choose a different blend mode. Blend modes hang out in the Transparency panel Blend Mode menu, as shown in Figure 10-11.

Figure 10-11: The Blend Mode pop-up menu in the Transparency panel.

Figure 10-12 shows three (of the 16 possible) blend modes at work on the same image — and they're completely changeable. If you try one and don't like it, just choose another from the menu.

Figure 10-12: Three blend modes in Illustrator.

Discovering How Strokes Work

Any path in Illustrator can pick up a stroke (. . . stroke . . . stroke! Sorry. Just daydreaming about going for a nice row on a lake). In Illustrator, a stroke is a line placed on a path. A stroke can be of any thickness, which Illustrator calls its weight. Strokes can be any color or pattern.

In Chapter 9, I discuss the specialized strokes that you can make with the Paintbrush tool. The Pen and Pencil tools also provide distinctive strokes of their own (Chapters 7 and 8, respectively).

In addition to color and weight, you can give strokes special attributes. These attributes include the specific look of corners (joins) and endings (caps) as well as whether the stroke has a pattern of dashes applied to it. To investigate all the advanced ways you can modify strokes, look at the Stroke panel shown in Figure 10-13. (Choose Window➪Stroke and choose Show Options from the Stroke panel pop-up menu.) To change how a stroke appears, select a path and play around in the Stroke panel to see what happens. I won't tell a soul.

Strokes are applied to the center of a path by default, which means that the strokes, especially those of larger weight, can ooze beyond the path. The path runs along the exact middle of the stroke. For more information on the relationship between strokes and paths, see Chapter 5.

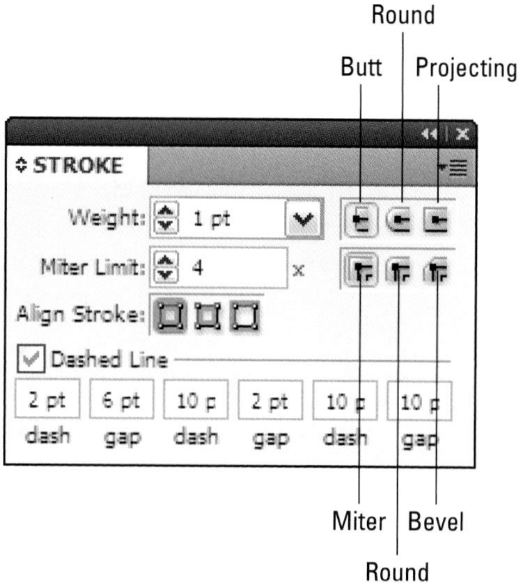

Figure 10-13: The Stroke panel displaying a full set of options.

Caps, joins, and dashes

A stroke can be (and often is) a continuous line of color that follows a path, even if the path is as convoluted as a strand of cooked spaghetti. But paths can also appear chopped up into dashes. You can tweak the shape of the dashes all at once, without having to fuss over every single one. You can set the shape that an individual dash (the basic unit of an open path) begins or ends with (its cap) and the shape of its corner points (its join).

Strokes can have any of three different caps and any of three different joins applied to them. Combine these with the almost-limitless combinations possible for dash patterns and weights, and you can see the incredible versatility of strokes. To access these additional options, choose Window⇨Stroke. In the Stroke panel that appears, select Show Options from the panel pop-up menu; refer to Figure 10-13.

Caps

Shaping the ends of the dashes that make up an open path can change the entire look of the path. For example, imagine a dashed line that's 500 dashes long. Then imagine that all 500 dashes have identical ends, shaped like one of the three shapes in Figure 10-14.

Figure 10-14: Three different caps on three paths.

Depending on which Cap setting you choose, you get three noticeably different capped lines. Here are the options:

- **Butt Cap:** Chops off the stroke at the ends.

- **Round Cap:** Extends the stroke past the ends (or around the dash location) with semicircular ends. (The radius of each semicircle equals half the stroke weight.)

- **Projecting Cap:** Extends the stroke past the ends (or around the dash location) with squared ends. (The amount of each extension equals half the stroke weight.)

To change how a line is capped, select it with any selection tool, and then click the desired cap in the Stroke panel.

Joins

The Stroke panel offers three different joins. Figure 10-15 shows how they appear on paths. Joins affect only corner points, not smooth points. (See Chapter 6 for more info on corner points.) They make corners appear sharp and pointy, blunt and rounded, or squared off.

Figure 10-15: Three different joins on a path (left to right): Miter, Round, and Bevel.

Depending on which Join setting you choose, you get three noticeably different corners. Here are the options:

- **Miter Join:** Causes the outside corner of the stroke to come to a sharp point

- **Round Join:** Causes the outside corner of a stroke to come to a rounded or smooth curve

- **Bevel Join:** Cuts off the corner so that the width of the stroke is the same at the bevel as on the rest of the stroke

If these terms look familiar, you're probably familiar with woodworking — or you actually paid attention in industrial arts class.

Dashes

Dashes break up the stroke into repeating segments of any length, with gaps between them, also of any length. You can set up to three different dash sizes — and three different gap sizes — in any stroke, as shown in Figure 10-16.

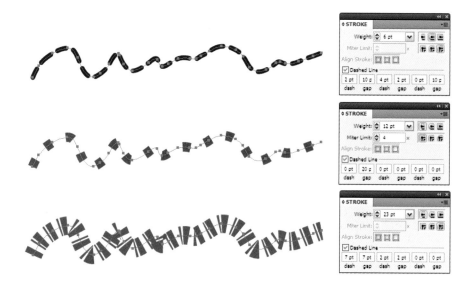

Figure 10-16: Three different dash patterns and the settings used to create them.

Dashes work with the Cap settings. (What the heck, call it a labor-saving device.) Whichever Cap setting you use applies to the ends of all the dashes, not just to the ends of the path.

To create a dashed line, follow these steps:

1. **Select the Dashed Line option in the Stroke panel.**

2. **Set a dash size in the first dash box.**

   Remember that the Round and Projecting Cap settings extend the dash from its center by half the width of the stroke. Therefore, if you use the Projecting Cap setting and your dash setting is 10 points (pt), on a line with a 20 pt stroke, the dash will be 30 pt long.

   Choose a Butt Cap setting when you want your dashes to be an exact length that doesn't vary with the width of the stroke. If you want an exact circle for a dash (or a dot), use a 0 pt dash. That creates a dot the width of the stroke.

3. **Set the gap size in the first gap box (the distance between the ends of the dashes).**

This setting can be a little confusing if you're using the Round or Projecting Cap settings because these extend the length of the dash past the end of the dash and into the gap, based on the width of the stroke, creating a gap that looks smaller than what you specified. The width of the stroke also affects the gap size. If you want a gap of 20 pt and you're using a 10 pt stroke, set the gap size to 30 pt.

Clipping Masks

No, clipping masks aren't special headgear that the barber wears to entertain young customers. Clipping masks are simple, yet incredibly handy, Illustrator features. Simply put, they hide things. Like Effects and Transparency settings, Clipping Masks are live functions that make no permanent change to path data. They make things look different, but you can take them away with a single command, and your paths remain exactly as they were before.

Clipping masks use objects to hide other objects, as shown in Figure 10-17. The top object (the masking object) becomes completely transparent. The underlying objects become invisible except for where the mask object is. The number of objects beneath the mask doesn't matter. Only the topmost object functions as the masking object. The top object's fill and stroke also don't matter, because the top object becomes invisible.

Clipping masks let you "fill" an object with any other object(s), making them the most extreme fill you'll find in Illustrator.

Figure 10-17: Original (left), the masking object in front of the artwork (middle), and the masked artwork (right).

To create a clipping mask, here's the drill:

1. **Create an object to be used as a mask.**

   Masks can be any shape or color. You can even use text as a mask.

2. **Position the object in front of whatever you want to mask out.**

3. **Select the object and all the objects behind it that you want to mask out.**

   Shift-click with the Selection tool to select multiple objects.

4. **Choose Object⇨Clipping Mask⇨Make.**

   The masking object and anything outside the mask disappear, leaving just what's inside and behind the masking object.

The things that seem to disappear after you apply the mask aren't really gone. They're just hidden. You can bring them back by choosing Object⇨Clipping Mask⇨Release. Sometimes that's more impressive than pulling a rabbit out of your hat.

Effectively Keeping Up Appearances, with Style(s)

*B*ack in the twentieth century, Illustrator was a straightforward program that offered relatively few (and relatively obvious) choices. You knew when you looked at a pink rectangle that it was made with four corner points joined by four paths and was filled with a single, solid pink color. But those days of blissful innocence are past. Now that pink rectangle might really be a red rectangle that some fiend faded to 50% Opacity via the Transparency panel. And that rectangle might not be a rectangle at all, but a graphic of an old shoe that has been disguised as a rectangle using the Effect⇨Convert to Shape⇨Rectangle command. In this world of illusions, where anything can appear to be anything else and nothing is as it seems, what's an artist to do?

The truth is, the ability of Illustrator to make objects *look* different without changing the original object is amazing. Illustrator lets you do incredibly powerful stuff that would be impossible otherwise, and more importantly, gives you incredible editability. Editability, you ask? That's one of the primary reasons to use Illustrator in the first place. The ability to go back at any time to change a small aspect of your artwork without having to redo all the work you initially put in is incredibly valuable.

Effects (and transparency) let you change the appearance of your artwork easily (again, without changing the underlying object). Illustrator has dozens of them, giving you power and flexibility beyond anything you can dream of.

In this chapter, you also discover a wonderful tool for cutting through (and taking control of) the illusions of Illustrator: the Appearance panel. The Appearance panel enables you to see exactly what secrets your artwork is hiding. If that were all it did, it'd be worth its weight in gold. But it does so much more! Beyond just seeing what's been done to an illustration, you also find out how to change the attributes of the illustration. For example, you can alter applied effects — or delete them altogether.

You also discover how to use the Appearance panel to target only the fill of an object (or just the stroke) when you apply Transparency or Effects settings. You also use the Appearance panel to perform casual miracles, such as assigning multiple fills and strokes to a single object.

To make matters even better, this chapter shows you how to save all the Appearance settings as a style. Styles are saved in the Graphic Styles panel. You can apply a style to any object. In addition to being a quick way to apply all these attributes to objects, styles can be updated in a way that also updates all objects with those styles applied.

The Effect Menu

The Effect menu (shown in Figure 11-1) contains more amazing things than you see on a government-sponsored tour of Area 51 (okay, bad analogy . . . but there's a lot of stuff there, really). Everything that you apply remains *live* — that is, changeable until you tell it to stop changing. Effects change the way an object looks but not the object itself. Applying effects is like telling the object to put on a specific costume, or changing the appearance of the world when you look through rose-colored glasses. No permanent change to the underlying object takes place.

Instead of rewriting the code for an object (which is what you tell Illustrator to do when you move a point), effects tack on extra code, leaving the original code untouched. You can change or remove the extra code, without affecting the original. It's sort of like when you put on a nice outfit — you're still the same person underneath, but you have snazzy duds on that make you look different.

Ah, yes, all things must change — and sometimes you get to change them. Contemplate the concept of *infinite editability* for a moment. An object in Illustrator is saying, "Turn me into anything." Illustrator provides the capability of changing appearance without manipulating points. You can simply get rid of them at any time, without putting a scratch on your original artwork, without having to redo it, without having to resort to Edit➪Undo, and without having to growl at the dog. Now that's progress.

Applying live effects to objects

Figure 11-2 shows the difference between manually changing an object as opposed to a live effect. A path (left) is manually "roughened" by adding points and moving them,

Figure 11-1: The Effect menu, fully of, erm, Effectiveness.

and the same path (right) roughened with the Roughen effect. The biggest difference is that the path on the manually changed object shows the additional points you had to put on the path, and where you moved them. The Roughen effect, found under the Effects menu, leaves the original path untouched, but still looks roughened.

Figure 11-2: A path (left) manually "roughened," and the same path (right) with the Roughen effect.

To apply an effect to a path, follow these steps:

1. **Select a path using a selection tool of your choice.**

2. **Choose an effect from the Effect menu.**

   For example, you can choose Effect➪Distort & Transform➪Pucker & Bloat. A dialog box opens for that effect, and you can enter the specific settings.

   You can always go back and change the settings if you don't like the result. (If only I could do that in real life.)

3. **Click OK to apply the effect to the path.**

Some effects (many of these are in the second section of effects that starts with the Artistic effect) only work when the document is in RGB Document Color mode. (See Chapter 1 for more on the various modes.) If an effect is grayed out (unavailable) after you select an object, your document is probably in CMYK (cyan, magenta, yellow, and black) mode. You can, however, work on artwork initially in RGB Document Color mode and change it to CMYK later.

3D Effects

Illustrator is technically a 2D product. Everything it creates exists (at least in final form) in 2D space. But hidden away amongst all the cool effects in the Effects menu is the 3D effect, which allows you to quickly extrude, revolve, and rotate items in 3D space. Figure 11-3 shows the 3D Extrude and Bevel dialog box, where you can see all sorts of fun 3D options (and there's all sorts of other ones that are hidden)!

Going into all the options for 3D is beyond the depth <cough> of this book, but simply stated, select any path with a solid color fill, choose Effects⇨ 3D⇨3D Extrude & Bevel and just start noodling around with the settings (make sure the Preview checkbox is checked) and you'll see the wonder that is 3D. Figure 11-4 shows a simple path in its original drawn form next to the same path that has been extruded, another that has been revolved, and another that has been rotated in 3D space.

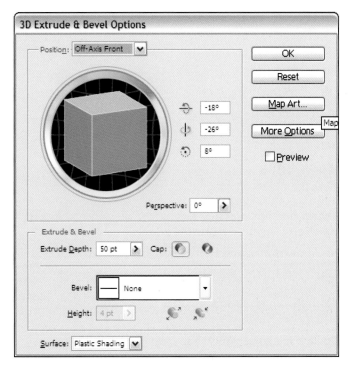

Figure 11-3: The 3D Extrude & Bevel dialog box is ironically presented to you in 2D.

Figure 11-4: From left to right: Original path, extruded path, revolved path and rotated path.

Removing and changing effects

To change or remove effects, use the Appearance panel, as shown in Figure 11-5. The Appearance panel is such an amazing panel that the majority of this chapter is devoted to it. For now, though, I just want to show you how to use the Appearance panel to remove and change effects.

Appearances aside (so to speak), removing an effect is as simple as following these steps:

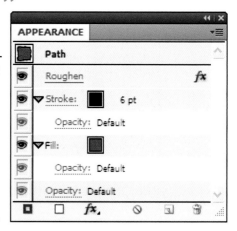

Figure 11-5: The roughened path from Figure 11-2 in the Appearance panel.

1. **Select the object that has the effect that you want to remove. (Unless the object is grouped, you can use the regular (black) Selection tool for selecting the object.)**

2. **If the Appearance panel isn't visible (it is by default), choose Window⇨Appearance.**

   In the Appearance panel, the selected object is listed as Object or Path. Beneath the object is a list that includes the stroke and fill of the object and all the effects applied to it.

3. **In the list, click the effect that you want to discard.**

4. **Click the trashcan at the lower right of the Appearance panel.**

   The effect disappears, and the object returns to its former appearance (before you applied the effect).

To change an effect, follow the preceding steps. However, instead of clicking the trashcan, double-click the effect in the Appearance panel. The particular effect's dialog box opens, where you can enter new settings. Click OK to apply the effect with the new settings.

Do *not* go back to the Effect menu to change the settings of an effect that has been applied to an object, even if adding the effect is the last thing you did. Instead of changing the settings on the existing effect, you actually apply *another* effect to the object on top of the existing one. While applying multiple effects to objects is often desired, it isn't if you're trying to edit the existing effect. So, as my Tip above states, just go back and start all over again.

Rasterization effects

Not all effects can be generated from path-based artwork. That's where the Rasterization effects come in. (Rasterization = the process of turning things into pixels or adding pixel-based imagery to your artwork.) These effects either change the original artwork into pixels or add new pixel-based images to achieve the desired effect. The effects in the second section of the Effect menu (from the Artistic effect down), as well as Drop Shadow, Feather, Inner Glow, Outer Glow, and Rasterize use pixels to achieve the change in appearance.

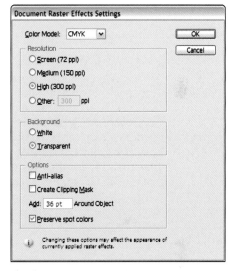

Figure 11-6: The Document Raster Effects Settings dialog box takes a bow.

You control various attributes of these rasterization-based effects by choosing Effect⇨Document Raster Effects Settings. The Document Raster Effects Settings dialog box appears, as shown in Figure 11-6.

In the Document Raster Effects Settings dialog box, you can set the following options:

- **Color Model:** This setting determines the color model used by the resulting graphic. Try to use the color model of your target output as much as possible. If you're creating a graphic print in grayscale, choose Grayscale. If you're bound for the Web, choose RGB. Choosing Bitmap turns your art into harsh black and white tones, if you're into that sort of thing. But most people aren't, and you should stay away from that setting. Refer to Chapter 1 for more about CMYK vs. RGB.

- **Resolution:** This setting determines how much information the resulting image contains. Try to match this setting with the graphic's purpose. For the Web, select 72 ppi (pixels per inch). For most ink jet printers, 150 ppi is sufficient. For high-resolution printing, 300 ppi is a good, all-purpose size.

✔ **Background:** Pixel-based images are always rectangular. If the graphic you're rasterizing is anything but rectangular, you have to add a background to make the graphic rectangular. The background can be white or transparent. White is fine for a stand-alone graphic, but if that graphic is in front of other objects, the white background obscures them. When that's the case, choose the Transparent setting.

✔ **Options:** The Anti-Alias option adds a slight blurring wherever different colors meet. Believe it or not, this setting usually makes the resulting graphic look better. Results vary from graphic to graphic, of course, so try rasterizing with and without the Anti-Alias option selected. The Create Clipping Mask option matters only if you select white for the Background setting; see the preceding bullet. In Illustrator, a *clipping mask* is a special graphic that hides parts of other graphics. When you select the Create Clipping Mask option, a clipping mask is added to hide the white parts added to make the graphic rectangular.

✔ **Add:** Typing a numeric value in this option box adds extra pixels around the graphic, just in case you need them. Hey, you never know! Nobody wants to run short of pixels, and this option actually helps prevent objects, such as drop shadows and other offset pixels, from getting clipped on the edges.

✔ **Preserve Spot Colors:** Checking this box will allow you to use spot colors in your document if it contains transparency. If you're using a spot color, keep this checked.

After you choose your settings, click OK. Any existing (or future) effects that use pixels will use these settings.

The Appearance Panel

The Appearance panel, shown in Figure 11-7, is where you go to see why your artwork looks the way it does. (However, the panel can't explain why anybody would put neon-pink paisleys all over the place.) You can view the Appearance panel by choosing Window➪Appearance. When the Appearance panel wafts into view, it bears a vast treasure of option information. In its basic state, the panel displays Fill, Stroke, and Opacity settings. In its more complex

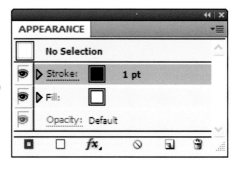

Figure 11-7: The Appearance panel.

state, the panel displays additional fills and strokes, and effects applied to those fills and strokes (as well as to the object itself).

Not to worry: This wealth of information isn't nearly as confusing as your income tax form. Here's why: All along, in the course of creating your artwork, you've been putting all these informational tidbits into the Appearance panel. You tell Illustrator to add info to this panel every time you set an option that changes the way your object looks (such as stroke, fill, and transparency).

The Appearance panel faithfully records all this information all the time, even if you don't look at it. (Good thing it doesn't record everything appearance related, like that incredibly fashionable bathrobe you're wearing as you read this.)

Reading the Appearance panel

The (much larger) Appearance panel shown in Figure 11-8 displays accumulated information about a particular object. What does it all mean? Is it important? Why oh why did Natalie ever leave the Maniacs? I'll answer the first questions, and leave the last one for a Behind the Music special.

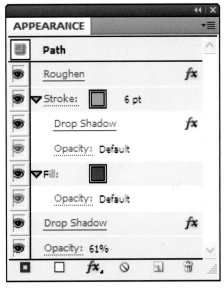

Figure 11-8: The Appearance panel displays info about the object, such as stroke and fill data.

To make sense of all the Appearance panel's information, peruse the following list of its features:

- **Target:** This feature identifies the type of graphic that the information in the Appearance panel refers to. Typically this feature reads Object or Path, meaning the information in the panel refers to (or will be applied to) an appearance that is or will be applied to a single selected object. When you select a group or a layer, the target reads Group or Layer. If text is selected, the target reads Type. The target section is always at the top. A tiny thumbnail image emulates the appearance of the graphic.

- **Global effects:** These effects apply equally to, and affect all aspects of, the entire object. Whenever you apply Effects or Transparency settings (as I described earlier in this chapter) without using the Appearance panel, you apply the effects as global effects. Although they're usually the first attribute you apply, they always appear near the bottom of the list in the Appearance panel.

Another way to differentiate global effects from other effects is how they line up with other items listed in the panel. Global effects appear in alignment with the Stroke and the Fill listings. Effects applied to a specific stroke are indented beneath the listing for that specific stroke. In Figure 11-8, Roughen is the global effect.

- **Strokes:** Objects can have more than one stroke only when you add them through the Appearance panel. (See the section, "Adding fills and strokes," later in this chapter.) Therefore, the first one (listed at the top) is typically the one also shown in the Tools panel. The target may have additional strokes listed here as well. Strokes can have effects applied to them specifically. In Figure 11-8, you see a single stroke with a weight of 6 points. See Chapter 5 for more information on strokes.

- **Stroke and Fill effects:** Effects can be applied directly to strokes and fills, instead of to the entire object, group, or layer. In this figure, a drop shadow has been applied directly to the fill.

- **Stroke and Fill Opacity:** Each stroke and fill can have various Transparency settings applied to it. Here, the fill has an Opacity setting of 61%.

- **Fill:** Each object (group or layer) can have multiple fills (like it can have multiple strokes). Each fill can also have any number of effects applied to it.

- **Eyeballs:** Every single line in the Appearance panel has an eyeball next to it. Super creepy, I know. But each of those eyeballs can be used to hide any one line of info for the selected object, or the object itself. Say you're working with an object that has three strokes, and you want to see the color of the middle stroke, but it's hard to see 'cause the top stroke is covering it. No problem! Just click the eyeball next to the top stroke, and it won't be visible while you're working on that middle stroke.

- **Opacity:** This feature is the transparency appearance for the entire object, group, or layer. In Figure 11-8, the Opacity is set to 61%, meaning the entire object has been faded to 61%. If no special Transparency settings were applied, this would simply read Opacity: Default. See Chapter 10 for more information on the Transparency panel.

The top-to-bottom order of the fills and strokes in the Appearance panel reflect a front-to-back order in the graphic. Strokes and fills on top in the panel appear in front of the strokes and fills that are lower in the panel. Effects run from top to bottom in terms of which effect is applied to the graphic first.

Most of the items in the Appearance panel can be moved up and down through the list into different positions, and this change is reflected in the actual graphic. For instance, you can move the Feather effect applied to a stroke so that it's applied to a fill. You can also move the Feather effect so that it applies to the entire object. To move something in the Appearance panel, drag it up and down through the panel, just as you move things in the Layers panel.

If a fill or stroke has an effect applied to it, the little disclosure triangle automatically appears on the left and points down, listing the attributes of that fill or stroke. When you have a whole lot of different effects applied to a fill or stroke, the panel can get cumbersome. Clicking the disclosure triangle hides the list of effects. You can access the list at any time by clicking the disclosure triangle again.

Adding fills and strokes

Chapter 5 explores fills and strokes in greater detail (and if you want to nip back there for more information, I can wait). When you apply a different stroke or fill to an object without using the Appearance panel, the fill or stroke replaces any existing fill or stroke. You don't have to settle for just one of each, though! From the Appearance panel, you can add as many fills and strokes as you want, as shown in Figure 11-9. This feature offers some interesting possibilities. For example, you can give a path three different colored strokes of different sizes, to create a striped path. Or you can apply a pattern fill over a solid-color fill. The Appearance panel is shown next to this figure so you can see exactly how it is constructed.

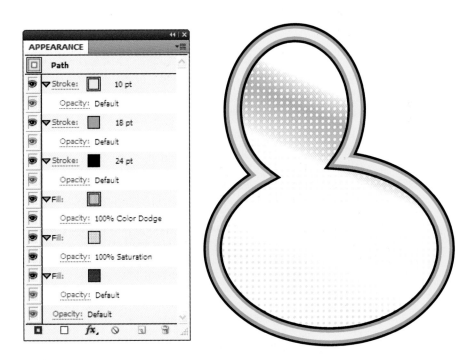

Figure 11-9: Multiple fills and strokes on an object.

Just follow these steps to apply an additional fill and stroke to an object:

1. **Create an object with a fill color and a thick stroke.**

   In this example, I drew a simplistic rubber ducky shape using the Pen tool. (See Chapter 7 for more information on the Pen tool.) I filled it with a solid color by clicking the Fill box in the Tools panel, and then by adjusting the sliders in the Colors panel. I next added a 24-point black stroke to the ducky by clicking the Stroke box in the Tools panel, and then by clicking a black swatch in the Swatches panel, and finally by choosing 24 points from the Stroke panel. (For more info on fills and strokes, see Chapter 5.)

2. **Choose the Add New Fill command from the Appearance panel pop-up menu or by clicking the white box at the bottom left of the Appearance panel.**

   Illustrator adds a fill, but you don't see any difference because the new fill is identical to the fill already there. The new fill is highlighted in the Appearance panel, however, and as soon as you select a new fill from the Color panel or the Swatches panel, you see the new fill over the old one.

3. **With the new fill still highlighted in the Appearance panel, change the fill to a pattern fill from the Swatches panel.**

   For this example, change the fill to the pattern called "Polka Dot Pattern" by clicking it in the Swatches panel. Then click on the Opacity link under that fill and change the blend mode to Saturation.

   If you don't know which pattern is the Polka Dot pattern, pause your cursor for a moment above each swatch. Its name pops up.

4. **Choose the Add New Fill command from the Appearance panel pop-up menu or by clicking the white box at the bottom left of the Appearance panel.**

   Illustrator adds another fill on top of the second one you created. With the new fill highlighted, change the fill to a gradient by clicking on it in the Appearance palette. Then click on the Opacity link under that fill and change the blend mode to Color Dodge.

5. **Choose the Add New Stroke command from the Appearance panel pop-up menu or by clicking the black framed square at the bottom left of the Appearance Panel.**

   A stroke appears on top of the original stroke. Like with the added fill color, the new stroke uses the same settings as the previous stroke, so you don't see an immediate difference.

6. **In the Color panel, change the color of the new stroke to green and change its stroke width to 18 points (pt).**

7. **Choose the Add New Stroke command from the Appearance panel pop-up menu or by clicking the black framed square at the bottom left of the Appearance Panel.**

   Another new stroke appears on top of the 2nd stroke. Change the color of the stroke to Yellow and change the stroke weight to 10 points.

After you add strokes and fills, you can move them around. Simply click them in the Appearance panel and drag up or down. While you drag, a black line appears in the panel, indicating where that fill or stroke will go after you release it.

Multiple fills and strokes work great with the Transparency panel. Each fill and stroke can have its own Transparency settings. This approach is a great way to blend fills and strokes together to achieve unique appearances. For example, if you apply a solid color fill over a pattern fill and then change the blend mode of the color fill to hue, you replace the color(s) in the pattern with the color of the solid color but still maintain all the detail of the pattern. See Chapter 10 for more information on the Transparency panel and blend modes.

Changing the appearance of groups and layers

You can change the appearance of groups or layers as well as objects. Groups are collections of separate objects that have been grouped together (using the Object⇨Group command) so that they act like a single object when you select them with the Selection tool. (See Chapter 3 for more information on the Group command.) Similar to grouping, layers are a method of organizing multiple elements of your graphic into separate areas. Chapter 13 discusses layers in depth.

To change the appearance, you need to *target* those groups or layers first. Targeting is a method of selecting a group or layer so that any changes made to the appearance affect all the objects in the group or layer. Changing the appearance of groups or layers creates a global appearance for all objects in the group or on the layer. Objects still maintain their individual appearance settings, but any group or layer changes are added to all the objects.

To change the appearance of a group by adding an effect, just follow these steps:

1. **Select a group by clicking it with the regular Selection tool.**

2. Add an effect to the group.

Any effect would work, but if I were you, I'd add a Gaussian blur by choosing Effect⇨Blur⇨Gaussian Blur. In the Gaussian Blur dialog box that opens when you choose the effect, set the Radius to 5 and then lick OK.

All the objects in the group become blurred. Just like that. Wow.

I applied the Gaussian Blur effect to the previous figure. (The figures for this book tend to be done in Illustrator, which is an amazing coincidence.) The panel (a placed image) and the original path were grouped and the effect was applied to it, resulting in the mess you see in Figure 11-10.

On the other hand, targeting a layer to apply an effect is a little more unusual, since you have to use the Layer palette to "select" a layer first, as shown in Figure 11-11.

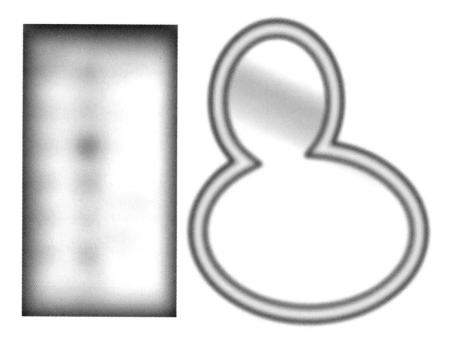

Figure 11-10: This is perfectly clear. When was the last time you had your eyes checked?

Target Layer Appearance button

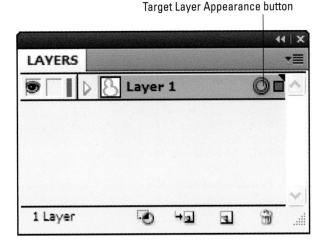

Figure 11-11: Targeting a layer to apply an effect.

Layers are a way to organize and arrange objects in your document. (Chapter 13 talks about layers in depth.) Every time you add an object to a layer, the appearance of that object changes to match the settings of the layer. When that object goes to another layer with different Layer Appearance settings, the object's appearance changes again.

To target and apply an effect to a layer, just follow these steps:

1. **Choose Window⇨Layers.**

   The Layers panel opens (refer to Figure 11-11).

2. **In the Layers panel, click the Target Layer Appearance button beside the layer that has the appearance you want to change.**

   The Target Layer Appearance button is the circle to the right of the name of the layer in the Layers panel. Clicking this circle targets the layer, so your changes affect that layer.

3. **Add an effect to the layer.**

   For this example, choose Effect⇨Stylize⇨Feather. The Feather dialog box opens. Set the Feather Radius to 5 and then click OK. All the objects in the layer are feathered. (Lay in a large supply of birdseed. Just kidding.). Figure 11-12 shows the Feather layer with the word "feather" feathered.

Figure 11-12: The word "feather" has been placed on its own layer and the layer has been given a Feather effect.

Applying effects to strokes and fills

Normally, whenever you apply an effect, it's applied to the entire object. However, to keep matters interesting (or confusing), you can also apply any effect to either a stroke or a fill. Whichever one you change, the other remains unaffected, as shown in Figure 11-13.

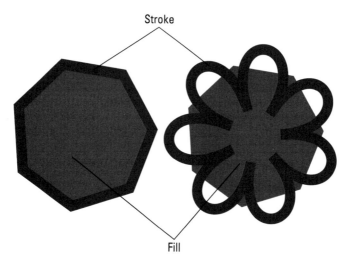

Figure 11-13: The Pucker & Bloat effect applied to the stroke, but not the fill.

To apply an effect to a stroke only or to a fill only, just follow these steps:

1. **Select an object by clicking it with the Selection tool.**

2. **Choose Window⇨Appearance to open the Appearance panel.**

3. **In the Appearance panel, select the stroke or the fill to which you want to apply the effect.**

   For this example, select the stroke.

4. **Choose an effect from the Effect menu.**

   For this example, choose Effect⇨Distort & Transform⇨Pucker & Bloat. The Pucker & Bloat dialog box opens. Drag the slider towards Pucker (to the left) or towards Bloat (to the right). The effect applies to the path and takes an appropriate place in the Appearance panel.

When you look at your artwork, you see that only the stroke has been puckered (or bloated, depending on what you chose). If you want to apply an effect just to a fill, follow the preceding steps, but select a fill instead of a stroke.

Going back to adjust settings

Any effect previously applied to an object, group, or layer can be modified. You can edit the effect by double-clicking it in the Appearance panel. After you do, the effect's dialog box appears, enabling you to edit the current values for that effect. If the effect dialog box has a Preview check box, place a check in it and watch your changes in real time!

Don't try to edit an effect you just applied by selecting that effect again in the Effect menu. Doing so applies the same effect a second time over the same path. Instead, double-click the effect in the Appearance panel.

Removing appearances

If you're tired of keeping up appearances (for example, you feel your artwork is too complex and want it to be cleaner and simpler, or you added so many effects that printing or drawing on-screen takes too long), Illustrator gives you three ways to remove them (from on-screen artwork, that is). You can take an appearance apart (one attribute at a time), trash the whole appearance except the basics, or zap everything at once. Here's how you accomplish each of these tasks:

✔ **To get rid of a single effect, transparency setting, stroke, or fill:** Select what you want to remove in the Appearance panel and then click the little trashcan icon at the bottom right of the panel.

✔ **To get rid of all effects, extra fills and strokes, and transparencies:** Click the Reduce to Basic Appearance button (the button with the circle with a slash running through it at the bottom center of the panel). This action strips away everything except one stroke and one fill color and resets the Default Transparency setting to a blend mode of normal and an Opacity setting of 100%. (See Chapter 10 for more details on blend modes and Opacity settings.)

✔ **To clear everything:** If you really want to clear the decks, leaving a path with no strokes or fills whatsoever, click the Clear Appearance button (the circle with a line through it at the bottom left of the panel).

Note that the Appearance panel always shows a Fill color, Stroke color, and default Opacity setting for an object, even after you throw them away. Throwing away a fill or stroke automatically sets it to None; throwing away a transparency sets it to the default Opacity setting, which is a blend mode of Normal and an Opacity setting of 100%.

If you're wondering what the last three buttons in the Appearance panel do, here's the skinny. The FX button provides superfast access to the Effect menu (the entire menu magically appears right at the button!). The dog-eared page icon is the Duplicate button. Select the appearance effect or attribute (stroke or fill) you want and click this button to create a duplicate. The trash can icon will delete any line item(s) you choose in the appearance palette.

Killing live effects until they're dead

Sometimes, you want to preserve the way an object looks, but get rid of all the things in the Appearance panel. One reason to do this is that all these multiple fills, strokes, and effects can take tremendous processing power when they are live. This situation can result in long print times, or long times redrawing whenever you make a change to your graphic. The drawback to live effects is that they are previews and need to be recalculated every time you make a change. You can kill these live effects so that they permanently change your graphic. You can no longer make individual adjustments to them or remove them, but all the calculations have been made and the graphic has been permanently changed. This results in a much simpler, if limited, graphic.

To permanently set all the live effects, choose Object➪Expand Appearance. The object expands, which is a completely counterintuitive way of saying the object gets simpler. All the settings made in the Appearance panel are really just previews. They haven't been applied to the graphic. Every time you make a change, that appearance needs to be completely recalculated. Expanding the object applies all those changes to it permanently, so the calculations don't have to be made again. The graphic is simpler, if less editable. Figure 11-14 shows the difference between live and, um, dead objects.

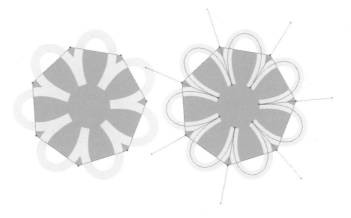

Figure 11-14: A live effect (left) and after Expand Appearance is applied (right).

Figuring Out Styles

Styles are collections of colors, transparency settings, effects, and additional fills and strokes that can be applied to any path, group, or layer. Just think of all that information in the Appearance panel. Saving it and applying it to different objects (without having to re-create all those settings) can significantly reduce the time and effort you spend. That's the advantage of using styles.

Another advantage is that any update in the style changes all the objects to which you apply that style. For instance, if you apply a style with a red fill and black stroke to a path, and later you update the style to an orange fill, the object you previously applied that style to changes to an orange fill and black stroke.

Applying styles to objects

Illustrator comes with a whole slew of premade styles that are stored in the Graphic Styles panel and in premade libraries that ship with Illustrator (see Figure 11-10), ready for you to use with just a click.

To apply a style to an object, follow these steps:

1. **Select an object.**

2. **Choose Window⇨Graphic Styles.**

   The Graphic Styles panel appears. Figure 11-15 shows styles from the default Style library as well as styles from other libraries included with Illustrator.

3. **Click a thumbnail style in the Graphic Styles panel.**

   Doing so automatically applies all the settings to the selected object.

Figure 11-15: Styles examples.

Creating and editing styles

You can create a style from any selected object in the document. You can also create a style based on the current Appearance panel settings. (The Appearance panel contains the settings for the last object selected, even if that object isn't currently selected.)

1. **Select an object (or not, as the case may be).**

   If you don't select a path, the style you create adopts the current settings in the Appearance panel.

2. **Open the Graphic Styles panel by choosing Window⇨Styles.**

   The Graphic Styles panel (shown in Figure 11-16) appears.

3. **Click the New Style button (the middle button at the bottom right of the Graphic Styles panel) or simply drag your object onto an empty space in the Graphic Styles panel.**

   A thumbnail representation of the new style appears in the Graphic Styles panel.

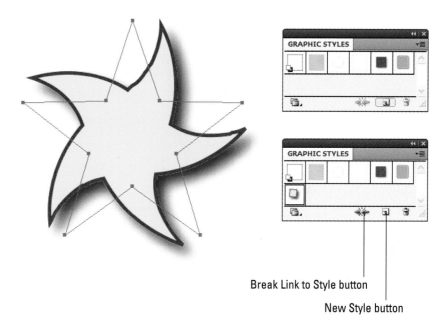

Break Link to Style button

New Style button

Figure 11-16: The Graphic Styles panel.

You have more than one method available to edit an existing style. Regardless of the method you use, Illustrator automatically updates all the objects that have that style applied to them to match the new style. The basic way to edit an existing style is to redefine it.

After you apply a style to an object, you can click the Break Link to Style button on the Graphic Styles panel to prevent Illustrator from updating the object to a new style if you redefine the existing one.

To redefine an existing style, just follow these steps:

1. **Create a basic shape and apply a style to it.**

   In this instance, I created a triangle by using the Basic Shapes tool. Then I chose Window⇨Graphic Styles and applied the style Bermuda to the triangle by clicking that style in the Graphic Styles panel.

2. **Edit the selected object as you normally would to create the new appearance that you want.**

   Change the fill and stroke, and/or add effects. In this case, I chose a darker fill color and added two strokes of different colors to the triangle by using the Add New Stroke command in the Appearance panel pop-up menu (which I describe in the "Adding fills and strokes" section of this chapter).

3. **After you're satisfied with the changes, open the Appearance panel by choosing Window⇨Appearance. With the altered object still selected, choose Redefine Graphic Style *Style Name* from the Appearance panel pop-up menu, accessed by clicking the triangle in the upper-right corner of the Appearance panel and shown in Figure 11-17.**

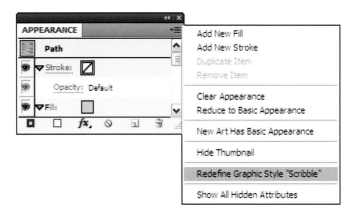

Figure 11-17: Redefining an existing style.

You're replacing a style, but you have to do it through the Appearance panel. Go figure! Because the name of the style I edited in this example was *Scribble,* the menu reads *Redefine Graphic Style "Scribble."* The menu changes to whatever name the style has been given.

Illustrator updates the style in the Graphic Styles panel with the changes — and updates any object in the document that has that same style applied to it.

Another way to edit an existing style is to replace it with another set of Appearance settings. Set the fill, stroke, and effects for an object to make it look the way you want. Then hold down the Alt key (Option on a Mac) and drag the object over the thumbnail of the style that you want to replace in the Graphic Styles panel. It might look as if you're dragging that entire object into the Graphic Styles panel, but you're just dragging its fill, stroke, and effects settings (in other words, its appearance). To let you know that the object is in the proper position to replace the existing style, a black border appears around the style. Release the mouse to update the style to the Appearance settings of the selected object. Illustrator also updates all objects that share the style.

Spotting the difference between graphic and text styles

The Illustrator graphic styles are different from its text styles. (Text styles are discussed in Chapter 14.) *Graphic styles* specify graphic attributes, such as fill color, stroke color, transparency, additional strokes and fills, and any applied effects. *Text styles* (Illustrator has two types: Character and Paragraph) specify text attributes, such as font, size, leading, alignment, and other Character panel and Paragraph panel settings.

The Illustrator graphic styles don't allow you to save text attributes, such as font and alignment, with them. However, you can apply graphic styles to text and text objects; the graphic styles just don't apply any text-specific attributes.

Applying graphic styles to text

Illustrator looks at text as a *picture* of letters and numbers — not as letters and numbers — and then applies a graphic style to that picture, as shown in Figure 11-18.

Figure 11-18: Text before (top) and after (bottom) a graphic style is applied to it.

To apply a graphic style to text, just follow these steps:

1. **Select text by using the Selection tool.**
2. **Display the Styles panel by choosing Window➪Graphic Styles.**
3. **Click a thumbnail in the Graphic Styles panel to apply that style to the text.**

   Illustrator applies the graphic style you select to the text object.

You can quickly apply a style to text or other objects by selecting the style you want and then clicking with the Paint Bucket (which is located in the same Tools panel slot as the Eyedropper tool) on anything you want to change to that style. (It's so much easier than dragging a real paint bucket. And you don't have to worry about the carpet. Is Illustrator great, or what?)

Part III
Taking Your Paths to Obedience School

By now, you're probably thinking that this whole Illustrator thing really is a lot easier than your pixel-based buddies had led you to believe. And because you can do so much more, why would anyone want to limit themselves to pixels, anyway? But you'll keep quiet on that around them and just continue to amaze and astonish them with your newfound skills, which in this section takes your art to the next, um, layer.

12

Pushing, Pulling, Poking, and Prodding

In This Chapter

▶ Understanding how transformations work

▶ Using the Scale, Rotate, Reflect, and Shear tools

▶ Moving and shaking (even stirring) objects and portions of objects

▶ Blending paths until they're confused and happy

*A*rt that you create in Illustrator can be modified in a number of ways. Perhaps the most powerful of these ways are transformations and distortions. These enable you to bend, move, and manipulate paths and other Illustrator objects like silly putty, shaping them to your every whim. (Power mongers, rejoice!)

In this chapter, you find out how to use the many Illustrator transformation tools to alter the shape of your artwork in any way you desire. For the more extreme stuff — we're talking real distortion here – check out Bonus Chapter 1, available for download from the Web site associated with this book.

Understanding the Five Transformation Sisters

You can do five fundamental things to paths: move, scale, rotate, reflect, and shear. Each of these transformations has both a tool and a dialog box associated with it. Move actually has three tools, if you count all the arrow tools (each of which are used to move selections).

The key to using all these tools (and their control-freak dialog boxes) is to select what you want to change first and then to apply the transformation. Use the Selection tool when you want to transform an entire object (Shift-click with the Selection tool to transform multiple objects simultaneously) or use the Direct Selection tool to transform just a few points at a time.

Move

Illustrator enables you to move objects simply by clicking and dragging them with any of the selection arrows. Figure 12-1, for example, shows an object moved from one spot to another. The original illustration (left) is modified (right) by using the Selection tool to move Joey the chit up into the air. (Suddenly the chit seems to defy gravity.)

Figure 12-1: The original illustration (left) is modified (right) by using the Selection tool.

Sometimes, you need to move a selection a specific amount. Suppose you draw a flower (or a weed, if your drawing skills aren't quite up to par yet), and you want to move this flower exactly one inch to the right.

To specify how much you want to move your object, follow these steps:

1. **Select your artwork and choose Object⇨Transform⇨Move.**

   The Move dialog box appears (see Figure 12-2).

   You can also double-click any of the three arrow tools to access the Move dialog box.

2. **In the Distance field, type how far you want the object to move; in this case, type** 1 in.

3. **Type** 0 **in the Angle field.**

   Setting the Angle field at 0 ensures that the object moves directly to the right without shifting up or down. Leave the other fields at their default settings.

4. **Click OK to exit the Move dialog box.**

Figure 12-2: The Move dialog box.

Okay, so you might wonder how Illustrator knows to move the flower just an inch to the *right,* instead of to the left. Well, Illustrator knows because the number you entered in the text field is a positive number. If you enter a negative number, the object moves to the left. In fact, the only way to move something to the left in the Move dialog box is to enter a negative number in the Horizontal text field. If you do that, the Angle field automatically changes to 180 degrees, which is to the left (0 degrees is to the right).

Tell Illustrator the appropriate measurement unit with these symbols: **in** for inches, **p** for picas, **pt** for points, **cm** for centimeters, **mm** for millimeters, or **px** for pixels.

Scale

To make something bigger or smaller in Illustrator, you *scale* it. Illustrator has a Scale tool, a Scale dialog box, and a Scale function as part of the bounding box that surrounds an object after you select it with the Selection tool. Not only can you make an object bigger or smaller, but you can also squish an item to change its size. For instance, you can make an item twice as high but the same width as it was originally. Figure 12-3 shows what happens when you scale an object.

Figure 12-3: The original artwork (left) scaled smaller (center) and larger (right).

The easiest way to scale art is not to use the Scale tool but to use the bounding box that appears around objects after you select them with the Selection tool. The bounding box enables you to scale and rotate artwork. To scale artwork, click and drag the handles (big, black squares) around the outside of the artwork.

If you hold down the Shift key while you drag the bounding box handles, you constrain the sizing of the bounding box (and the artwork) so that the width and height are scaled proportionately. This is typically a good thing because it prevents your artwork from getting really, really fat or really, really skinny while you scale it.

Holding down the Shift key while you use any of a variety of tools keeps the object constrained. For instance, with the Rotate tool, holding down the Shift key constrains rotation to 45° increments (a nice angle sideways, another nice angle upside down, another nice angle sideways the other way, and finally one more lovely angle straight up).

The bounding box is nice and all, but you don't find Illustrator Knights of the Galaxy using it because they like doing things the hard way (you know, greater evidence of artistic prowess, more prestige). The Scale tool is definitely more difficult to use than the bounding box for resizing artwork, but the Scale tool also has all sorts of capabilities that the bounding box doesn't have, such as scaling from a specific origin, using specific values, and copying as you scale. Locate these buried treasures by double-clicking the Scale tool in the Tools panel.

As a certain short, green, levitating philosopher once said, "Try not. Do. Or do not. . . ." Well, okay, you can just try the technique, as shown in Figure 12-4, if you want to. (The galaxy isn't at stake here.) Figure 12-4 shows the original artwork selected (left); the light blue preview that appears when you drag with the Scale tool (center); the final scaled artwork (right).

To scale your artwork with the Scale tool, just follow these steps:

1. **Select your artwork using the regular Selection tool.**

2. **Choose the Scale tool.**

   The Scale tool icon is supposed to look like a small box being resized into a bigger box. Really. (Call it artistic license.)

3. **Click at the corner of the artwork and drag.**

   By default, the Scale tool scales from the center of the selection. When you drag, a light blue preview of your artwork appears, indicating the size and shape that your graphic will be after you release the mouse.

   Drag away from the graphic to enlarge it; drag toward the center of the graphic to shrink it.

4. **Release the mouse button when the art is the size you want.**

   The artwork scales to that size.

Figure 12-4: Original artwork (left), light blue preview (center), and the final scaled artwork (right).

All you accuracy addicts out there (you know who you are) can double-click the Scale tool in the Tools panel to indulge your habit: The Scale dialog box appears and offers a nice blank space in which you can type an exact scale percentage. (Some folks just have a hankering to know what an object looks like at 183 percent or 0.5597 percent of its current size.) You can also access this dialog box by choosing Object⇨Transform and choosing your desired transformation.

But wait, there's more! You also have an option for choosing a Uniform or Non-Uniform scale change. Well, no, choosing Uniform won't dress up the object in khakis. Instead, the object acts as if you pressed some super Shift key and ends up looking like a bigger or smaller version of the original, identically proportioned (nary a squish anywhere). A Non-Uniform scale change enables you to enter separate scale percentages for horizontal or vertical measurements. In addition to scaling objects themselves, you can also scale patterns and/ or strokes and effects, if your object(s) contains any of these attributes. See Chapter 5 for more on patterns and strokes and Chapter 11 for more on effects.

Not content with scaling from the center? The two-click method of using the Scale tool might soothe your yearning for alternatives. It enables you to move the origin point around the screen before scaling. The *origin point* is a place tacked to the Artboard around which the rest of the artwork scales. Normally, the origin point is in the middle of the selection, but you can put the origin point anywhere, even outside the selection! Just select the Scale tool from the Tools panel and click once before you do the click-and-drag routine to scale the object. Illustrator resets the origin point to the location where you single-clicked.

If you drag back across the origin point (or the middle if you didn't set one) while using the Scale tool, you might well flip the artwork over. That's a little disconcerting, but as long as you don't release the mouse button, you can always drag back and fix it. If you do release the mouse button, you can undo (choose Edit⇨Undo).

Rotate

Spinning your artwork around in circles is a good way to whittle away an afternoon. Sometimes, I just sit, click, and spin, watching the artwork rotate on-screen. It's mesmerizing. Then again, I don't really get out all that much.

You can use the funky corner arrows in the bounding box (which shows up when you have something selected with the regular Selection tool) to rotate things around or you can use the aptly named Rotate tool. The Rotate tool (like the Scale tool) enables you to set the origin point, which is the location the artwork rotates around. Double-clicking the Rotate tool also enables you to set a specific angle of rotation. Figure 12-5 shows artwork before and after it's rotated with the Rotate tool.

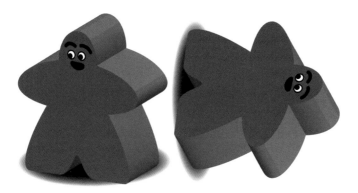

Figure 12-5: The original artwork (left) and after it's rotated (right).

Reflect

With the Reflect tool, you can flip a selection over any axis, making a mirror image. Figure 12-6 shows original artwork before and after it's flipped over a 90° axis.

Figure 12-6: Reflecting the artwork with the Reflect tool.

To use the Reflect tool to create a mirror image, just follow these steps:

1. **Select the artwork to be reflected.**

2. **Choose the Reflect tool from the Tools panel.**

3. **Press and hold the Shift key. (Release it after you release the mouse button in Step 5.)**

   The Shift key constrains the reflection to a 45° angle, which makes a horizontal reflection easier to accomplish. (Who knew it took so much work to be a beam of light? Other than Einstein. . . .)

4. **Click the far-right edge of the selected artwork and drag to the left.**

5. **Release the mouse button (and then the Shift key) after the artwork "flips" over.**

But that's not all! If you act now and double-click the Reflect tool, you get the Reflect dialog box (shown in Figure 12-7) absolutely free! Here are its exciting capabilities:

- ✔ **Horizontal:** Select this radio button to flip the image upside down while you reflect it.

- ✔ **Vertical:** Select this radio button to flip the image over while you reflect it.

- ✔ **Angle:** Select this radio button to rotate the image to a specified, um, angle while you reflect the image.

Shear

Most programs call this *skew,* but Illustrator takes the high road and uses a lofty aviation term. It's commonly used for creating cast shadows (the kind that fall away from an object, like your own shadow does on a sidewalk on a sunny afternoon, also known as perspective shadows) or cast reflection (like a still lake reflecting autumn trees).

Figure 12-7: The Reflect dialog box.

The Shear tool can be tricky to use because it can quickly zip out of control and turn your artwork from a mild-mannered logo into something resembling Timothy Leary's nightmares. When you click and drag with the Shear tool, everything on the side of the origin point moves to where you drag it while everything on the other side of the origin point moves an equal distance in the opposite direction. The artwork between distorts accordingly, and you get a slanted version of your artwork. If you drag too far or in the wrong direction, it's back to the land of funky spastic visions of inkblots.

 To make the Shear tool easier to use, always use the two-click method. Before you drag with the Shear tool, click at the edge of the selected artwork to set the origin point. When you do this, you have to pay attention only to your artwork shearing in one direction. The overall effects are the same, but you don't have to worry about the artwork shearing in both directions.

To use the Shear tool

1. **Select the artwork to be sheared.**

 2. **Choose the Shear tool from the Tools panel.**

   The Shear tool hides behind the Scale tool in the Tools panel. Click and hold the Scale tool, and the Shear tool pops out from behind it.

3. **Click once at the edge of the artwork to be sheared.**

   This sets the origin point, making the Shear tool easier to control.

4. **Drag with the Shear tool.**

   The artwork *shears,* or distorts, to look slanted, as shown in Figure 12-8.

Figure 12-8: Original artwork (left) and after shearing (right).

Additional Transformation Tidbits

All this transforming might seem like some pretty amazing stuff. What's really amazing is the bevy of little extras that Illustrator has thoughtfully provided to make transforming easier and faster. The following sections in this chapter show you how to use these extras. Here's a list of what you can do:

- **Use the Transform panel.** This panel keeps all the transformations in one handy place, where you can apply them by typing in numerical values.

- **Copy while you transform.** Rotate a copy of your artwork.

- **Transform each piece of artwork separately.** The Transform Each dialog box enables you to apply transformations to individual objects, instead of to everything at once. This feature is useful, believe it or not.

- **Repeat the last transformation.** Do it again . . . and again . . . all with a simple menu command (or keystroke).

- **Transform a portion of a path.** That's right, you can select just a few points and move, scale, rotate, reflect, or shear them. (This capability is especially useful if you want to give that virtual caterpillar a Mohawk.)

The Transform panel

The Transform panel, shown in Figure 12-9, is a one-stop shopping location for all your transformation needs. Access the panel by choosing Window⇨ Transform. The panel's quite powerful, as long as you don't mind the math.

By entering values in the Transform panel's fields, artwork can be moved, scaled, rotated, and sheared. The panel pop-up menu has options for reflecting (Flip Horizontal and Flip Vertical) as well as options for scaling strokes and effects and transforming the object, the pattern, or both. The W and H (width and height) fields can take both *absolute measurements* (sizes specified in inches, centimeters, and so on) or *relative measurements* defined by percentages. Just type the little extra bit after the number that specifies what kind of measurement the number represents — **in** for inches, **cm** for centimeters, or % for a percentage. You can also type in the rotation and shear degrees in the two boxes at the bottom (or choose a preset from the drop-down menus).

Figure 12-9: The Transform panel in all its glory.

If you hate to crunch numbers, rejoice! The Transform panel does the math for you! For instance, if you want an object to be one-third as wide as it currently is, just type **/3** after the current value in the text box for width, and the artwork will shrink to $^{1}/_{3}$ of its original width.

Copying while transforming

All five Illustrator transformation functions enable you to copy objects as well as transform them. To accomplish this dazzler, Illustrator applies the transformation to a copy of the original selection, just as if you used cut-and-paste to copy the object, pasted it directly on top of the original, and applied the transformation. In Illustrator, you can do all that in one step.

When using the transformation tools, you can press Alt (Option on a Mac) to make a copy of your selection while transforming. Just press Alt (Option on a Mac) after you start dragging (not before) and hold it down until after you release the mouse button. Illustrator creates a duplicate of the selection.

Illustrator users do this sort of thing so often that they invented a couple of terms (*Alt-drag* for PCs, *Option-drag* for Macs) to mean *copy an object*. (Nine times out of ten, it means *move a copy.*)

Figure 12-10 shows how a sample of type looks after you transform it with the Shear tool while holding down Alt (Option on a Mac). To get this cool cast shadow with the Shear tool, I copied the text object and filled with a gradient. The result is a cast shadow that appears in front of the original type (which Illustrator treats as an object).

Figure 12-10: Get a cool cast shadow with the Shear tool.

If you're using a dialog box to accomplish a transformation, click the Copy button instead of OK to create a *transformed duplicate* of the object. The original artwork stays untransformed.

Transform Each

The Transform Each dialog box (see Figure 12-11), accessed by choosing Object➪Transform➪Transform Each, does two things: First, it brings most of the transformations together into one dialog box. Second, it applies transformations to each of the selected objects separately, instead of all at once.

Oddly enough, this approach results in an effect that bears almost no resemblance to transforming every-thing at once. Figure 12-12 shows the results of regular rotation versus the results of rotation using the Transform Each dialog box. (Just don't say I didn't warn you.)

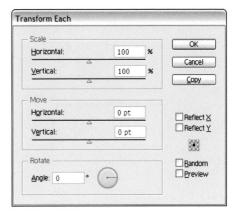

Figure 12-11: The Transform Each dialog box.

Transform Again

After you transform something, you can repeat the transformation quickly by choosing Object⇨Transform⇨Transform Again; the keyboard shortcut is Ctrl+D (⌘+D on a Mac). This action simply repeats the previous transformation — whether by tool or dialog box or panel — and applies that transformation to the current selection. You can even deselect something, select something else, and apply the same transformation to the new selection.

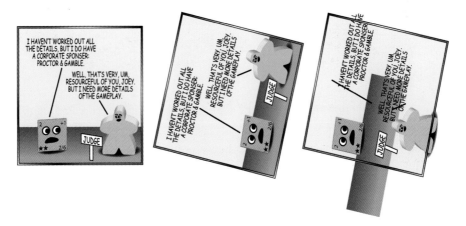

Figure 12-12: Original artwork (left) after it's rotated with the Rotate tool (middle) and using the Transform Each dialog box (right).

The Transform Again command also works with copying selections, as shown in Figure 12-13. Here, the little "Clarks" around the circle were made with the Transform Again function by rotating a copy around the center in 18° increments.

Partial transformations

If you select just a section of a path, you can apply the five basic transformations to it, just as you do with an entire object. The result can be quite ordinary (as when you move a few points around) or rather unexpected (as when you scale, shear, or reflect just a few points), as shown in Figure 12-14.

Figure 12-13: Repeat a transformation to the current selection.

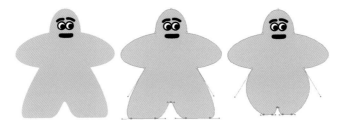

Figure 12-14: Moving and scaling a portion of a path.

The following steps select, move, and scale *just a few points* on a path (with some interesting results):

1. **Using the Direct Selection tool, click and drag over a portion of a path.**

   While you click and drag with the Direct Selection tool, a rectangular marquee appears. Only the points inside this marquee are selected.

2. **With the Direct Selection tool still selected, click a selected (solid) point and drag.**

   All the selected points move along with the one you click and drag. Be sure to click directly on a point that you selected (indicated by a solid point); otherwise, you'll accidentally drop the selection and select something else.

3. Release your mouse, choose the Scale tool, and then click the same point as Step 2 and drag.

Dragging toward the middle of the selected points brings the points closer together. Dragging away moves them farther apart.

Don't click too near the middle of the points, or they get all cantankerous and hard to control.

Blending: The Magic Transformation

This section covers what may well be the oddest feature in Illustrator. Illustrator can blend one path into another. For instance, you can blend the shape of a fish into a lowercase letter *f*. The result is a series of paths that slowly transform from one path into another. In addition to the shape changing from one path to another, the color (and style, if one exists) changes as well.

Sound familiar? No surprise. The results look a lot like the morphing effect you see in every werewolf-vampire-alien-shapeshifter movie made in the past 20 years.

Only paths can be blended together. The paths can be open (lines, curves) or closed (shapes such as circles and squares). They can also contain either solid colors or gradients. You can select any number of paths and blend them together, as shown in Figure 12-15.

Figure 12-15: Creating a blend between three objects.

To create a blend that takes the artwork from one path to another, just follow these steps:

1. Create two paths on opposite sides of the document.

2. Choose the Blend tool from the Tools panel.

3. **Click one path, click the other path, and watch the blend appear.**

The number of objects between the two original paths depends on how different the colors are.

Figure 12-16: The Blend Options dialog box.

4. **(Optional) To specify the number of steps between the paths, double-click the Blend tool.**

5. **In the Blend Options dialog box that appears, as shown in Figure 12-16, select Specified Steps from the Spacing drop-down menu and enter the number of steps you want between the two paths. Click OK.**

Illustrator creates the number of objects you specify between the two original paths.

Other options are available in the Blend Options dialog box besides the Specified Steps option. The Smooth Color option lets Illustrator automatically calculate the number of steps for the blend, which allows for a smooth transition of color and shapes. The Specified Distance option specifies the distance between steps in the blend based on the edge of one object to the edge of the next object. You can also specify the orientation of your blend — either with the Align to Page orientation or the Align to Path orientation. The icons for each give you a visual of each orientation.

You can also edit your blends with selection tools, such as the Arrow or Lasso tools, or with the Rotate or Scale tools. If the blend still doesn't meet your expectations as you make your edits, you can undo a blend by choosing Object⇔Blend⇔Release.

13

Organizing Efficiently

In This Chapter

▶ Arranging and stacking images

▶ Using the Layers panel

▶ Changing the stacking order of objects with the Layers panel

▶ Naming objects, groups, and layers

▶ Organizing artwork with groups

▶ Letting Smart Guides do the work for you

▶ Working with guides

▶ Aligning objects

A good way to think about how Illustrator objects relate to one another is to consider Illustrator objects like construction paper cutouts. You can arrange them any way you want, but in all likelihood, some will overlap. Each piece of paper can then be tucked behind another piece or pulled out in front of another piece. Doing so results in totally different results, even though the paper cutouts never really change.

In this chapter, I focus primarily on stacking objects — tucking them behind each other or bringing them forward to upstage each other — and show you how to deal with stacking as easily as possible. In addition, a later section scrutinizes precision placement and aligning of objects.

Stacking Illustrator Artwork

Illustrator automatically accomplishes front-to-back positioning for you in a straightforward, logical way. Each new object that you draw, place, or paste is positioned in front of the last object that you drew, placed, or pasted, resulting in a stack of artwork.

Unless you apply transparency (as I detail in Chapter 10), objects positioned in front of other objects tend to knock out the portions of the objects that they overlap. Figure 13-1 shows Illustrator objects (cards) stacked in three different arrangements. The cards are in the same locations, but their stacking order is different. The result is completely different artwork in each example.

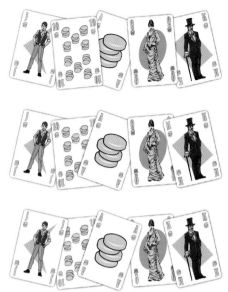

Figure 13-1: These arrangements of cards are a result of changing the stacking order of the objects.

Stacking order

Illustrator treats on-screen objects as if they were playing cards stacked neatly on a table (or not so neatly, as in Figure 13-1). (Think of yourself as standing next to the table and looking straight down on them. All the individual cards cannot be seen. You only see the topmost card.) *Stacking order* is the order of objects in the stack. The order of the objects in the stack is typically determined by when they're created or placed in the document, although you can change this order by using an Object⇨Arrange command. (Read more on the Arrange commands in the upcoming section "Moving art up (front) or back (down) in the stacking order.") The first object created sits at the bottom of the stack. In Illustrator, this is referred to as the *Back*. The next object created is in front of that object, and the most recent object created sits on top of all the others. The topmost position is considered to be the *Front*.

Figure 13-2 shows a top down view of a stack of cards and an imaginary side-edge view of that same stack as it would appear from the side.

Even when two objects appear visually side by side and don't overlap in any way, Illustrator still considers one object to be in front of the other — as if each object that you create in Illustrator were painted on a separate piece of transparent plastic. Often, the only time you can know the stacking order is when you move one object in front of another. That's the only time you need to know the stacking order because stacking order makes a difference only when objects overlap. When objects overlap improperly (like if a big yellow triangle hides the word *YIELD* that you really want in front of the triangle), you turn to the Arrange commands to change stacking order, as spelled out in the next section.

Figure 13-2: From above (left) and from the side (right).

Moving art up (front) or back (down) in the stacking order

Illustrator offers the following five commands to move objects up and down through the stacking order:

- **Object⇨Arrange⇨Bring to Front:** This command brings selected artwork to the top of the layer you're working on (more about layers in the next section) by putting that artwork in front of the other objects.

- **Object⇨Arrange⇨Send to Back:** This command moves selected artwork to the bottom of the layer you're working on by putting that artwork behind the other objects.

- **Object⇨Arrange⇨Bring Forward:** This command brings selected artwork forward (that is, upward in the stack) one step at a time.

- **Object⇨Arrange⇨Send Backward:** This command puts the selected artwork farther back (that is, downward in the stack) one step at a time.

- **Object⇨Arrange⇨Send to Current Layer:** This command moves the selected artwork from the layer it resides on to the layer selected in the Layers panel. For more on layers, see the section "Using the Layers panel" coming up in this chapter.

Illustrator uses stacking order to keep track of all the objects on-screen, even when they don't overlap. The Bring Forward and Send Backward commands affect the stacking order, regardless. Whether you send an object backward or bring it forward, you may not see any difference if nothing's overlapping. Don't panic! The object really did move in the pecking order.

Managing the Mess

Although the commands for moving artwork may seem fairly flexible at first, that's true only if you keep the number of objects limited. After you start creating artwork with dozens (or even hundreds) of objects in it, the first four commands start showing their limitations and causing frustration. For instance, think of the hassle of putting an object in a precise order when you have a hundred different levels in the stack ("Move it from level 94 to level 63? Sure, no problem." Right.), not to mention the challenge of selecting one object from among hundreds!

That situation is where the Layers panel comes in. Not only does it enable you to organize your artwork into layers, but it also gives you a much more flexible method of arranging your artwork within the stacking order. You can also do fiendish things to layers, such as hiding them so you can't see them, or locking them so you can see them but can't change them or duplicate them (along with their artwork) in a different document. This flexibility brings a great deal of sanity to working with complex illustrations.

Imagine that you're creating an image of a flock of birds in a maple tree. Your client wants to see the tree change according to the four seasons. She also wants to see the tree with and without the birds. You have 1 tree, 50 birds, and hundreds of leaves — and the whole image is set in spring. Oh, and the client is coming over to see the finished artwork in 15 minutes! Do you panic? No, you use layers! You separate the tree, birds, and leaves into separate layers. Then you can hide and reveal the bird layer to show the tree with and without the birds. Hide the layer with the leaves on it, and you have your maple tree in winter! To simulate seasons, duplicate the leaves layer twice. Then, again using the Layers panel, you can select all the leaves in one layer and change the fill colors to summer colors. Then go to the third leaf layer and change those colors to fall colors. By showing one layer while hiding the other two, you can create your fall, spring, and summer trees. There you have it! Eight pieces of artwork from one piece, in about as much time as it takes to describe it!

Using the Layers panel

The Layers panel, shown in Figure 13-3, provides you with the means to do as much (or as little) organization as you want. You can split your artwork into layers, sublayers, and sublayers of those sublayers. Then you can view, hide, select, rearrange, or delete any number of the layers and sublayers.

Thumbnails

The thumbnails on the Layers panel show what objects are on each layer. You can quickly select everything on that layer by clicking the Target circle. In addition, clicking the Target circle (to the right of each layer) enables you to apply Transparency settings and effects to that layer, as I discuss in Chapter 10.

Is the thumbnail too small to get an accurate view of the artwork? Select the Panel Options option from the Layers panel pop-up menu. The thumbnail size is determined by the row size. Choose from small, medium (the default size), or large; or choose the Other setting and type in any pixel size for your thumbnails.

I call it layer cake . . .

If you haven't opened the Layers panel before, you might be surprised to find that you've been working with layers all along. Whenever you create a new document, Illustrator automatically creates a layer to contain your artwork.

When you work with multiple layers, you might have to get accustomed to the Arrange commands, such as the Bring Forward and Send to Back commands. These commands work within layers but don't move objects from one layer to another. After you select an object and choose Object⇨Arrange⇨Bring to Front, Illustrator brings the object to the front of the layer that it currently occupies — but not all the way to the front of the document. So, if another object is hanging around in a layer in front of the selected object and you use the Bring to Front command, the selected object might still be behind another object in the document. If this happens, you can use the Object⇨Arrange⇨Send to Current Layer command, or you can use Steps 3 and 4 in the following list to move artwork into another layer.

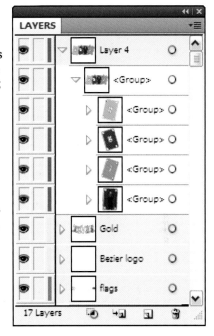

Figure 13-3: The Layers panel with multiple layers.

A good way to get a feel for the Layers panel is to break a piece of existing artwork into several layers, as shown in Figure 13-4.

To separate your artwork into multiple layers, just follow these steps:

1. **Decide how you want to organize your artwork.**

   You might want to split it into similar elements — such as type, pixel images, graphics, and a background.

2. **Create the additional layers you need for your artwork by clicking the Create New Layer button — click once for each additional layer.**

   The Create New Layer button is the third button from the left at the bottom of the Layers panel; it looks like a sheet of paper with the bottom-left corner folded up to reveal a second sheet of paper underneath it. You can also choose the New Layer option from the Layers panel pop-up menu.

3. **With the Selection tool, select the graphic element in your artwork that you want to move to one of the other layers.**

   After you select the art, a little square appears to the right of the layer that currently contains the selected artwork.

4. **To move the art to another layer, click and drag the little square up or down in the Layers panel to the layer you want.**

   When you release the mouse button, the artwork has already changed layers. You might not see any apparent change in the artwork, but moving the artwork into a new layer changes the color of the selection highlights (the tiny, on-screen squares and lines that appear along the points and paths after you select something with any selection tool). The color changes to the selection highlight color for the new layer. It's a dead giveaway. Figure 13-5 shows a document (with objects selected) right next to the Layers panel for that document. Note how the color paths/points for objects on each layer have the same color as their corresponding layers in the Layers panel.

5. **Repeat the previous two steps until all your artwork is in the correct layers.**

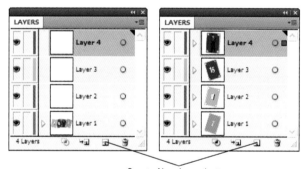

Create New Layer button

Figure 13-4: Placing existing artwork into multiple layers.

Changing the stacking order of layers

Layers, like individual objects, have a stacking order. This order is reflected in the Layers panel. The contents of layers at the bottom of the panel appear in back of the contents of layers at the top of the panel. To change the stacking order of a layer, click the name of the layer or its thumbnail and drag upwards or downwards in the Layers panel. While you drag, a black bar appears between layers to indicate where the layer will be moved to after you release the mouse. When this black bar is at the position you want the layer to occupy, release the mouse. The layer and all its contents move to that position.

Figure 13-5: The objects on each layer have paths and points colored the same as the layer that they are on.

Lock and Unlock, View and Hide

Well, no, I'm not suddenly writing rhythm-and-blues lyrics. You can lock layers by clicking the Lock/Unlock toggle button (the square just to the right of the eyeball icon — it's empty when unlocked and shows a little padlock when locked). Clicking it causes it to do the opposite of whatever it's currently doing. If a layer is unlocked, for example, clicking the Lock/Unlock button locks the layer. If a layer is already locked, clicking the Lock/Unlock button unlocks the layer. So far, so good. But potential frustrations lurk.

When a layer is locked, you can see it, but you can't select it or alter it in any way. If you try to select anything in a locked layer, you select only the object behind it. After you get accustomed to this state of affairs, you find that layers are a great way to get things out of the way that you aren't working on and to preserve any artwork that you don't want accidentally changed.

Just to the left of the Lock/Unlock button is the View/Hide button (which looks like an eye). Why hide all that work? One word: safety. This button not only hides the artwork in the layer, but it also locks the artwork so you can't accidentally change it. The View/Hide button is also a great way to get things out of the way and to prevent accidents. It's also a great way to create multiple versions of artwork by showing and hiding different elements. (You know — trees with several sets of leaves for different seasons, or football players with several uniforms, depending on their contracts. . . .)

Hidden artwork is always locked artwork. If it weren't locked, you could change that poor, hapless object without meaning to — because you can't see hidden artwork. (Wow. Sometimes obvious stuff is so comforting.)

Copying layers (quickly and completely)

You can copy a layer — along with all the artwork it contains — by clicking the layer and dragging it on top of the Create New Layer button, which is just waiting around at the lower edge of the Layers panel, hoping that somebody will give it something to do. This technique is a great way to create multiple versions of artwork. You can duplicate one element many times, and then change the appearance for each layer. Show and hide the layers to compare and contrast the different versions.

To create a new sublayer (a layer within a layer), click the Create New Sublayer button at the bottom of the Layers panel (the little piece of paper directly to the left of the trash can icon), or select the New Sublayer option from the Layers panel pop-up menu.

Viewing objects and groups

When you click the little triangle to the far left of a layer's name, you see an instant panorama of the groups and objects on that layer, as shown in Figure 13-6.

Using your options on layers, groups, and objects

You can give each layer, group, and object in Illustrator a name. If you don't name them, they wander around despondently, lugging their default names (such as <path> and Layer 1). Naming layers can be a great help for locating different objects. (Those teensy thumbnails can be awfully hard to distinguish.) Naming the layers provides you with instant recognition.

To change a layer's name, double-click that layer in the Layers panel. To change the name of a group, double-click that group in the Layers panel. And finally, to change the name of an

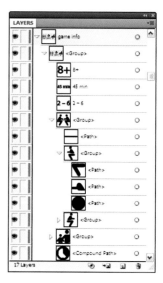

Figure 13-6: View a layer's contents.

object, double-click that object in the Layers panel. (Is there an echo in here? Nope, just consistency — part of good software design.) The Layer Options dialog box appears, as shown in Figure 13-7.

The Layer Options dialog box offers several other options beyond just naming layers:

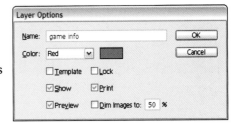

Figure 13-7: The Layer Options dialog box.

✔ **Name:** Use this text box to type in a descriptive name for the layer.

✔ **Color:** Set the selection highlight color here. Changing this option doesn't change any color in the artwork — just the color used to show that something is highlighted.

✔ **Template:** Selecting this check box enables you to give the layer a special designation and the following unique set of behaviors (which tells you that the layer is a template):

- *The layer is automatically locked* so nothing on it can be selected or changed.

- *By default, pixel-based artwork shows as dimmed,* which allows you to focus on your own artwork better while still being able to see the template artwork. Think of the layer as virtual tracing paper. You can, however, uncheck (deselect) this option if you so desire.

- *The names of the Template layers are italicized,* so they're easy to spot in the Layers panel.

- *Template layers do not print,* and they aren't included with your artwork when you use the Save for Web & Devices command.

- *You can create a different version of a particular piece of artwork* and put the existing artwork in a Template layer where it's out of the way. It won't print, but you can still see it.

✔ **Lock** and **Show:** These options can be checked and unchecked to enable you to perform the same function as selecting the Lock/Unlock and View/Hide buttons in the Layers panel.

✔ **Preview:** Selecting this check box allows you to see your artwork in Preview mode. When unchecked, it displays the current layer's artwork in Outline view; all other artwork in the document remains in Preview view.

✔ **Print:** This option can be checked or unchecked to make the layer printable or not printable.

✔ **Dim Images To:** This option enables you to dim pixel-based artwork to any set percentage. You might want to do so for tracing purposes so that you can focus on your Illustrator artwork while using the faded pixel artwork as a guide.

You can move objects, groups, and layers around inside the Layers panel, doing all sorts of strange things to your artwork. You can move objects from one layer to another, move groups inside other groups, and even nest layers by dragging them inside each other. Try doing this and watch out for surprises.

Imposing Slavish Conformity with Groups

Grouping objects is a great way to organize your artwork because it gives several objects a common address, so to speak, where Illustrator can find them. After you click any one of them with the Selection tool, you automatically select all the objects in the group.

To create a group of objects, select the objects that you want to include and then choose Object⇨Group. You won't see any physical change in the artwork, but from that point onward, all objects in the group are selected at once (provided that you use the regular Selection tool to select them).

The main difference between layers and groups is that grouping organizes objects by *their relationships to other objects* rather than by their position inside a layer. As any former high-school student can tell you, belonging to a group means having to conform to its rules. Consider these rules, for example:

- **Grouped objects must exist in the same layer.** You accomplish this by selecting two objects in different layers and grouping them. The bottom-most object gets moved into the layer that the topmost object inhabits.

- **Groups can be grouped.** You accomplish this by selecting two or more groups and choosing Object⇨Group. If you have two groups called *Football Team* and *Cheerleaders,* for example, you can group them in another group called *Stadium.*

- **Grouped objects can be ungrouped.** You accomplish this by selecting the group and choosing Object⇨Ungroup. (Or maybe you can get an object in the group to do something uncool. . . .)

See Chapter 6 for more information on selecting groups.

Lining Up

Illustrator provides several ways to make things line up as neatly as possible. Instead of just eyeballing the things in the line (which sounds sort of icky), you can have Illustrator help you make sure everything lines up just right. In fact, so many ways to align things exist that you don't need to figure out all the different methods. Just pick the one that makes sense to you and use it.

Two of the more-arcane-but-useful functions in Illustrator are tricky to find and use, but are worth the effort:

- **Snap to Point:** This function (choose View⇨Snap to Point) snaps your cursor to a nearby point (on a path) whenever you're near to it. This function is perfect for butting objects up against each other.

- **Constraining via Shift.** This function (hold down the Shift key after you make your selection) constrains movement of objects to 0, 45, or 90 degrees (and all sorts of combinations thereof).

If you want your objects to move in a constrained fashion, make sure that you hold down the Shift key after you make your selection and keep holding it down until after you release the mouse button. If you hold the Shift key down before you make your selection, you add that selection to anything else you already selected. If you let go of the Shift key before you let go of your mouse button, you release the constraint, and the object is positioned someplace far from where you want it to be.

Guides that are truly smarter than most of us

What if Illustrator knew what you were thinking? Science fiction? Maybe. But Illustrator is smart enough to know what you want to align — if you turn on Smart Guides, that is (by choosing View⇨Smart Guides). These little helpers come out and start drawing temporary guides for you all over the place. Suddenly you can align objects in all sorts of ways.

Here's how this feature works. When the Smart Guides feature is on, it watches you work. When your cursor passes over different objects, Smart Guides draws lines from the points that you drag over, showing you how they align, and highlights the paths of objects as you pass over them. Beware, though: After you start using them, it's really, really hard to stop. Figure 13-8 shows the highlighting of a path when the cursor is placed over it. The cursor was placed over the collar object, causing it to "light up" with the layer color (red) because Smart Guides was turned on.

Let the rulers guide you . . .

You can create a guide of your own if you drag out from one of the rulers (click the ruler and drag it into the document). Think of these guides as individual grid lines. You can use them to align artwork horizontally or vertically wherever you want without having your whole screen become littered with grid work like you do whenever you choose View⇨Show Grid.

Figure 13-8: Using Smart Guides.

Unlike Smart Guides, the guides you create on your own give you no additional information about your artwork. They're just lines that hang out
behind your artwork to use as a point of reference, like the blue ones shown
in Figure 13-9. When View⇨Snap to Grid is turned on, objects snap to guides
as well (even if you aren't using a grid).

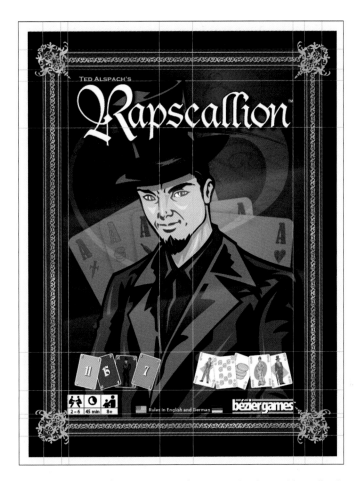

Figure 13-9: Guides (bright blue lines) were used to keep objects lined up while being placed.

You can drag out as many of these guides as you want or need. To move a guide that you dragged out, choose View⇨Guides⇨Lock Guides and toggle the option off. Then click and drag the guide that you want to move. You can also press the Delete key after clicking a guide to remove it altogether. This action lets you customize your guides so that they're in the exact position you need to help you with the specific artwork you're creating.

Lock your guides after you move them by choosing View⇨Guides⇨Lock Guides and toggling the option on.

I'm a path, I'm a guide

You can turn any path into a guide by selecting the path and choosing View⇨Guides⇨Make Guides. That means circles, squares, wavy lines, or an entire logo can be used as a guide . . . basically anything you might want to quickly align to. You can also turn any guide back into a path (even the ruler guides) by selecting it and choosing View⇨Guides⇨Release Guides. Guides need to be unlocked and selected for this to work.

If you need to move or delete a single guide, you can press Ctrl+Shift (⌘+Shift on a Mac) and then double-click the guide to unlock it and change it into a path. (Just press the Delete key afterward to make it disappear.)

You can always clear out all the guides in a document by choosing View⇨Clear Guides.

Alignment

The Illustrator Align panel enables you to align and distribute selected objects just by clicking a button. Open the Align panel (shown in Figure 13-10) by choosing Window⇨Align. The little pictures on each button in the panel show what the button does after you click it.

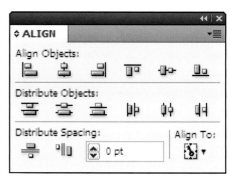

Figure 13-10: The Align panel.

The top row of buttons aligns objects. You can align objects horizontally or vertically. If you align objects horizontally to the left, Illustrator aligns the leftmost points in the objects. If you center objects horizontally, Illustrator aligns the centers of the objects.

The final location of the objects might seem a little random at times because the Align command aligns them to a point that is the average of the locations of the objects. For instance, if you align two objects vertically by their centers — and one object is on the right side of the page and the other is on the left side — the objects will align somewhere near the center of the page. To get them exactly where you want them, you may need to click and drag the objects with the Selection tool after you align them. Still, the Align panel saves you a whole lot of time getting there.

The bottom row of buttons distributes objects. In other words, these buttons move selected objects so that they are the same distance apart. The Distribute Objects option takes the two objects that are the farthest apart and distributes the remaining objects between these two objects.

Using the Align panel is a good way to align things you created in Illustrator and simply need to straighten up a bit. If everything you created is all helter-skelter (or just helter work with), Align adjusts your artwork until it looks just right. Or left. Or centered. (It's pretty handy and politically neutral.)

If you think the buttons on the Align panel look familiar — that you've seen them before — you're probably right. Most of the Align panel buttons are available in the Control panel at the top of the screen, as shown in Figure 13-11. For most of your aligning work, you can simply click the button you need there, without ever having to open the Align panel.

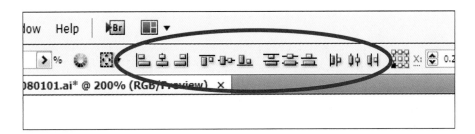

Figure 13-11: The Control panel's Align buttons.

Part IV

Practically Speaking: Type, Print, and Files

The 5th Wave   By Rich Tennant

"Why don't you try blurring the brimstone and then putting a nice glow effect around the hellfire."

*O*ne picture is worth a thousand words. But if you create those words in Illustrator, each word — no, each letter — is a work of art. Which means a sentence is worth about 17 billion words. (I'm estimating, seeing as how I don't have a calculator handy.)

In this part, you master creating type, and then you'll become the expert you always knew you could be when it comes to the practicality of printing, taking your art to the Web, and working with other applications.

If you do the math of pictures being worth words, and words being knowledge, and knowledge being power, then by the end of this part, you'll be the most powerful person in the universe!

Introducing Letters and Such
(Type 101)

In This Chapter

▷ Uncovering why Illustrator has so much type stuff

▷ Mixing fonts effectively

▷ Spacing out lines of type

▷ Changing the space between letters

▷ Stretching and squishing type

▷ Using type as a mask

▷ Turning type into paths

*T*ype is undoubtedly one of Illustrator's strongest areas. All the things that Illustrator does best — logos, advertisements, posters, and Web-page graphics — depend upon text and typography. Many Illustrator features interact with type in some way; and the program's type capabilities are pretty straightforward — that is, after you know where they are and what they can do.

In this chapter, I discuss Illustrator type. (If you're already familiar with controlling type in Microsoft Word or some other piece of word-processing software, you're already familiar with many of these terms.) To ease the journey, this chapter covers locating the Illustrator controls — and deciphering the Illustrator way of doing things. Finally, I describe how to get the most out of type and how to turn Illustrator from a glorified word-processor into an astounding type-modifying tool that can do just about anything to type you could think of.

.g around paths is so.
of typing within an area,
around the outside of
shapes) rather tha
shape. This te
referred to as
or a type wrap
have a special to
ing type around
you do have t
command with
type and the path se
how text flows around a shap
14-25.

JOE-BOB

Using the Word Processor from Outer Space

If you think of Illustrator type capabilities as an extended word-processing program, you're in the right ballpark; people frequently mention Illustrator's amazing typographical control. The basics of type (such as fonts, size, and alignment) work much the same in Illustrator as they do in most software programs. Illustrator also packs some advanced typographical capabilities, such as saving files in four of the most universally recognized file formats (PDF, EPS, GIF, and JPEG). What sets this program apart from the rest is that you can do wonderful things with type and use it just about anywhere.

Controlling type in Illustrator

Illustrator has a variety of places where you can work with type options, such as the Type menu; and the Character, Paragraph, Character Style, Paragraph Style, and OpenType panels. Ninety-five percent of what you need, however, resides on the Character and Paragraph panels, shown in Figure 14-1. These two panels are essential knowledge for Illustrator users, which is why I devote much textual real estate to them later in this chapter. For now, though, I'd like to point out that a good grasp (so to speak) of the Type tool(s) in the Tools panel is equally important. The next section tells why.

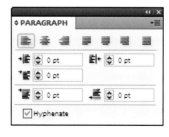

Figure 14-1: The Character and the Paragraph panels.

The Type tool(s)

You don't need anything but the Type tool to create type although the Type tool by itself won't let you change anything about your type.

Several type tools hide behind the standard Type tool. Although they're convenient for quickly creating type on a path, area type, or vertically oriented type, you can get away with using only the standard Type tool — if you know a few clever shortcuts. To make type on a path with the standard Type tool, just click any open path with it; the type flows on the path. To make type flow within an area, just click a closed path with the standard Type tool, and your type fills the path.

Starting with the Type tool, follow these steps to create type:

T.

1. **Choose the Type tool (which looks like a letter *T*) from the Illustrator Tools panel.**

2. **Click where you want the text to start.**

   A flashing insertion point appears. (If you accidentally click and drag at this point, you create a text box that contains your type. For more information on the text box, see the next series of steps.)

3. **Start typing.**

This process is the most basic way to create type. What you actually do in the preceding steps is create *point type,* which is a single line of type that doesn't *wrap* (move to the next line) automatically, as shown in Figure 14-2. You have to press Enter (Windows) or Return (Mac) if you want to add a line beneath this line; otherwise, the line you're typing continues to infinity.

Point type looks like this.

Figure 14-2: Point type in Illustrator.

You can also create *area type* (type that's confined within a closed shape) with the Type tool, like the type shown in Figure 14-3. Just follow these steps:

Area type fits nicely into a rectangle or other closed shape.

Figure 14-3: Area type in Illustrator.

1. **Choose the Type tool from the Tools panel.**

2. **Click and drag with the Type tool.**

   While you drag, a rectangular marquee grows from the cursor. You can type text only inside the area of the marquee.

3. **Release the mouse button.**

   A flashing insertion point appears in the upper left of the text box.

4. **Start typing.**

   When you reach the right edge of the text box, the text wraps to the next line.

In both cases, you create a type object. You can treat this type object like any other Illustrator object. (After you select it, the familiar path and point symbols show up to indicate the selection.)

With both point type and area type, you can always get to the next line by pressing Enter (Windows) or Return (Mac) on the keyboard.

The Character panel

The Character panel (choose Window⇨ Type⇨Character) is where you make changes to individual characters (letters, numbers, and punctuation). Figure 14-4 shows the expanded Character panel (all options displayed) with all the pieces labeled. The drop down menus next to each entry field allow for quick access to commonly-used values.

To make text changes via the Character panel, first select the text you want to change. You can select text in three ways:

✓ **Click the text with the regular Selection tool.** This action selects all the text in the text object. Even though the text isn't highlighted (rather, it has a simple underline, or the outline of a rectangle), you can still change the size, font, and alignment.

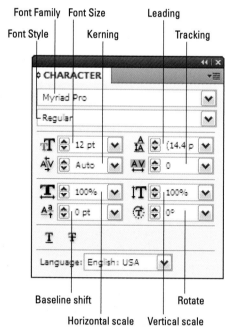

Figure 14-4: The Character panel in Illustrator.

✓ **Click and drag the Type tool across the type that you want to select.** When you click and drag, a black box appears behind the selected text to indicate that the text is selected (*highlighted*). Only highlighted text is changed.

If you click and drag too far away from your targeted text, you make a new text box instead of selecting the text.

Pay attention to the Type tool cursor because it always alerts you as to what the tool is going to do. When the cursor is in position to create a new text box, a dotted rectangle appears around it. If it's in the right place to select text, the dotted rectangle disappears. To select text, click and drag when you see only the I-beam text tool cursor with no box around it.

✏ **Double- or triple-click with the Type tool.** Double-clicking a word selects the entire word. Triple-clicking selects the entire paragraph in which the word appears.

The Paragraph panel

The Paragraph panel (shown in Figure 14-5) is where you make type changes that affect whole paragraphs. If you haven't dealt with this feature in other software, you might be in for a bit of a tussle. To view the panel, choose Window⇨Type⇨Paragraph. Then things start to get a little strange.

To Illustrator, a paragraph consists of the type contained between hard returns, which typically look like this: ¶. Even if you type only one letter, press Enter (Windows) or Return (Mac), and type another letter, Illustrator considers each of those letters as separate paragraphs.

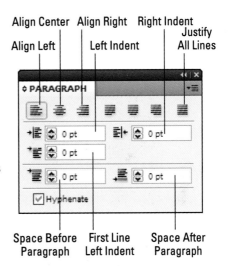

Figure 14-5: The Paragraph panel in Illustrator.

You don't have to select an entire paragraph for the Paragraph panel functions to make changes. Paragraph panel changes affect the entire paragraph, regardless of what you select. For instance, even if you highlight only a single letter, changing a paragraph option affects the entire paragraph — not just that single character. In fact, you don't even need to select anything to make paragraph changes. Just click the paragraph you want to change with the Type tool (you see a blinking insertion point where you click), and paragraph changes you make then affect the entire paragraph. All options in the Paragraph panel are designed to affect an entire paragraph, regardless of the selection, and are discussed later in this chapter in more detail.

Introducing the Strange Land of Type

Although much of Illustrator might seem new and different, it describes type with a language steeped in centuries of tradition (not to mention years of Illustrator history), so while some of the terms may sound strange, feel confident that you could discuss a lot of these concepts with Gutenberg's buddies.

Fonts, typefaces, and font families

Although maybe you've heard these terms used interchangeably, fonts, typefaces, and font families actually have distinct meanings. For this book's purposes, I deal primarily with fonts. *Fonts* are sets of common letterforms that give consistent, distinct designs to the entire alphabet, all the numbers, and a boatload of symbols. Figure 14-6 shows a variety of fonts.

Myriad Pro Black Condensed Italic

Arial Black

Bauhaus 93

Bickham Script Pro

Forte

Harrington

Kabel LT Std Black

Magneto Bold

Rage Italic

Figure 14-6: Several different fonts.

You change fonts in Illustrator quite easily by following these steps:

1. **Using either the Type tool or a selection tool, select the type you want to modify.**

2. **Choose Window⇨Type⇨Character.**

The Character panel appears. The family name of the selected font appears at the upper left of the Character panel. Below the Font Family name is the Font Style box, with a downward-pointing triangle just to the right.

3. **Click the downward-pointing triangle next to the Font Style box.**

   A pop-up menu presents you with a list of all the fonts on your computer, as shown in Figure 14-7.

4. **Pick a font from the list and click its name.**

   After you release the mouse button, the selected text changes to the font you chose.

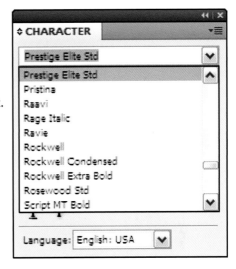

Figure 14-7: A scrollable list of fonts appears in the Character panel.

Illustrator doesn't have buttons for making fonts bold and italic. (Grumble.) However, programs with such features are usually faking it because not every font family has genuine bold and italic versions. If a program takes the non-italic version and tilts it (or the non-bold version and thickens it), the resulting false impression can waste money. The *faux* bold and italics might look okay on-screen, and even print out okay on an inkjet printer. But when an image-setter (a professional high-resolution printer) rejects them as fake, they show up on the page as the ordinary non-bold, non-italic fonts that they are — *after* you had costly films made.

While you peruse the list of fonts, notice that the font styles appear in sub-menus of the main list. This feature shows you related versions of a particular font. For instance, Figure 14-8 shows samples of three font styles in the Myriad Pro font family. All are in the same submenu of the Myriad Pro menu item. Font styles in the same font family have a similar look and work well together.

Myriad Pro is nice.
Myriad Pro Black is better.
Myriad Pro Light Condensed Italic is wordy.

Figure 14-8: These font styles are part of the Myriad Pro font family and look good placed together.

Serif and sans serif

Fonts are generally divided into two categories: serif and sans serif. *Serif* fonts have little doohickeys — *serifs* — on the tips of letters and numbers. *Sans serif* fonts don't have them. (In this case, *sans* means "not gonna happen here.") Figure 14-9 shows examples of serif and sans serif fonts.

Dr. Serif
Mr. Sans Serif

Figure 14-9: Serif (top) and sans serif (bottom) fonts.

Why choose serif or sans serif? Traditionally, serif fonts are used for large areas of small text because the serifs make the text easier to read. Sans serif fonts are used for larger type in headlines because they stand out more boldly. However, as wider ranges of fonts have become available to wider ranges of users, more people are breaking the traditional font-choice rules. Traditional usage isn't always the case anymore. Books and magazines still use serif fonts (more than sans serif fonts) for long passages of text, but you can find many exceptions to the rule. Sans serif type is often easier to read on-screen; those little serifs are frequently just too small to display properly on low-resolution computer screens.

When you're creating for print, a wise idea is to print your Illustrator text throughout the creative process. The printed page can differ slightly from what you see on-screen. If you're creating text for Web graphics, consider yourself lucky; when you have your graphics and the text looking good on-screen, mission accomplished!

To make Illustrator show as closely as possible what your text will look like on the Web, choose View➪Pixel Preview.

The biggest Don't Do It that I can think of

Back in 1987, when Illustrator and PageMaker just hit the scene, many computer users without an artistic bone in their bodies created documents and graphics. They got carried away with the computer's magnificent ability to mix and match fonts. The printed results often looked short of professional: busy, trashy, and hard to read. Lately, font madness has struck again — with Web pages — so your loyal author makes this impassioned plea:

*D*on't use **too** m**any fo**n**ts** *on the* s*ame page* the w**A**y I just did.

What's too many? Well, the awful no-no I just inflicted on the page has five. If you run out of fingers (on one hand) while counting fonts, you have too many. The classic limit is three fonts (including any bold or italic versions of the main font you're using).

Exploring Size, Leading, and Other Mysterious Numbers

The world of type has a lot of measuring associated with it. You have to keep in mind point size, leading, x-height, kerning, baseline shift, tracking, horizontal scale, vertical scale, em-width, and other matters that only the Secret Brotherhood of Typesetters really cares about. All these numbers affect the appearance of your type. Some of these measurements are important; some of them aren't. The following sections let you in on which is which — and on how to understand and use each type setting in Illustrator. Figure 14-10 shows the Character panel settings for each of the different blocks of type, using an abbreviated view of the Character panel.

Measuring can be just plain odd

The size of type is measured in *points*. An inch has 72 points (pt). A quarter-inch is 18 points (pt). That's the easy part. The hard part is that type isn't measured from top to bottom. Rather, type is measured from its ascenders and descenders for the entire font. You know those cute little tails that hang down from the lowercase *g, j, p, q,* and *y?* Well, those tails are *descenders;* the *ascenders* are the upper parts of letters, such as the tall parts of lowercase *d* and *k* and of UPPERCASE letters.

Some words, such as *anon* (all lowercase, no ascenders or descenders), seem to have a smaller type size than words such as *Mr. Ripley,* even though they're the same type size. Type is measured from the uppermost point to the lowermost point that is possible to create using that font. Even if you aren't using any ascenders and descenders in the words that you're typing, the font size has to leave room for them (see Figure 14-11) in case words, such as *Rumpelstiltskin* or *syzygy,* show up in the sentence.

Things get really wacky when you mix different fonts. Each font can have completely different heights for its ascenders and descenders, creating the appearance of completely different font sizes, even though the actual space from the topmost point to the lowest point for both entire alphabets is identical.

For another example, sneak a peek at the mishmash of fonts I stuck in the earlier section, "The biggest Don't Do It that I can think of." They're all 12 pt fonts.

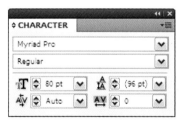

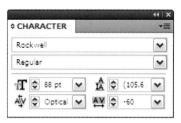

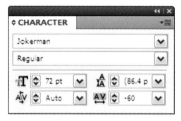

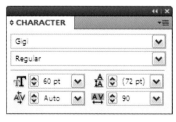

Figure 14-10: Character panel settings for different type blocks.

You can set the point size of your type in the Character panel, right below the font. Pick a value from the pop-up menu or type in a value in the field provided and then press Enter (Windows) or Return (Mac).

Two good guidelines are that capital letters are about two-thirds the point size, and lowercase letters without descenders or ascenders (like a lowercase *a*) are about one-half the point size. So if you want a letter *a* that's one inch (72 pt) high, you have to specify it as 144 pt (two inches) tall.

Ascenders
ajfopTJQZ
Descenders

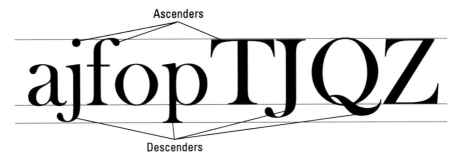

Figure 14-11: Font size allows enough space to accommodate all the possible ascenders and descenders in a font.

Measuring can be just plain annoying

The space between rows (lines) of letters has an even stranger story. This space is its *leading*. Second, the space is measured not between the descenders of the line you're on and the ascenders of the line below (which would make sense), but rather, between the *baseline* of the line you're on and the baseline of the line above the line you're on. The baseline is the line on which most letters rest (those that don't have descenders). Figure 14-12 shows how leading appears in a typical paragraph.

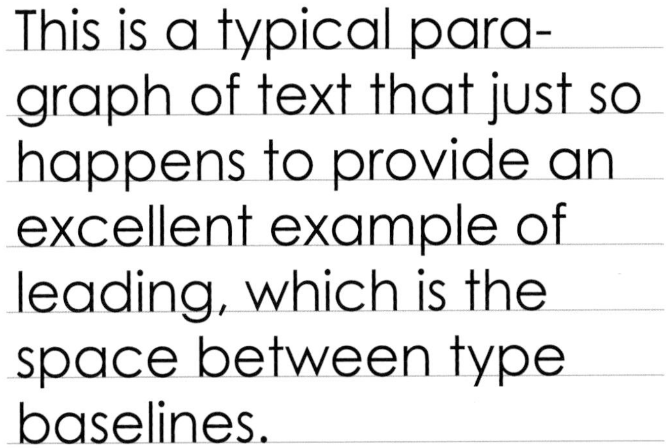

This is a typical para-
graph of text that just so
happens to provide an
excellent example of
leading, which is the
space between type
baselines.

Figure 14-12: Leading is the space between the baselines of type.

You set the leading in the spot to the right of the font size in the Character panel. If a number appears in parentheses, that's the automatic value of the leading — 120 percent of the point size, rounded up to the next half point.

If the amount of leading matches the point size, the descenders of one line touch the ascenders of the line below. In the majority of cases, that's a *large* no-no.

Spacing out while staring at type

Yet another thing to worry about (or ignore, if you choose to) is the space between individual letters that are next to each other. This space can be called two things (specifically to confuse the novice):

- **Tracking:** The space between letters in a series of letters
- **Kerning:** The space between two specific characters

Figure 14-13 shows the difference (sorta) between these two.

tracking

kerning

Figure 14-13: Tracking (top) and kerning (bottom, between the K and e).

Change the kerning by placing your cursor where you want to change the space between two characters. Change the tracking by highlighting a series of characters. Then change the appropriate field in the Character panel, as indicated in Figure 14-14.

Typically, you can leave these values alone. However, when setting short sets of large type, for example, the type can look much better when it's kerned more tightly. Many rules and guidelines exist for proper kerning and tracking, but the best designers set these by eye. If the type looks good, it's probably kerned correctly.

Putting type on the rack

You can stretch your type to make it wider or taller. By changing the values in the Vertical Scale and Horizontal Scale boxes (shown in Figure 14-15), you can reshape type into all manner of oddness. (If you don't see these boxes in the Character panel, double-click the title tab of the panel to expand it.)

In general, this sort of modification is frowned upon, unless used sparingly and only to produce a small degree of change. Stretching type distorts it, making it more difficult to read, and also tends to really irritate the original designer of the typeface.

Moving on up and down

Whereas leading sets how far apart the lines of text are, the baseline shift controls the vertical position of the text after it's been moved via the leading value. Use the field at the bottom of the Character panel to change the baseline shift. Positive numbers move selected text up; negative numbers move selected text down. Figure 14-16 shows a paragraph with a word of text that has a shifted baseline.

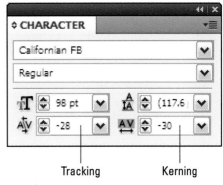

Tracking   Kerning

Figure 14-14: Changing the kerning and tracking values in the Character panel.

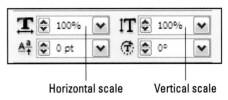

Horizontal scale   Vertical scale

Figure 14-15: Vertical Scale and Horizontal Scale of the Character panel.

Here we have the word "odd" being baseline shifted up for no apparent reason.

Figure 14-16: Using baseline shift within a paragraph.

Adjusting Entire Paragraphs

The Paragraph panel provides controls for modifying all the text in a paragraph at once. These controls are quite different from those in the Character panel. (Don't want any silly old consistency to spoil the fun, now do we?)

Changing the alignment of a paragraph

At the top of the Paragraph panel are seven buttons that set the alignment of paragraphs. Although the buttons are tiny, if you squint hard enough at them, you can see that the tiny graphic image on each one mimics the alignment that they create. Position the cursor over the button without clicking and a tooltip appears and tells you what it is.

To align a paragraph, click anywhere inside it with the Type tool; then click the alignment button in the Paragraph panel. By default, paragraphs align to the left side with their right edge *ragged* (uneven). Choose the Align Right setting, and the opposite is true (right edge smooth, left edge ragged). Try the Align Center setting for ragged left and right edges with centered lines of text. Use the Justify Full Lines setting for straight left and right edges (except for the last line if it's not a full line). Finally, the Justify All Lines setting keeps all lines (including the bottom one) even on both the left and the right. Figure 14-17 shows examples of these alignments.

Changing the space around the paragraph

The Paragraph panel in Illustrator offers options for adjusting the space around a paragraph, plus an option to set how far from the left edge of the paragraph the first line starts. Figure 14-18 shows these options.

Use the Left Indent setting for modifying the position of the left edge of the paragraph. The larger the number, the farther to the right the left edge moves.

Use the First Line Left Indent setting to move the first line of the paragraph left or right relative to the left edge of the paragraph. Use a negative number to make the first line come out from paragraph's left edge, as shown in Figure 14-19. Use a positive number to push the first line in to the right of the paragraph's left edge.

Use the Right Indent setting to adjust the paragraph's right edge. The larger the number, the farther to the left the edge moves.

Use the Space Before Paragraph setting adjusts the amount of space before the current paragraph. If you select a bunch of paragraphs, changing this setting puts space between each one of the paragraphs.

The text in this particular paragraph is set to Align left. Really, I wouldn't kid you about something so seriously serious as that.

The text in this particular paragraph is set to Align center. Really, I wouldn't kid you about something so seriously serious as that.

The text in this particular paragraph is set to Align right. Really, I wouldn't kid you about something so seriously serious as that.

The text in this particular paragraph is set to Justify with last line aligned left. Really, I wouldn't kid you about something so seriously serious as that.

The text in this particular paragraph is set to Justify with last line aligned center. Really, I wouldn't kid you about something so seriously serious as that.

The text in this particular paragraph is set to Justify with last line aligned left. Really, I wouldn't kid you about something so seriously serious as that.

The text in this particular paragraph is set to Justify all lines. Really, I wouldn't kid you about something so seriously   serious   as   that.

Figure 14-17: Text results of different text alignments in Illustrator.

Use the Space After Paragraph setting to adjust the amount of space after the current paragraph. If you select a bunch of paragraphs, changing this setting puts space between each one of the paragraphs. If you enter a value for Space Before *and* Space After, you'll get the sum of both values between your paragraphs.

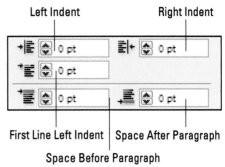

Left Indent   Right Indent

0 pt   0 pt

0 pt

0 pt   0 pt

First Line Left Indent | Space After Paragraph

Space Before Paragraph

Figure 14-18: Controls for changing the amount of space around a paragraph.

Normally this paragraph would
be simply flush left. However, I
used a negative number in the
Paragraph panel's First-line left
indent setting in order to get
the first line to move outside of
the paragraph, a very snazzy
trick.

Figure 14-19: Bring out the left edge of a paragraph with a negative number.

With the basic options available in Character panel and the Paragraph panel, you can create astounding feats of typestry. These two panels provide the core for nearly everything you do with type in Illustrator. Using them, you can equal or surpass just about anything you can create on a single page in any word-processing or page-layout application.

Using Type as a Mask

Illustrator enables you to do a remarkable number of things to your type, but some modifications seem forbidden. For example, if you try to fill type with a gradient (read through Chapter 5), the type just turns black. And what if you want to get really fancy and fill text with another piece of artwork that you create in Illustrator? There's just no way you can do that!

Or is there?

By using the Clipping Mask feature (read more about this in Chapter 10), you can create the appearance that text is being filled with a gradient, artwork, or anything that you can put the text in front of. And what can't you put text in front of? Absolutely . . . nothing! (Say it again, y'all. . . .)

A *clipping mask* is a special feature of Illustrator: It uses the front-most object (the *clipping object*) to hide the objects behind it in a unique way. Everything outside the clipping object is hidden, and the fill and the stroke of the clipping object become transparent, enabling you to see whatever's behind and apparently filling the clipping object. A *type mask* is what you get when you use type as your clipping object. This might sound strange but makes a lot more sense after you create a type mask of your own.

Creating a type mask is simple. Here's how:

1. **Create the artwork you want to fill your type with.**

   This can be absolutely anything. The only catch is that it must be bigger than the type that you want to use as fill.

   For example, if you want to fill your text with a gradient, create a rectangle (or any other object, provided that it's larger than your type) and fill it with a gradient (see Chapter 5), or create the artwork that you want to fill the type with. You can even use a pixel-based image, such as a scanned photograph of your loved one. The only stipulation is that whatever you fill the text with must be larger than the text. Think of the text as a cookie cutter and the object you're filling the text with as cookie dough. You cut away everything outside the text.

2. **Create type in front of whatever you want to fill the text with.**

   Create your type by using the ordinary Type tool. From the Character panel, choose a font size large enough that the type is almost (but not quite) as large as the artwork behind it. If you already created your type, select it with any selection tool and choose Object⇨Arrange⇨Bring to Front and drag it in front of your object.

3. **Use any selection tool to select the text and the object or objects behind the text and then choose Object⇨Clipping Mask⇨Make.**

   To select multiple objects, just hold down the Shift key while clicking each of them with any selection tool.

   After you choose Object⇨Clipping Mask⇨Make, the fill and stroke of the text disappear and are replaced by the contents of whatever is behind the text. Anything outside the area of the text becomes invisible, or masked-out, like the example in Figure 14-20.

With type masks, the text is still ordinary text. You can highlight the text, change the font, type in different words, and so on, while retaining the masking properties.

Any time you want to make the text stop masking out what's behind it, select the text and choose Object⇨Clipping Mask⇨Release.

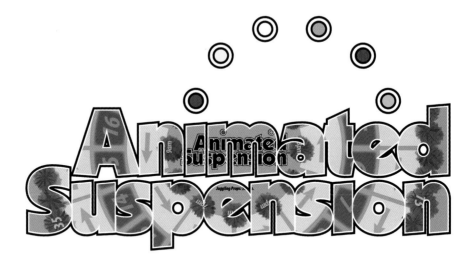

Figure 14-20: The type mask in action: The text of the logo masks out anything outside the type area.

Converting Type to Paths

The type possibilities in Illustrator are nigh infinite. To make them truly infinite, you need take only one step — convert the type to paths. You gain absolute control over every point of every letter of every word of type.

Edit carefully and spell-check the text before you convert it. After you convert text to a path, you can't edit it as type. You also can't highlight it with the Type tool and retype it, change the font, or anything editorial like that.

Here are some reasons why you'd want to make this conversion:

- **To manipulate type like you do any other object in Illustrator:** Type stops being type and becomes just another Illustrator path, at which point you can do absolutely anything to it that you can do to other paths, specifically using the Direct Selection tool on individual points and segments of those paths.

- **To bypass the need for the font files associated with the type:** If you give someone a graphic file containing a font that isn't installed on the recipient's computer, the graphic won't display or print properly if opened in Illustrator or placed into a page-layout program. However, converting the type to paths creates a file that displays and prints exactly as you created it, regardless of the fonts installed on the recipient's computer.

This action is also a good way to make sure that the text can't be retyped. You should always convert text to paths for any logo that you send to other people, which helps guarantee that the logo always looks how you created it.

To convert type to paths, as shown in Figure 14-21, follow these steps.

1. **Use the Selection tool to select the type that you want to convert to a path.**

   Okay, you're altering type, so you should be able to do this by using the Type tool — but you can't. This is just one of those little frustrations that have been around for years in Illustrator.

Figure 14-21: Left: The letter A as type. Right: The letter A converted to paths.

2. **Choose Type⇨Create Outlines.**

   All the points that make up the type suddenly appear, enabling you to edit the type as you would edit any other object in Illustrator (as shown in Figure 14-22). Here's the same letter A from Figure 14-21 after the points are moved and a gradient fill is applied. Why the name *Create Outlines?* Only some long-gone Adobe programmer knows for sure. A better name may be *Create Paths from Text*, which is what this command really does.

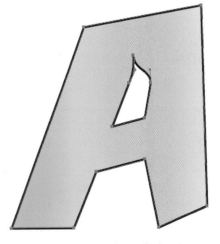

Figure 14-22: The same letter A after the points are moved and a gradient fill is applied.

Type Styles

Illustrator has the concept of styled type, through paragraph and character styles. Styles are just a fancy name for a collection of character or paragraph attributes that allow you to make several changes at once.

For instance, maybe you want to use the exact same font, point size, and justification for all your type in a document. Instead of changing each of the settings each time you create a type object, use a *style* to change all the settings at once. Even better, if you decide that the initial font, or size, or justification needs changed, simply update the style, and all the type with that style applied changes instantly!

Of the two types of type styles in Illustrator, Paragraph styles are much more common and powerful. Not only do they contain all the attributes you find in the Paragraph panel, but also all the character attributes as well. Character styles contain only character attributes (and are useful for type within paragraphs, where you don't want an entire paragraph to change).

To unleash all that power, you'll first need to call up the Paragraph Styles panel by choosing choose Window⇨Type⇨Paragraph Styles from the main menu. Then, to actually create a paragraph style, set up your type just the way you want it to appear, and then click the New Style button in the Paragraph Styles panel (the little piece of paper directly to the left of the trash can icon; see Figure 14-23). To apply that style to type, select a type object or make a selection with the Type tool, and then click the name of the style once in the Paragraph panel.

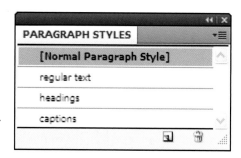

Figure 14-23: The Paragraph Styles panel.

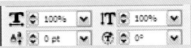
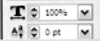

Printing Your Masterpiece

In This Chapter

▶ Working with printing in mind

▶ Sizing artwork to fit a page

▶ Printing black-and-white illustrations

▶ Printing color illustrations

▶ Understanding the strange issue of color separations

*W*hen designing your artwork, keep in mind how it will look if it will be printed. If you know what medium you're going to print your artwork on, you can save yourself time in the long run. For instance, say you create a stunning logo, full of vibrant colors and subtle hues and reflections. Well, you probably can't use that logo in a black-and-white context. In this chapter, I provide some great ideas to keep in mind while you create your artwork — and you can also refer to this chapter when you arrive at the printing process.

If you just want to print, read the next section. If you want to discover all the stuff behind what goes into printing, check out the upcoming section "What You See Is Roughly What You Get." Or, if you want the nitty-gritty about setting up Illustrator for printing (plus even more details on printing), skip ahead to the section "Setting Up Your Page to Print (You Hope)."

Printing Quickly

If you have a printer hooked up to your computer or network, you can print just about anything that you can create in Illustrator.

Before you print, make sure that your artwork is inside the *printable area,* which is indicated by a dotted gray line. Anything outside the dotted line doesn't print. If you don't see a dotted gray line, choose View⇨Show Page Tiling. To hide the line, choose View⇨Hide Page Tiling.

To print your artwork, choose File⇨Print. When the Print dialog box appears, press Enter (Return on a Mac), or click the Print/OK button. You now have a printed version of your Illustrator creation. Pressing Enter (Return on a Mac) without adjusting any settings in the Print dialog box is known in the trade as *running with the defaults. Defaults* are settings that are made automatically when you install Illustrator, and they work just fine for printing artwork from Illustrator. When your creations don't print as you expect them to, however, you need to adjust the other settings, which I discuss throughout this chapter.

What You See Is Roughly What You Get

Whatever you create on-screen, you can print (theoretically). And what you print looks pretty much like what you see on your monitor. Note that I say *pretty much* and not *exactly*. Here's why:

- **Resolution differences:** Your monitor resolution is much lower than your printer resolution. If you think everything you print will look better than it does on-screen, you'd be correct — in most cases.

- **Aliasing differences:** By default, Illustrator displays art and text on your monitor as *anti-aliased* (the edges where colors meet blend together, producing a more visually appealing image on-screen). Printed pages are not anti-aliased, and images print crisply and cleanly, with no blurring of edges. Figure 15-1 shows the crisp edges of Rocky the Meeple on the left, compared with a zoomed-in screen representation of Rocky. Note that the pixelized edges on the right image are anti-aliased, smoothing out the curved edges of the blue meeple.

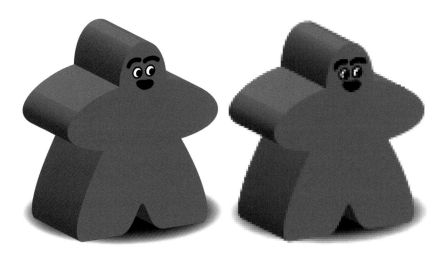

Figure 15-1: Crisp printed meeple, left vs. blurred anti-aliased screen meeple, right.

✏ **Color differences:** Your monitor displays color images by lighting up little red, green, and blue phosphorescent squares called *pixels,* whereas printing produces color images by applying dots of ink on paper. Creating colors by completely different physical processes causes a major difference between what you see on-screen and what you get in print.

With these points in mind, you should regularly print your artwork during the creation process to make sure that the printed result is as close as possible to what you're designing on-screen. That way, you can modify your artwork to avoid surprises when you print the final product. After some practice, you develop an eye for what a printout will look like, even when you're working entirely on-screen.

Setting Up Your Page to Print (You Hope)

Long ago in the Dark Ages, people slaved over drafting tables, among matte knives and ink bottles, struggling to create graphics while gagging on glue fumes. At last, at the dawn of the new millennium, computer systems forever replaced those ancient torture devices. These days, you can whip up a document in Illustrator, feed pure white paper into a printer, and *let 'er rip!* (Uh, maybe I ought to rephrase that.)

Quick printing

Use the Document Setup dialog box (shown in Figure 15-2) to set up your page so that it prints properly. You can view the Document Setup dialog box by choosing that option from the File menu.

The easiest way to print is to choose File⇨Print and press Enter (Return on a Mac) after the Print dialog box appears.

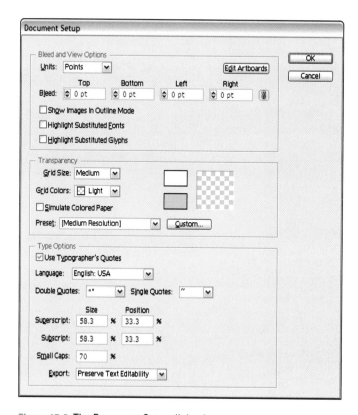

Figure 15-2: The Document Setup dialog box.

Changing Artboard size

To change the size of your document, you can either click the Edit Artboards button in the Document Setup dialog box, or click the Artboard tool in the Tool panel. Doing either action makes your screen look decidedly unusual, as shown in Figure 15-3.

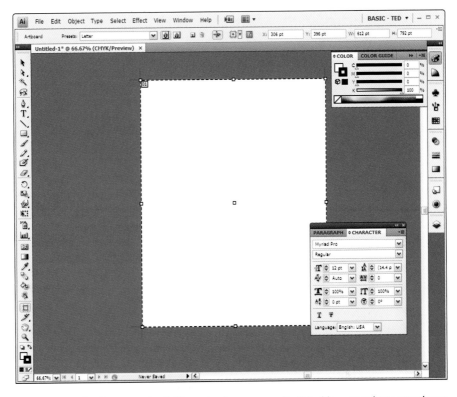

Figure 15-3: Adjusting page size in Illustrator is an unusually disturbing grayed-out experience.

Here, you can drag any of the handles along the edge of the page to adjust the size of the Artboard, or enter in values along the Control Panel (at the top of the work area) in the W and H fields, for width and height, respectively. When you're done making changes, click any other tool in the Tools panel to be returned to the normal, healthy-looking Illustrator screen.

Printing Mechanics

After you make sure that your page size settings are correct (typically they're fine unless — ahem — somebody mucks them up), you're ready to commit your masterpiece to paper.

Printing composite proofs

Printing a composite proof is really printing what you see on-screen to a single sheet of paper. You do this kind of printing all the time. If you have a color printer, your result looks really close (hopefully) to what's on-screen. If you have a black-and-white printer, you get a black-and-white version of what's on-screen.

The other kind of printing is called *printing separations,* which means generating a separate sheet of paper (or, more likely, film) for each ink to be used when the artwork is printed. I discuss separations in more detail in the section "All about Way-Scary Separations" later in this chapter.

You can print composite proofs by following these steps:

1. **Choose File⇨Print from the menu.**

   The Print dialog box appears, as shown in Figure 15-4.

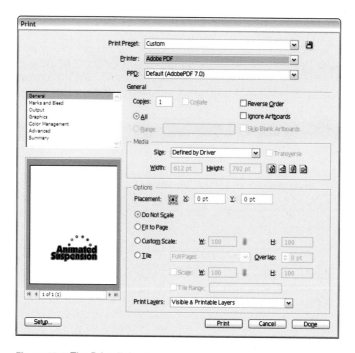

Figure 15-4: The Print dialog box.

2. **Select the appropriate printing options (as I detail in the next section "Important printing options").**

3. **Click Print.**

Important printing options

The Print dialog box has all sorts of options, but only a few of them are worth noticing. Fortunately, the default settings are usually what you want anyway — for example, one copy of whatever you send to the printer of your choice. However, for situations in which the current setting is not what you want, the following handy options are lurking in the Print dialog box:

- **Name (Windows)/Printer (Mac):** This drop-down menu near the top of the Print dialog box indicates the printer that you intend to use. If you have only one printer, this setting is most likely correct all the time. If you have more than one printer, you can see which one you're currently using. You can change the printer setting here as well.

- **Number of Copies (Windows)/Copies (Mac):** This option shows the number of copies of your artwork that you want to print, each on a separate sheet.

- **Range:** This option controls which Artboards (sure, they're pages, but Illustrator is more sophisticated than that and calls them Artboards) will print. If you plan on printing all artboards, leave the All radio button selected.

All about Way-Scary Separations

Separations print a separate page for each color of ink that you use in a document. Printing separations is a good way to double-check your work before you send it to a service bureau to be made into film or plates. If you never do that, skip this section.

If you do send your work to a service bureau to be made into film or plates, printing separations can save you a lot of time. For example, suppose you plan to print a job using black ink and the spot color Pantone 185. After printing separations, you get pages for cyan, magenta, yellow, and Pantone 185, rather than just pages for black and Pantone 185. You know immediately that some of the colors you used were created as cyan, magenta, yellow, black (CMYK) process colors, not as spot colors. On closer examination of the pages, you see that the black type you used exists on all pages, and you know that the type was specified as Registration, not as Black. Registration and Black look identical on-screen, but Registration is a special color that's used exclusively by printers (for those little marks that help center the content on the page). Registration is totally unsuitable for artwork. (Ack! No! Don't print that ink drawing in Registration! You'll only get a page full of gunk.)

I could fill a book with information about looking at separations to find out information about potential problems in your artwork. The book would be painfully long and boring, however, and one I don't want to write. My advice: Print separations and leave it at that. Perhaps the best place to find out more about separations is your service bureau. The people there can help you examine your separations. In fact, many service bureaus require that you provide laser print separations when you place a print order so they know the file is properly prepared.

The concept behind printing separations from Illustrator is straightforward. Because printing in color requires different inks, which are applied to paper sequentially on a printing press, each ink gets its own printing plate. Illustrator generates film, paper, or even the individual plates themselves — one for each color of ink.

Traditionally, full-color artwork is printed using four different inks (and therefore four plates): cyan, magenta, yellow, and black (CYMK). If you have a CMYK document in Illustrator, you're working in the environment that's perfect for full-color printing. Check out Figure 15-5 for a composite image and the four separations used to create it.

Figure 15-5: The original artwork (center) shown as four separations.

Separations are not in color

Separations don't print in color; they print in black and white. It doesn't matter to the printing press what color each plate is because the color is determined by the ink that's used with a particular plate.

Printing separations

Okay, anybody except a jet pilot might find the Output section of the Print dialog box (shown in Figure 15-6) a bit intimidating. Don't panic at the sight of that very strange list that appears, though. Instead, create the artwork that you want to separate. (Be sure to save any changes before you continue.) Then use the following steps to set up your document for separation printing.

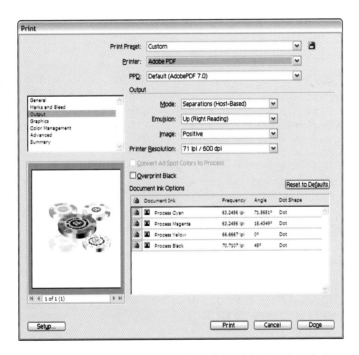

Figure 15-6: Use the Output section of the Print dialog box for printing separations.

1. **Choose File➪Print and click Output from the list on the left.**

   The Output options in the Print dialog box appear.

2. **Choose the Separations (Host-Based) option from the Mode drop-down menu.**

   The ink check boxes become enabled.

3. **Make sure that the settings (Emulsion, Image, and Printer Resolution) are correct.**

   If you aren't sure whether they're correct, leave the default settings as they are and check with the representative from your offset printing company.

4. **Click the icon to the left of any color that you want to print.**

5. **Click the Print button after you finish making changes.**

By the way, if you need a quick refresher on the uses of CMYK and RGB (red, green, blue), sneak a peek at Chapter 1. I won't tell a soul.

16

Moving Files Into and Out of Illustrator

Although you can certainly take a file from concept to final printing using only Illustrator, you probably shouldn't. It's a specialized program, created to be one small (but vitally important) part in a production cycle.

In a typical production cycle, text is created in a word-processing program (such as Microsoft Word), scanned images are edited in an image-editing program (such as Photoshop), and vector-based graphics are created in Illustrator. Finally, all these elements are combined in a page layout program (such as Adobe InDesign) or a Web-design application (such as Adobe Dreamweaver).

Attempting to make Illustrator perform all aspects of the production cycle is like trying to build a house with only a hammer. Yeah, you could probably do it, but the task takes you a lot more time to complete, the result looks really awful, and you're a lot more tired and frustrated than if you'd used the right tools for the job in the first place.

Don't get me wrong. Illustrator is a strong link in that production cycle. You can save Illustrator files in nearly *three dozen* different file formats! If you create something in Illustrator and save it properly, you can open your creation in just about any application that ever supported graphics on any platform — even bizarre and forgotten computer platforms, such as Amiga!

The bottom line is that Illustrator is designed to create files for use in other programs as well as to receive graphics files created in other programs. Harnessing the full power of Illustrator means making the program work well (and play nicely) with other programs — in other words, getting files into and out of Illustrator.

In this chapter, you find out how to make Illustrator play well with others by bringing files that weren't created in Illustrator into your Illustrator document and by moving Illustrator files into other applications.

Bringing Files Into Illustrator

You can bring graphics or text into Illustrator in several different ways, but the most straightforward, Joe-Friday way is to use the Place command from the File menu. Every type of graphic or text that can be inserted in Illustrator can be placed with this command, making it the one-stop location for all file importing. The "Getting Files Out of Illustrator" section (later in this chapter) contains a list of the most common file formats that Illustrator can both export and import.

When you place artwork into Illustrator, you usually have the option of either *embedding* or *linking* the artwork. Each of these processes has different implications for file size and storage:

> ✔ **Embedding:** Makes the placed artwork part of the Illustrator file, even though the artwork was created elsewhere. That way, you need only the single Illustrator file for your artwork to print properly.
>
> Embedding can dramatically increase the file size.
>
> ✔ **Linking:** Creates a link in the Illustrator document to the placed artwork. The file size of the Illustrator document is smaller as a result, and any change to the linked file is automatically reflected in the Illustrator document. Linking also enables the file to be updated outside of Illustrator (while maintaining the link). In order for linked files to print properly, both the Illustrator file and all linked files must be present.

To place a graphic in an Illustrator document, follow these steps:

1. **Choose File⇨Place.**

   The Place dialog box appears, as shown in Figure 16-1, from which you choose the file that you want to place.

Figure 16-1: Select a document to embed or link with the Place dialog box.

2. **Select the file that you want to place.**

   If you don't have any files lying around, look in the Sample Files folder (located in the Adobe Illustrator application folder) and pick one of those files.

3. **Choose whether to link or to embed the file.**

   - *To create a link between the file you want to place and the Illustrator file,* make sure that the Link check box (lower left) is selected.

     Creating a link is the default setting.

     To embed the file you want to place in the Illustrator file, deselect (clear) the Link box.

4. **Choose whether to use the graphic as an artistic element (the default) or a template.**

   If you select the Template check box (lower left), Illustrator creates a special layer for the pixel-based image. (See Chapter 13 for more on layers.) This layer is *locked* (you can't change anything on the layer); and the graphic is dimmed in the document after it is placed, making the graphic 50 percent lighter. Template layers also don't print and aren't included in the artwork when you use the Save for Web & Devices command. Template layers are especially useful when you plan to use the pixel-based image as a guide for tracing in Illustrator.

5. **Choose to replace an already placed graphic or add the graphic as new.**

   This check box option is available only after you place a graphic in the file and that graphic is selected. You have the option of replacing that graphic with the graphic that you're about to place or bringing the new graphic in as a separate graphic. Just select the Replace check box to replace the selected graphic, or leave the check box clear to leave the selected graphic alone.

6. **Click the Place button.**

Deciding whether to link or embed

If you're just playing around to see how the program works, it doesn't matter whether you link or embed. If you're working on a production with tight deadlines and making rapid changes to your document and money is on the line, I recommend that you link whenever possible. Linking makes the chore of changing placed images much easier.

When you embed something, it exists totally within a single Illustrator file: Your artwork is locked down. You can't do anything to it other than move it, scale it (and other such transformations), or run a Photoshop filter/effect on it. That's all, folks — and that isn't much. You can't edit your artwork in another application; because it's embedded in Illustrator, it won't respond to other applications. The term *embedding* is quite literal — it's stuck in there. You can't get your artwork out unless you pry it out with the Export command. (More on that in the section "Getting Files Out of Illustrator," later in this chapter.)

Here's an example. You send a completed job to your service bureau, but it can't be printed because your five pixel-based images are embedded — two in RGB (red, green, blue) mode and the rest in CMYK (cyan, magenta, yellow, black). The images need to be in CMYK for the job to print properly. Illustrator can't convert pixel data from RGB to CMYK. (Illustrator can only convert vector data.) You need to use Photoshop to convert the pixel images. If the images are linked, however, the folks at your service bureau can change them by opening the image in Photoshop, making the change, and then updating the link — a quick process that takes about a minute on a fast computer.

Because the images are embedded, however, you have two options. You can deliver the original pixel-based graphics to the service bureau (assuming that your company has one, that you didn't send the job over at the last minute, and that the service bureau is still open). Or you can rack up bad karma if you make the staff at the service bureau do this for you. This situation entails separating each image into its own layer in Illustrator, exporting the entire document as a Photoshop file; opening the document in Photoshop; deleting all the other layers; cropping the image to the right size; changing the color mode; saving the image; going back to Illustrator; and replacing the graphic. Whew! And this assumes that the service bureau staff actually knows how to do this, which not many people do.

If you know beyond a doubt that your images are perfect, pristine, and final, and never need changing in any way, you can embed them. If your feet touch the earth like the rest of ours do, link your images.

The only hassle that comes with linking is that you have to provide all the linked images with your Illustrator file whenever it leaves your computer because your file won't print properly without them. This procedure is a minor hassle, however, considering the amount of hassle it saves!

Managing links

Whenever you place an image into Illustrator and link it, the image isn't actually in your document — just like how Katie Couric isn't actually in your house when you watch the news on TV. What you see in Illustrator is a preview of the file — an image of the image, so to speak. Think of the actual file as broadcasting an image of itself to Illustrator while the file itself sits somewhere else on your hard drive. You look at the preview on-screen; and when the document prints, the actual file supplies the image for the document. If the actual file gets moved, modified, or deleted, you have a problem — especially if you're printing — because Illustrator uses the preview image instead of the real file. The preview image in Illustrator contains just enough

Figure 16-2: Use the Links panel for total link control.

info to be displayed on-screen, but not nearly enough info to print with any quality. Fortunately, Illustrator provides you with a powerful tool to help you manage links: the Links panel. You can find the Links panel by choosing Window⇨Links. What you get looks remarkably like Figure 16-2.

The Links panel shows you all the placed images in your document; alerts you if anything is amiss; and enables you to update, edit, or replace the images — all with the click of a mouse.

The Links panel includes embedded images as well, even though they aren't technically links.

To use the Links panel, you must first understand what the panel is telling you. The Links panel informs you about the status of the graphic through alerts. *Alerts* are tiny icons that appear beside the names of the graphics in the Links panel. They look a little like buttons, but they are strictly informative: Alerts warn you when a potential problem exists with the link. You can fix most problems by clicking the graphic within the Links panel, and then by clicking the Replace Link or Update Link buttons at the bottom of the panel (more on these options in just a second).

The alerts provide the following information:

- **Embedded:** The Embedded icon (a rectangle overlapping a triangle) indicates that the image data is completely contained within the Illustrator document and is *not linked* to an external file. This situation isn't necessarily a problem, but it can be. See the earlier section, "Deciding whether to link or embed." No "un-embed" button exists. The only way to turn this embedded image into a linked file is to click the Update Link button at the bottom of the panel, locate the original file on the hard drive, and replace the file with the Link option checked.

- **Missing:** A question mark inside a red octagon (or stop sign) shows that the actual image file is missing. This information is good to know because the linked image still shows up in Illustrator even if the information that the file needs to print properly is missing. You can fix this image by clicking the Replace Link button. (More about this in a moment.)

- **Modified:** A triangle with an exclamation point (sort of like an emphatic yield sign) indicates that the actual linked image has been changed outside of Illustrator. This information is also vital because Illustrator still displays the original image.

- **No icon:** Everything is okay. Okay, so this isn't really an alert. (Yeah, that would be pretty silly — Warning! Everything is normal!) Still, it's worth noting that when nothing is wrong with a linked image, the panel shows just the filename of the image, its thumbnail, and nothing else.

After you identify the problems with the linked graphics, you can manage them by using the buttons along the bottom of the Links panel (refer to

Figure 16-2), by clicking the problem graphic in the Links panel, and then by clicking one of the following four buttons:

- **Relink:** This is the first button from the left. Click this button when your image is missing or when you want to swap the selected graphic with another graphic on your hard drive. After you click this button, the Place dialog box opens. Choose a different file or locate the missing file on your hard drive, and then click Place. The new image replaces the old one.

- **Go to Link:** Second from the left, this button is handy for locating and selecting linked graphics. Click the linked graphic in the Links panel and click the Go to Link button. This action selects the graphic in the document as if you clicked it by using the Selection tool. Clicking this button also centers the view on the graphic, making the graphic easy to spot whenever you have a lot of other graphics in the document.

- **Update Link:** Click this third button whenever you see the Modified warning beside a link. This action updates the selected link with the latest information from the original file.

- **Edit Original:** This fourth button is available only for linked images — not for embedded images. After you click this option, the selected image opens in the original application that created it.

The Edit Original option is a great way to modify images. After you place a Photoshop image, for example, click this button to launch Photoshop and open the image. In Photoshop, you can make the necessary changes and then save your image. When you go back to Illustrator, it asks whether you want to update your modified image. Click OK to update the information.

Your goal, as you work with placed images, is to avoid all question marks and exclamation points in your Links panel. Fix these problems by using the buttons at the bottom of the panel.

The Links panel offers a few more tidbits through its pop-up menu to help you manage links. Click the triangle in the upper-right corner of the panel (refer to Figure 16-2) to access the Links panel pop-up menu. Here you find Replace, Go to Link, Update Link, and Edit Original commands that duplicate the functions of the buttons along the bottom. You also find various Sort commands, such as Sort by Name, which alphabetizes the linked images within the panel. You can also reorganize the panel by using Show commands, such as Show Embedded, which hides all linked graphics. The Show and Sort commands are useful only when you have several linked images, which is rare in an Illustrator document. The two most useful things in the Links panel pop-up menu (shown in Figure 16-3) are the Embed Image and Information commands. Here's how you use them:

✔ **Embed Image:** Click a linked image in the Links panel and choose the Embed Image command to embed the image into the Illustrator file.

✔ **Information:** Click an image in the Links panel and choose the Information command to open the Link Information dialog box. This dialog box is strictly informative. You can't make any changes here, but you find out lots of information about the selected graphic, such as the image's location on the hard drive, the image's file size, the image's file type, when the image was created, and a whole lot more. You can also access this dialog box by double-clicking the name of the link.

| Relink... |
| Go To Link |
| Edit Original |
| Update Link |
| Placement Options... |
| Check In Link... |
| Versions... |
| Embed Image |
| Reveal in Bridge... |
| Link File Info... |
| Link Information... |
| ✔ Show All |
| Show Missing |
| Show Modified |
| Show Embedded |
| Sort by Name |
| Sort by Kind |
| Sort by Status |
| Panel Options... |

Getting Files Out of Illustrator

Files that are *native* to Illustrator (files saved in the Illustrator format within Illustrator) can't be read by every application. However, these files are Portable Document Format (PDF)–based, so any application that can read PDFs generated by Acrobat 5 or a later version can also read Illustrator files. For the applications that can't read Illustrator-native files, Illustrator can export a number of different file formats.

Figure 16-3: The Links panel pop-up menu.

To decide which format to use, consider the eventual use of the file. For instance, if you're posting your artwork on a Web page, you probably want to use either JPEG or GIF formats. (Find out more about these formats in Chapter 17.) If you want to place your file in a Microsoft Word document, you can use EPS, EMF, or BMP formats. (More on those formats in a moment.)

Typically, the manual that accompanies your software describes which file formats it accepts. Illustrator supports the export of 20 different formats (including variations of individual formats), so just choose a format that works in the target application from the list of available formats.

To export your artwork in a certain format, choose File➪Export from the File menu, choose the format you want from the Format list, and save the file. Some Export formats open an additional dialog box for that specific file format after you click Save. You'll also find various file formats under the Save for Web & Devices command, such as PNG, GIF, and SVG as well as JPEG and SWF, which are also found under the Export command.

Not all file formats support vector-based data! (See Chapter 2 for details.) If you use EPS, PDF, Flash, or SVG, you preserve your paths; but most other formats convert your Illustrator files to pixels.

The following list is a brief summary of the most useful file formats available in Illustrator:

- **EPS:** Encapsulated PostScript files are accepted by most software packages. Raster and vector-based data are preserved in EPS files.

  For more information about vector-based and pixel-based graphics, see Chapter 2.
- **GIF:** Graphics Interchange Format files are commonly used on the Web for files with few colors (good for solid-color logos and text).
- **JPEG:** Joint Photographic Experts Group files are highly compressible files that are used on the Web. They're especially good for photographs.
- **PNG:** Portable Network Graphics files are the most flexible of the Web formats, providing support for compression and detail in a single file format.
- **TIFF:** Tagged Image File Format files are the industry standard for pixel-based images for print work.
- **PDF:** Portable Document Format files are designed to keep the look and feel of the original artwork and can be read by anyone with a copy of the free Adobe Acrobat Reader (www.adobe.com).
- **PICT:** PICT files are the built-in Macintosh pixel format. Export any graphics to be viewed on Mac screens as PICT files.
- **BMP:** BMP files are the built-in pixel format of Windows. Use the BMP format to export any graphics that will be viewed on Windows screens.
- **EMF:** Enhanced MetaFile formatted files are perfect for embedding graphics in Microsoft Office applications, such as Word, Excel, and PowerPoint.
- **PSD:** Photoshop Document files are native Photoshop files, which can contain Photoshop layer information.
- **Flash:** Flash files are a vector-based graphic format for the Web.
- **SVG:** Scaleable Vector Graphics files are the up-and-coming Web standard of vector-based graphic formats.

Whenever you export files, use the same name as the original document file but with a different extension (the two, three or four letters after a filename, traditionally required by Windows and DOS computers). These letters tell you the format of the file just by looking at its name.

Working with Illustrator and Photoshop

Illustrator and Photoshop, both from Adobe, provide unique and useful integration capabilities. You can take files from either application and put them directly into the other application in five ways: dragging and dropping; copying and pasting (almost identical to cutting and pasting); placing; exporting and importing; or opening. Each method produces slightly different results to meet your every need, whim, or desire. (Well, okay, just the desires that center on moving files between graphics applications. You have those all the time, right?)

Making life easy: Copy and paste, drag and drop

The copy-and-paste and drag-and-drop methods of getting a file from one program to the other are incredibly easy. Open a file in Photoshop, and then open a file in Illustrator. Make a selection in either program, choose Copy from the Edit menu, and then go to the other application and choose Paste from the Edit menu. Or simply click a selection in either program and drag the selection from that one application into an open window in the other application. In Illustrator, you can use any selection tool to do the dragging. In Photoshop, you need to use the Move tool.

After you move graphics this way, they appear at the height and width that they were when created in the other program. After you drag a graphic from Illustrator to Photoshop, the graphic rasterizes automatically. (*Rasterize* is a two-dollar word for the process that converts vector-based data into pixel-based data.)

Whenever you copy and paste a graphic from Illustrator into Photoshop, the Paste dialog box appears, as shown in Figure 16-4. Choose from the four radio buttons there to select your pasting preference: Smart Object, Pixels, Paths, or Shape Layer.

Your first impulse might be to paste the graphic as paths. After all, Illustrator uses paths — not pixels — so you expect this method to preserve

Figure 16-4: Pasting Illustrator data into Photoshop.

your original Illustrator files as they are. Unfortunately, although Photoshop uses paths similar to Illustrator's paths, they work very differently in Photoshop than they do in Illustrator. For example, paths in Photoshop can't have strokes or fills, although paths can be used to fill or stroke an image in Photoshop and to do other important Photoshop-specific things. You just can't use the path to print or display information on the Web.

Another option is to paste your graphics as a shape layer, which allows vector-based data to be retained without rasterization. In order to retain the vector-based data of shape layers, however, they must reside in a layered file, which limits your file formats to TIFF, PDF, or native PSD. Paste the Illustrator graphic as pixels if your end goal is to create and save a pixel-based Photoshop image.

The best option tends to be Smart Object. This allows the pasted object to remember that it's from Illustrator. If you double-click the object in Photoshop, you can edit it in Illustrator, paths and all. So while the illustrator objects display in Photoshop as existing in pixel-space, there are really vector objects in there that can be changed.

Copying and pasting or dragging and dropping from Photoshop to Illustrator is easier than going from Illustrator to Photoshop (and that's pretty darn easy). You don't have to worry about the paths-to-pixels issue. Just make your selection and drag it by using the Move tool; or copy the image, go to an open Illustrator document, and paste the image. That's it!

Don't assume (even if it is quite logical) that because moving Illustrator files into Photoshop rasterizes the files, moving Photoshop files into Illustrator must "vectorize" them. This isn't the case. The pixels in a Photoshop file stay pixels, subject to all the laws and limitations of pixels anywhere else. For example, Illustrator vector-based data prints out at the highest quality no matter how much you scale, skew, rotate, or distort the data. Pixel-based data within Illustrator starts to *degrade* (data gets blurry or worse) if you enlarge it or shrink it. Rotating, skewing, or distorting the pixel-based data has similar negative effects. Although you don't have to worry about resolution for vector-based data, you do have to make sure that your pixel data has a high enough resolution: namely, 72 points (pt) per inch (ppi) for the Web and anywhere from 150 ppi to 300 ppi or higher for print.

When you drop or paste into Photoshop, the artwork appears inside a preview box, as shown in Figure 16-5. I cannot overstate the handiness of this preview box. While inside the preview box, the graphic isn't really in Photoshop yet. You can position the graphic, rotate it, and then scale the preview. Then double-click inside the preview box (or press Enter for Windows, or Return for Mac), and Photoshop rasterizes the graphic at the best quality possible. If you rotate and scale the image after it's been rasterized, you blur and otherwise degrade the image.

 Photoshop graphics that are dragged and dropped or copied and pasted into Illustrator files are always embedded.

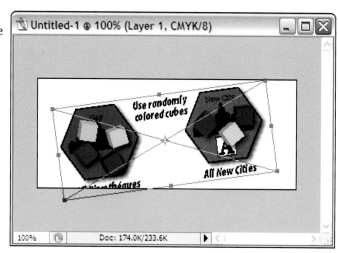

Figure 16-5: The Place preview box in Photoshop.

Placing files

Placing files into Photoshop or Illustrator is one of the more versatile ways to bring data into the application. Each application provides a variety of options that aren't available by using any other method.

Placing Illustrator files in Photoshop

To place an Illustrator file into Photoshop, open a Photoshop file and choose File⇨Place. Select a saved Illustrator file (it doesn't need to be open) from the Place dialog box and click OK. The file opens in Photoshop inside a preview box just like it does when pasting or dropping, which you can read about in earlier sections.

Placing Photoshop files in Illustrator

Placing Photoshop files into Illustrator is identical to placing any other graphic into Illustrator. See the section "Bringing Files Into Illustrator," earlier in this chapter.

Now opening in an application near you

Native files can be read by the "opposite" application. In other words, Photoshop can read Illustrator files, and Illustrator can read Photoshop files. One advantage of this capability is that you don't need to have any document already open.

To open a Photoshop file in Illustrator, choose Open from the Illustrator File menu and select the Photoshop file. The Photoshop file opens in a new document within Illustrator, in the color mode of the Photoshop file.

To open an Illustrator file in Photoshop, choose Open from the Photoshop File menu and select the Illustrator file. The Photoshop Import PDF dialog box appears, as shown in Figure 16-6. If you saved a file as an EPS or if you exported it in an Illustrator 10 or earlier format, this dialog box's name is Rasterize Generic EPS Format. If you save the file in Illustrator CS format, this dialog box is Rasterize Generic PDF. Otherwise, these dialog box options are identical, no matter which name you see.

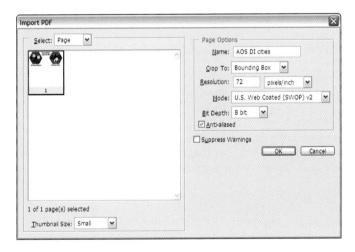

Figure 16-6: Use the Import PDF dialog box to refine your graphic settings.

In the Import PDF dialog box, you set the resolution and color mode of your graphic. Your exact settings should reflect, as closely as possible, the final purpose of the graphic. You should determine whether the graphic is going to be viewed on-screen (Web, multimedia) or if it's going to be printed (desktop or offset). The more you alter these settings after you rasterize the graphic, the more you degrade it.

Exporting a graphic

Exporting is almost the opposite of placing. Instead of bringing a graphic into an application, you're getting it out of an application. Exporting has two big advantages. First, you don't need a copy of the other application to create the graphic in that format. Second, Illustrator layers export as separate

Photoshop layers, instead of as one flattened graphic. (Layers don't stay intact when pasting, dragging, or placing an Illustrator file into Photoshop. See Chapter 13 for more info on Illustrator layers.) Sadly, Photoshop layers don't export to layers in Illustrator although you can get Photoshop layers by using the Open command on a Photoshop file.

You can export any path that you create in Photoshop as an Illustrator file. To export paths from Photoshop, choose File⇨Export⇨Paths to Illustrator. The Export Paths dialog box opens from which you specify those paths to export. Select a path and click Save, and an Illustrator file is created that contains your path.

Exporting from Illustrator is much more powerful than exporting from Photoshop because you can choose to export all your Illustrator layers as separate Photoshop layers. This option provides great versatility in case you want to further edit your graphics in Photoshop.

To export your Illustrator graphic as a Photoshop file, choose File⇨ Export. Name the file in the Name field and choose Photoshop (PSD) as your format. After you click OK, the Photoshop Export Options dialog box appears, as shown in Figure 16-7.

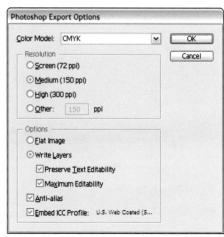

In the Photoshop Export Options dialog box, you determine color model; resolution (for more on resolution and which is best for what purpose, see Chapter 2), anti-aliasing; and whether to export the graphic as a single, flattened layer or as multiple layers. Select the Write Layers radio button to export the Illustrator layers as Photoshop layers. If you instead opt for the Flat Image option, you export the file as a single, flattened layer.

Figure 16-7: Set resolution in the Photoshop Export Options dialog box.

When in doubt, select the Write Layers option. You can easily delete or flatten the layers in Photoshop (by using the Photoshop Layers panel) if you decide you don't want them.

You also have the option of exporting your file with slices and image maps for use on the Web. For more on Illustrator and the Web, see Chapter 17. Also, you can export your image with compound shapes. When you bring compound shapes into Photoshop, they become editable clipping masks. Conversely, your Photoshop clipping masks become editable compound shapes when brought into Illustrator.

Using Adobe Illustrator with Nearly Everything Else

Illustrator works great with Photoshop and InDesign. But what happens when you want to use Illustrator with other products? To make your Illustrator files compatible with as wide a range of applications as possible, you need to go with the standards. Standard file formats are the formats that the majority of applications can use. Whenever you save something using a standard file format, you're almost guaranteed that anyone can open it, regardless of platform or application, just as long as he or she is using an industry standard application, even if it isn't one from Adobe, such as QuarkXPress.

For Web graphics, the standard formats are GIF, JPEG and Flash. As of this writing, PNG and SVG don't have the universal acceptance needed to declare them standards. Keep an eye on them, however; times change fast. For more information on saving files in these formats, see Chapter 17.

For printing hard copy, the original standard format for vector-based graphics was EPS, but it's now shifted to the more-flexible PDF. The Illustrator options for EPS appear in the EPS Format Options dialog box (see Figure 16-8). Virtually all page layout, word-processing, and graphics applications accept EPS files. InDesign and QuarkXPress accept EPS files and work well with the file format.

Fortunately, saving EPS files is vastly simpler than saving for the Web. Choose File➪Save As, name the file there, and choose Illustrator EPS for the format. Click Save, and the EPS Format Options dialog box opens. (Refer to Figure 16-8.) Typically, running with the defaults (just click OK without changing any settings) works fine. In case you want something different, bone up on the other settings in this dialog box:

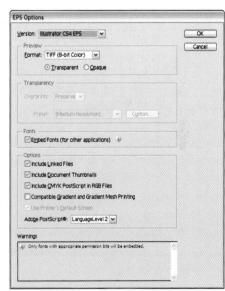

Figure 16-8: Set compatibility, preview, and other options in the EPS Format Options dialog box.

✔ **Compatibility:** You can open and edit Illustrator EPS files just like you do any other Illustrator files. Suppose a friend is helping out with a graphics project and doesn't have the latest version of Illustrator. To give an EPS file to this person for editing, set the Compatibility option to match whatever earlier version your friend is using. Otherwise, leave the file set to the current version of Illustrator that you're using.

Saving your file to be compatible with an earlier version can alter your graphic. For example, Illustrator 3 doesn't support gradients. If you used gradients, they get broken up into separate objects for every different color in the gradient. The graphic looks the same, but editing can be a problem. The fact that you can save files in the Illustrator 3 format is a testament to Illustrator's compatibility with other applications. Illustrator 3 was outdated back in 1993! (That's the computer equivalent of being fluent in ancient Greek.)

✔ **Preview:** Use these options to set how the Preview image displays when linked (Format) and whether the Preview image is transparent or opaque.

- *Format:* This option determines how you create the Preview image, which displays when the graphic is linked to a document in another application. Preview doesn't affect how the image is printed — only how it displays on-screen. Choose the TIFF (8-bit Color) setting for Windows (which most Mac applications can read) or the Macintosh (8-bit Color) setting for Macs (which most Windows applications can read). However, if your PC has problems reading the Mac file, change your preview to the TIFF (8-bit color) setting.

- *Transparent or Opaque:* These radio button options exist only when you choose the TIFF (8-bit color) setting for your Preview image. Select one to determine how transparent areas in your graphic are handled. Typically, you want to set this to the Transparent option, but if you're using the graphic in any Microsoft Office application, you need to select the Opaque option for full-compatibility.

✔ **Include Linked Files:** Select this check box to embed any linked files in your image.

✔ **Include Document Thumbnails:** In the Open dialog box of some applications, you get a thumbnail picture of the file, which lets you see the picture before you open the file. Select this check box to create one of those thumbnails.

✔ **Include Document Fonts:** Select this check box to build any fonts that you use in your document into the EPS file. Although selecting this option increases file size, it also ensures that your document displays and prints properly if the fonts don't exist on the computer used to open the file.

- ✓ **CMYK PostScript:** If you use any RGB colors in your document, this option enables them to print on a four-color, CMYK PostScript printer. This check box is a good one to select, just in case.

- ✓ **PostScript:** Choose levels here to set the PostScript level at which the file prints. *PostScript* is the language that printers use. You want to use the highest level that the printer is capable of. Today's printers support Level 3, but these files don't print properly on really old (pre-2000) printers. If the file doesn't print, try using a lower level. Be aware that lower levels can print more slowly and with less quality than Level 3. (But hey, that's better than not printing at all!)

If you save your file with Illustrator CS4 compatibility, you can't save it with Level 1 PostScript. Export the file as an Illustrator 8 file (or an earlier version) to change to Level 1.

- ✓ **Transparency:** This setting appears whenever you set the Compatibility option to any version prior to Illustrator 9. (Transparency was introduced in Illustrator 9. See Chapter 10 for more info.) This feature enables you to make an object semitransparent so that an object beneath it shows through as a blend of the two objects. (Think of a semitransparent red circle overlapping a blue circle, making the overlapped portion appear purple.) Because this is an Illustrator 9 feature, earlier versions don't support it. When you save an Illustrator CS4 file as Illustrator 8 or earlier, use a Transparency option to determine how to translate transparent objects into something that earlier versions can understand.

Choose from two radio buttons to either discard or flatten transparency: Preserve Paths and Preserve Appearance, respectively. The Preserve Paths option discards transparency altogether, keeping the same shapes that you originally created but making the graphic look very different. For example, a red and blue overlapping circle would look just like that, with no purple area where the two overlap. Select the Preserve Appearance option to create new shapes to maintain the look of the transparency. For instance, new paths are created for the purple area where the two circles overlapped. The Preserve Appearance option is almost always the way to go; it keeps your artwork looking exactly the way you created it.

If you use the Transparency option when you save an Illustrator document in an older format, you might get some strange and unexpected results. Save in the latest format (Illustrator CS4) if you can.

After you complete your settings, click OK. Your Illustrator file is saved as an EPS file, ready to use just about anywhere!

After you master saving your Illustrator artwork as an EPS, you can create graphics that are compatible with every major print publishing application available. Saving graphics as GIFs or JPEGs (which I cover in Chapter 17) enables you to make artwork that can be displayed in nearly every Web browser in existence. Add the ability to move files back and forth between Illustrator and Photoshop, as well as the many export options, and you can create graphics that work anywhere.

Putting Your Art on the Web

In This Chapter

- Designing for the Web in Illustrator
- Differentiating between raster and vector formats on the Web
- Saving JPEG, GIF, and PNG for the Web
- Exporting Flash and SVG
- Creating slices

*I*llustrator is the perfect tool for creating and designing graphical elements for Web pages. That statement might surprise you seeing as how most Web graphics are pixel-based, whereas Illustrator is a vector-based graphics tool. In Illustrator, however, the big advantage to creating Web graphics is in the resolution independence of vector-based graphics (as I discuss in Chapter 1). You can create a graphic once, scale it to be any size you need it to be (even use it for print in addition to the Web), and it will always be a high-quality rendition of your creation.

In this chapter, you peer into the myriad ways of preparing Illustrator graphics for the Web and see how to determine the options that best meet the needs of individual graphics. You also find out about how vector-based file formats, such as Flash and SVG, help you put vector-based graphics on the Web while preserving the advantages of vector-based graphics (such as small file size and maximum quality, no matter at what size you view or print the graphics) in the process.

From Illustrator to the Web

When you create a graphic in a pixel-based program, such as Photoshop, you have to decide upfront how big you want the graphic. If you want to enlarge the graphic, you add pixels; if you want to make the graphic smaller, you throw away pixels. Either way, messing with the size means you end up with a blurry, lower-quality image like the zoomed-in eye section of the otherwise incredibly handsome face on the left in Figure 17-1. With Illustrator, though, you don't have these problems. Even though you ultimately create pixel-based graphics, your graphics don't become pixel-based until you save or export them. You can save the Illustrator file many times at different sizes, and each one will be at the best possible quality!

Figure 17-1: Left: Standard size and resolution. Right: Zoomed in for lower resolution.

The differences between creating for the Web and creating for print happen when you save your graphic. Whenever you create artwork in Illustrator for the Web, you work like you always would. The key difference is in how you save your work after you create it. The only other difference that you might find is in the color choices whenever you create a graphic for the GIF file format. (More on that in a moment.) Otherwise, the creative processes for Web and print are identical.

Because you view Web graphics on-screen, you have a much better idea of how they will look after you put them on a Web site than you would if you were going to print them. Colors on-screen (and on the Web, which is always displayed on a screen) consist of red, green, and blue (RGB) pixel combinations. So if you create graphics just for the Web, RGB documents are your best bet. If you create things for both screen and print, RGB gives you the greatest flexibility. (For more on RGB, see Chapter 1.)

Using Web colors only

Suppose you're in a room full of Web designers, and you hear them talk about *Web-safe color space* and the *Web panel*. You look around discreetly. A dapper man in a dark suit steps out from behind the potted plant and tells you, "You're traveling through another dimension . . ." and a weird piano riff starts to play.

Granted, Web design can seem pretty weird. At least the number of colors is relatively small. *Web-safe color* refers to a set of 216 colors that look the same in all Web browsers and on all computer platforms. If you've been creating for print for any length of time, you might be used to using an almost unlimited range of colors. Comparatively speaking, a mere 216 colors might seem limited at first, but there's method in the madness.

One key benefit of the GIF file format is that you can specify exact colors to use in your artwork *after* the artwork is created. The catch is that you can only choose from the 256 colors that the GIF format supports. (Other modes, such as RGB support up to 16.7 *million* colors. Yikes!) So how do you get 216 out of 256? Well, unfortunately, only 216 colors actually display the same on all Web browsers and computer platforms. That's what makes them *Web safe*.

So, what happens if you use a color outside of those 216? Whenever a computer encounters a color it can't display, it *dithers* the colors. The computer takes the colors that it can display and tries to emulate the missing color, putting alternating squares of the colors that it *can* display close together. If you look at the monitor from a distance and squint, you see a color that looks very similar to your original color.

Dithering is especially noticeable in large areas of solid color. The effects vary from computer to computer and browser to browser. Sometimes the effects aren't noticeable at all. Sometimes you get an obvious plaid or striped pattern. Other times, you get plaids and stripes together (and that is such a fashion *faux pas*).

Bottom line: If it's critical that your colors display consistently (and without dithering) to as many viewers as possible (as in the case of a corporate logo on a home page), use Web-safe colors. Use these Web-safe colors when you save your Illustrator graphic for the Web or when you first create your graphic in Illustrator. You can change the colors in your previously created Illustrator artwork by choosing File➪Save for Web & Devices. Or you can start out using Web-safe colors to build your artwork (which might save some hassle down the line) by choosing Window➪Swatch Libraries➪Web. Doing so gets you the Web color panel shown in Figure 17-2, home to the 216 Web-safe colors.

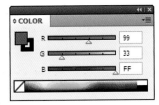

Figure 17-2: The Illustrator Web color panel.

Just click any color in this panel and add it to your Swatches panel so that you can use it just as you do any other color. If you use colors only from this panel, you ensure that your artwork uses only Web-safe colors. However, many Illustrator features (such as blends, color filters, and transparencies) can quickly turn even these colors into unsafe colors. Illustrator likes millions and millions of colors . . .

Don't let all this talk of Web-safe colors make you gun-shy. In some situations, Web-safe colors are vital: in logos and large on-screen areas of solid color, for example. In other situations, though, they just don't matter. Dithering is most obvious in large areas of solid color; if your graphic comprises many small parts, the dithering won't really be noticeable.

Using the Save for Web command enables you to decide at any time whether to use Web-safe colors when you save your illustration. (See the section later in this chapter, "Creating Web-Specific Pixel Graphics.")

Working in Pixel Preview mode

The majority of graphics created for the Web are pixel-based. The two most widely supported graphics file formats on the Web are JPEG and GIF, and these formats save only pixel data, not vector data. (See Chapter 2 for more on this crucial distinction.) When your graphics are in either of these formats, the majority of Internet users will be able to view your graphics. Fortunately, Illustrator can save graphics as both JPEGs and GIFs. Because pixel-based and vector-based images can look quite different, Illustrator has a special preview mode designed for when you're creating graphics for the Web: Pixel Preview mode. In Pixel Preview mode, you can see what your vector artwork will look like when it's turned into pixels for display on the Web. That way, you get a better idea of what the final artwork will look like on the Web (rather than waiting to be surprised when you see it in the browser for the first time).

To turn on Pixel Preview mode, choose View⇨Pixel Preview. You might not notice anything different on-screen until you zoom in closer than 100%. Try 200% to really see the pixel detail. Figure 17-3 shows Pixel Preview turned off and turned on at 200%.

This approach is much more convenient than using the File⇨Save for Web & Devices command to convert your graphic into pixels to see how it will look, and then having to resave it if it looks awful. With Pixel Preview mode, you can edit the graphics "live" while you're viewing the pixels.

Figure 17-3: Pixel Preview turned off (top) versus Pixel Preview turned on (bottom).

Choosing a file format

Deciding what file format to use is almost as perplexing as picking between paper and plastic in the checkout line. Annoyingly, no single correct answer exists when you have to decide which file format to use for the Web. What works best for your purpose normally turns out to be a compromise between what you want and what you can have.

Well, okay, what can you have? You can choose from five file formats to put your graphics on the Web: GIF, JPEG, PNG, Flash (SWF), and SVG. The basic difference is in how each format presents your artwork. Consider this thumbnail comparison:

- **GIF, JPEG, and PNG** require that vector-based files be converted to pixel-based artwork. The results look sketchier but load faster since the files are compressed.

- **Flash (SWF) and SVG** preserve the paths you create in Illustrator even though sometimes they come with gigantic file sizes.

Each format has unique benefits and drawbacks. And here they come now.

GIF file format

GIF is a great format for traditional Illustrator graphics — which means almost no gradients, blends, or fine details. GIF (Graphics Interchange Format) uses a maximum of 256 colors, but typically, you want to use even fewer. The fewer colors you use, the smaller your files.

GIF works best with simple graphics that have large areas of solid color. GIF compression encodes an area of solid color as if it were one big pixel. The more solid colors you have (almost regardless of how much on-screen area they cover), the smaller the file size. If you use gradients, soft drop shadows, or really complex graphics, you introduce more instructions into the file, and the file gets a lot bigger.

In the process of compressing all the different colors in your image (sometimes thousands or millions) down to 256 or fewer, you can get banding and dithering. *Banding* happens when a range of different colors gets compressed into one solid color and looks like a big stripe in your image where you didn't intend to put one. *Dithering* is Illustrator's way of simulating missing colors by putting tiny squares of the remaining colors close together, as shown in Figure 17-4. This type of dithering is separate from any additional dithering that happens when you don't use Web-safe colors; see the previous section, "Using Web colors only."

Figure 17-4: This image was saved with fewer colors, resulting in dithering.

GIF files differ from JPEG files in two important ways: GIFs can have transparent areas, and you can specify the exact colors you want (such as Web-safe colors) when you save the file.

GIF is one of the most widely recognized graphics formats for the Web. If you use a GIF file, you virtually guarantee that all your site's visitors can open it in their browsers.

JPEG file format

JPEG is among the most widely recognized graphics formats for the Web. Anything that you save in JPEG format can be viewed by almost everyone. The JPEG format (created by the Joint Photographic Experts Group) provides the best compression possible for digitized photographs by throwing information away. Don't fret too much about this situation. JPEG does so intelligently: examining the image and removing data where the human eye is least likely to notice the absence. What this amazing feat of mathematics means to you as an artist, however, is that your graphics files should start out with a lot of information — so that if you have to throw out a lot of the information, you still have a lot left. Unlike GIFs, JPEGs can't have transparent areas and offer no way to specify exact colors.

Complex images with lots of gradients, blends, and soft shadows make good JPEGs. Alas, this format is really lousy for graphics that have big areas of solid color. You can't hide the loss of information. Basically, if the image looks good as a GIF, it might look bad as a JPEG — and vice versa. Fortunately, you can decide which format works best by using the Save for Web command.

PNG file format

PNG (Portable Network Graphics) format has a split personality — PNG-8 and PNG-24. The graphics quality that you can get with simple GIFs is also available with PNG-8 graphics. PNG-24, on the other hand, is as adept at handling complex images as JPEG. PNG-8 and PNG-24 files can have transparent areas. Also, PNG-24 compression is *lossless,* which means no reduction in image quality. *Lossy* compression actually has less detail, substituting pixels when it is shown on screen; lossless keeps each pixel intact and simply uses math for the compression.

Why don't you just use PNG for everything? Well, first, PNG offers no way to control how much compression is applied to the image; you can't make the image smaller (like you can with a JPEG). More importantly, PNG isn't as universal as JPEG and GIF; you don't see PNG format nearly as often on the Web. If you use this format, not all your visitors can view the graphic on their browsers. Some visitors with older browsers might need to install a special piece of software (a *plug-in*) so their browsers can read PNG graphics. This situation creates enough hassle that some visitors turn away from Web pages using PNG graphics to avoid downloading and installing the PNG plug-in.

If your primary concern is image quality, use PNG-24. If you want the maximum number of people to view your work on the Web and the maximum control over file size, use GIF or JPEG.

Flash (SWF) file format

The Flash (or SWF) file format, created by Macromedia, is one of the cooler things that happened on the Web. Flash (now owned by Adobe) is the current standard for vector graphics on the Web. Not only does it support vector-based graphics, but it also supports animation, sound, and interactivity. Of course (as per Murphy's Law of Innovation), something so cool can't be perfect, and Flash has its blemishes, too. Nearly every browser requires a plug-in to view a Flash file, which limits your audience from the start. Last, Flash files don't play well with others. If you try to tie the Flash files into other non-Flash aspects of your Web site, you might run into difficulty.

SVG file format

SVG (Scalable Vector Graphics) format was a proposed standard for vector graphics that has slowly been fading away since Adobe purchased Macromedia. Like with Flash graphics, most browsers need a plug-in to read SVG files.

So which file format is best, already?

Sorry, but I can't tell you which file format is the best choice for you to use. That answer depends on what you need the file format to do and what trade-offs you're willing to live with. That's the most practical answer for now. However, a summary can help ward off the Too-Many-Choices headache, so here goes:

- **Maximum compatibility:** Use GIFs and JPEGs if you want maximum compatibility with as many people as possible.
- **Simplicity:** Use GIFs for simple graphics with large, solid colors or for transparency.
- **Complexity:** Use JPEGs for more complex graphics with gradients and images and so forth.
- **Maximum quality:** Use PNG for maximum-quality complex graphics and transparency when compatibility isn't an issue.
- **Web considerations:** Use Flash when you need to publish vector-based graphics on the Web and want as much compatibility as possible (but don't require as much compatibility as with GIFs and JPEGs).
- **La vida loca:** Use SVG when you want as many bells and whistles as possible and are willing to throw compatibility to the wind.

If we're all lucky, everyone will eventually adopt SVG as the standard, and we won't have to worry about issues, such as which file format to use. (Of course, you gotta ask yourself: Do I feel lucky?) Until then, choosing the right file format is a juggling act that balances features, quality, and compatibility.

Creating Web-Specific Pixel Graphics

Most graphics on the Web are not vector-based but pixel-based because of compatibility issues due to different browser versions and different platforms (Mac, Windows, etc) out there. Regardless of which pixel format you use, Illustrator gives you the same dialog box from which to export your artwork. Choosing File⇨Save for Web & Devices displays the Save for Web & Devices dialog box, as shown in Figure 17-5.

Even if the Save for Web & Devices dialog box appears a bit intimidating at first, it's actually quite easy to use. Although you do have to wade through a lot of settings, the dialog box provides you with a preview of the image so you can see how the settings affect the image's quality. The dialog box also gives you the file size and an estimate of how long the graphic will take to download — both important considerations when creating graphics for the Web.

The dialog box is slightly different, depending on the file format you're working with, but the following few features remain consistent in any format you use:

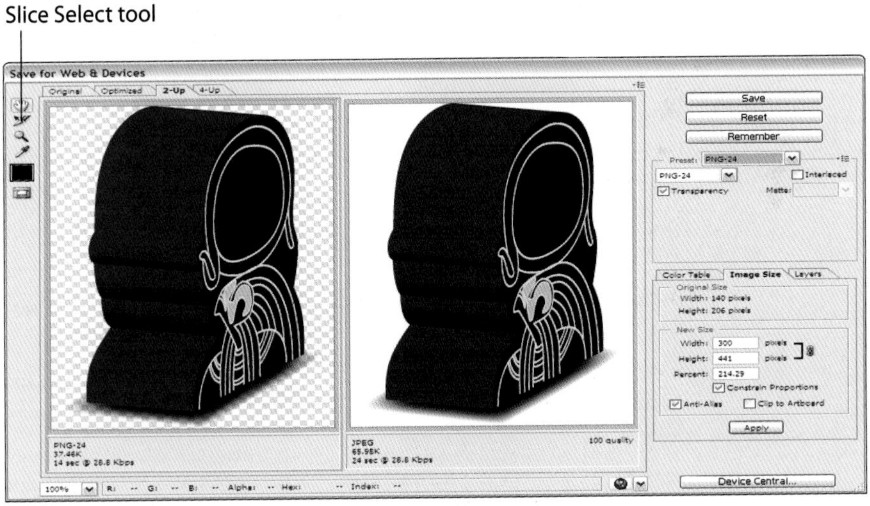

Slice Select tool

Figure 17-5: Preview your image in the Save for Web & Devices dialog box.

✔ **Original, Optimized, 2-Up, 4-Up:** These tabs let you view the image at different settings. Click the Original tab to view the image before any settings are applied. Click the Optimized tab to see how the image will look after you save it with the current settings. Click the 2-Up and 4-Up tabs to see the image at multiple settings at once. These last views are the most useful. Your goal when saving your image, no matter what format you use, is always to come up with a version that resembles the original as closely as possible while maintaining the smallest file size (and lowest download time). The ability to compare the image at different settings with the original is vital to achieving this goal. To use the 2-Up and 4-Up settings, click either of the tabs. Then click one of the images to select it. Any settings you make apply only to that selected image. Click a different image to apply different settings. Illustrator saves whatever image is selected (at whatever settings) after you click OK.

✔ **File Size and Download Time:** These features tell you how large your file is and how long that file will take to download over different connection types. This information is very important. Think of every second required for a graphic to download as another second the viewer has to get bored and click away from your page. Weigh this download time against the quality of the graphic and ask yourself whether having those extra colors, a little less banding, or a better-looking graphic is worth the download time.

✔ **File Format:** This drop-down menu is where you choose the format — GIF, JPEG, PNG-8, PNG-24, SWF, or SVG.

✔ **The remainder of the settings:** The remainder of the fields around the File Format menu deal with the file settings and the unique settings of that format. After you choose a format, the remainder of the settings change to match the features of that format. These settings are covered in depth under each file format in the next few sections of this chapter.

✔ **Color Table:** This tab shows you the exact colors used when you save the file in GIF or PNG-8 format. Here you can delete colors (or shift non-Web-safe colors to Web-safe colors).

✔ **Image Size:** This tab lets you set the size (in pixels) of the image as you save it. This setting is the actual physical size of the image as it displays in the browser, not the file size.

✔ **Layers:** Illustrator allows you to export your file as Cascading Style Sheet (CSS) layers. An advanced feature, CSS layers, enables you to selectively hide or show layers on your Web page. They also allow for transparent overlapping slices.

✔ **Slices:** The Slice Select tool, located below the hand on the left side of the Save for Web & Devices dialog box, enables you to select slices you made to your object in Illustrator. Slicing your artwork divides your artwork into individual pieces allowing your file to load in sections on your Web page. Slices also enable you to assign features, such as rollovers and links, to individual slices.

Saving a graphic as a GIF file

To save your graphic as a GIF, follow these steps:

1. **Choose File⇨Save for Web.**

   The Save for Web & Devices dialog box appears.

2. **Select GIF from the File Format drop-down menu (refer to Figure 17-3).**

3. **Click the 2-Up or 4-Up tab at the top of the graphic.**

   After you choose either 2-Up or 4-Up, the first graphic is your original image and the second is selected as the Optimized image. As you change your file settings, this graphic updates to preview those changes. Clicking the third or fourth graphic (in 4-Up view) lets you make different settings and simultaneously compare and contrast them to find the best settings. Adjust your settings to find the best balance of small file size and best image quality. Every setting you change affects both of those things. Watch the image carefully to see how the changes affect it.

4. **Adjust the settings for the graphic, as shown in Figure 17-6:**

   - *Color Reduction Algorithm:* This delightfully descriptive setting (the drop-down menu beneath the File Format menu) simply means that you take the many colors in your image and reduce them to 256 or fewer colors. How do you want to do that? Your choices are Perceptual, Selective, Adaptive, Web, or Custom. The first three are pretty much the same. The Perceptual setting makes the colors as close as possible to whatever colors the human eye perceives in the original image (so they say). The Selective setting does the same thing but uses as many Web-safe colors as possible. The Adaptive setting makes the remaining colors as mathematically close to the original as possible. The Web setting uses the closest Web-safe colors to the colors that are in the image. The Custom setting is for power users who want to create their own color-reduction algorithms.

     Your choices are really between the Perceptual and Web settings. The Perceptual setting gives you an image as close as possible to your original creation. The Web setting gives you an image that looks the same no matter what computer or Web browser it's on. Unfortunately, the Perceptual setting usually looks great, whereas the Web setting dithers things substantially. But look at the Web choice this way: This is as bad as the image is going to look. With any other setting, the graphic is going to look better or worse unpredictably. With the Web setting, you know exactly how much dithering is going on, and nothing more will happen to the image — and the file size is definitely a little smaller.

- *Dithering algorithm:* This is the actual shape of the dithering pattern. The No Dither setting won't dither the image at all. The Diffusion setting randomizes the dithering pattern to make it less noticeable. The Pattern setting dithers in a fixed grid. The Noise setting is even more random than the Diffusion setting, making any dither even less noticeable. Sadly, the settings that produce the least noticeable dithering also create the highest file sizes. The Noise setting produces the largest files, and the Diffusion setting the second largest. The Pattern setting produces small files with noticeable stripes. The No Dither setting produces obvious bands of color in the image. Notice the weird curved shapes in Figure 17-6. A No Dither setting causes these to appear. Here again, your goal is to strike a balance between the smallest size and the best quality.

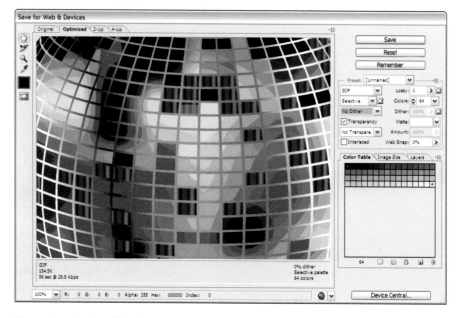

Figure 17-6: Saving a GIF with a limited number of colors and the No Dither option enabled.

- *Transparency:* How do you want to treat the parts of your image that have no graphics? Do you want them to be transparent or filled with the Matte color (explained later in this list)? Check this box to make them transparent.

- *Interlaced:* This setting makes the file larger so that it seems to be downloading faster, which seems like a contradiction. When a graphic is interlaced, it first loads a very low-resolution version to the Web browser, and then the full-resolution version. Graphics seem to load faster, but the Interlaced setting is just soothing the user by showing something useful happening. Without interlacing, the whole page has

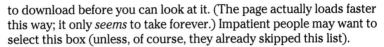

to download before you can look at it. (The page actually loads faster this way; it only *seems* to take forever.) Impatient people may want to select this box (unless, of course, they already skipped this list).

- *Lossy:* This setting reduces file size by as much as 40 percent by eliminating pixels (at the expense of image quality). Use as much Lossy as you can get away with, but don't ruin your image.

  The Lossy setting won't work with the Interlacing setting turned on.

- *Colors:* This setting is the total number of colors used in the image. Sometimes, reducing the number results in a smaller image, but doing so doesn't usually have as much effect as the Dither and Lossy settings.

- *Dither:* If you select the Pattern, Noise, or Diffusion settings for a dither method, you can use this setting to turn down the amount of dithering. Lower amounts result in smaller graphics with more noticeable dithering patterns.

- *Matte:* If you don't choose the Transparency box, the Matte color fills areas of your image where there are no graphics. If you're using transparency and know what color you plan to use for the background of the Web page, you can set the Matte color to the background color, and the pixels at the edge of your graphic will blend with the background, creating a more visually appealing image. If you don't know what the background color will be, set the Matte color to None. Otherwise, the edge pixels might blend to a different color from your background, producing an obvious fringe around the graphic as if it were snipped hastily out of a different background.

- *Web Snap:* If you aren't using the Web setting for your color reduction algorithm, you can use the Web Snap setting to convert some of the colors (starting with those used most in the image) to Web-safe colors. This setting is a great way to achieve a balance between quality and compatibility. By changing just the largest areas of color to Web-safe colors, you can avoid the dithering problem in places where it will be most noticeable. The higher the setting, the more colors Illustrator converts to Web-safe colors.

After you make your settings on several images and decide which image works best for you, click that image, and then click OK. The graphic saves as a GIF, ready for you to use on your Web page.

Saving a graphic as a JPEG file

In Illustrator, JPEGs are easier to make than GIFs. You need to worry about only one setting: Quality. Of course, quality can be specified in two ways. (Simplicity? Well, almost.)

To save your artwork as a JPEG, follow these steps:

1. **Choose File⇨Save for Web.**

   The Save for Web & Devices dialog box appears.

2. **Choose JPEG from the File Format drop-down menu.**

3. **Click the 2-Up or 4-Up tab at the top of the graphic.**

   For more on viewing options, see the earlier section, "Saving a graphic as a GIF file."

4. **Choose a Quality setting.**

   You can choose the Quality setting in two ways, but the effects are identical: by choosing it from the Quality drop-down menu, or by entering a number into the Quality field.

   - *The Quality drop-down menu:* The menu offers you a choice of four preset values: Maximum, High, Medium, and Low. These options refer to the quality level of the image, not the amount of compression applied. A Maximum quality level produces (as you may expect) the largest file sizes and the highest-quality images.

   - *The Quality field:* In this field, just to the right of the drop-down menu, you type in any value from 100 (maximum quality) to 0. Use the lowest Quality setting possible that doesn't destroy your image. You might notice that the loss of quality in your image shows up as weird patterns that weren't there before. These patterns are especially noticeable where two large areas of different colors meet. Notice the weird horizontal and vertical bands *(artifacting)* in Figure 17-7. A little of this is tolerable in the name of smaller files, but too much becomes distracting.

   Note: Entering settings in the Quality field is identical to choosing values from the Quality drop-down menu. In the menu, the values of Maximum, High, Medium, and Low correspond (respectively) to settings of 80, 60, 30, and 10 in the Quality field.

5. **Adjust the other settings.**

   - *Progressive:* Like interlacing for GIFs, the Progressive setting creates the illusion that the image loads faster on Web browsers by loading a low-resolution version of the graphic first and then turning it into a higher-resolution image. In actuality, the image takes longer to load because Progressive files are larger, but viewers feel as though the download is going faster because they see things happening while they wait, rather than waiting for the whole download before they see anything.

   - *Blur:* Blur is a fairly useless setting. The goal is to reduce the artifacting in the image by blurring it. Unfortunately, the setting blurs the whole image, not just the artifacts, creating problems where none existed before. Leave this set to 0 (zero) and ignore it. (Unless, of course, you're feeling a little misty.)

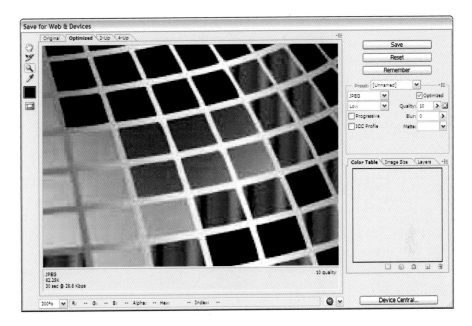

Figure 17-7: Saving a JPEG from the Save for Web & Devices dialog box.

- *Matte:* JPEGs can have no transparent areas, so wherever no graphic exists, Illustrator fills in with this color. A setting of None fills in with white.

Saving a graphic as a PNG-8 or PNG-24 file

The settings for PNG-8 are identical to those for GIF except you don't get a Lossy option. (Read through the earlier section, "Saving a graphic as a GIF file.") Put PNG-8 wherever you see GIF. No settings exist for PNG-24, except Transparency, Interlacing, and Matte options; what you get is what you get. Choose the PNG-24 file format, and the compression scheme does its thing. Either you like the result (and click OK), or you don't (and choose GIF or JPEG instead).

Creating Web-Specific Vector Graphics

Vectors have several advantages over pixels. One of the chief advantages is their small file size, especially for basic graphics such as logos and buttons. Another advantage is their ability to be scaled without any loss of quality.

Saving a graphic as a Flash file

Flash is a very versatile format developed by Macromedia (which Adobe acquired, so it's now *Adobe Flash*). Not only can you use Flash to show vector graphics on the Web, but you can also animate and add sound and interactivity to them. In Illustrator, you can create the graphic and do limited animation with it. Beyond that, you have to use another application (such as Adobe Flash or Adobe After Effects) to take full advantage of the format. For this reason, the Flash (SWF) setting in the Export dialog box is really intended to prepare artwork for export to one of these other applications, rather than to create artwork to go directly to the Web. Not that you can't put a Flash file created in Illustrator directly on the Web. You certainly can, but then you're tapping into just a fraction of what Flash can do.

Still, if you want your Illustrator artwork on the Web as vector data, Flash is the way to go. The one drawback to the format is the need for a browser plug-in in order for people to see your graphic in their browsers. This situation can make your graphic inaccessible to some people. However, Flash is such a popular format that most people have the plug-in installed in their browsers. Chances are quite good that many people will be able to see your work without problems.

If your primary concern is that your graphic appears on the Web with no-holds-barred top quality (and print with the best possible quality to boot), use the Flash format.

To save a graphic in Flash format, just follow these steps:

1. **Choose File⇨Export.**

   The Export dialog box appears.

2. **Specify a name, location, and file format for your document.**

   In this case, choose Flash (SWF) from the file format drop-down menu.

3. **Click OK.**

   The SWF Options dialog box appears.

4. **After you complete all your settings, click OK to save your file in Flash format.**

You can export Flash (SWF) files that include symbols. When opened in a Flash application, the symbols are included in the Symbol library of the application.

Saving a graphic as a SVG file

SVG files, once heralded as the Next Big Thing by Adobe have faded away at this time, as Adobe focuses on supporting their Flash format. However, some mobile devices and most browsers with the required plug-ins support SVG. Here are the steps for saving a graphic as an SVG file:

1. **Choose File⇨Save.**

   The Save dialog box appears. The SVG file format can be saved directly rather than exported. You can also open an SVG file directly into Illustrator. And if that isn't enough, Illustrator lets you open SVG files that were created in other SVG-savvy applications.

2. **Choose SVG (SVG) from the Format drop-down menu. Specify a name and location for your document.**

3. **Click Save.**

   The SVG Options dialog box appears, as shown in Figure 17-8.

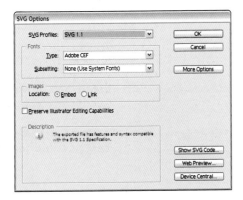

Figure 17-8: Saving an SVG file with the SVG Options dialog box.

4. **Establish your desired settings and click OK to save your file in SVG format.**

Slicing and Dicing Your Graphics

If you're an avid Web surfer, you've probably encountered a site or two where the graphics appear on-screen in separate chunks. In the Web world, these chunks are referred to as *slices*.

In Illustrator, slices can be applied to objects (vector- or pixel-based or text), groups of objects, or layers. And when any of these are edited, the slices are automatically updated. While Illustrator provides several methods for creating slices, the easiest is by dragging the Slice tool (found in the bottom half of the Tools panel) and dragging it around areas that you'd like to create slices out of. The on-screen result in Illustrator will look something like Figure 17-9.

Figure 17-9: Dragging the Slice tool around objects in your illustration results in an onscreen display of slices.

When you save via the Save for Web & Devices dialog box, the slices will be saved with your image.

Part V
The Part of Tens

*A*h, yes, the part of being tense. And who wouldn't be, knowing that there are only a few small sections of this book left to read?

What? Oh. Never mind. This part (Part of Tens, that is) contains two chapters full of lists to help you customize Illustrator and to be even more productive than you are now.

Ten Production-Enhancing Tips

*I*f you can picture something, you can probably create it in Illustrator. The only trick is knowing *how* to create it. People who use Illustrator rely on thousands of little tricks to make their lives easier, make production faster, avoid unnecessary hassle and expense, and generally make their world a better place to live. Well, those thousands of tricks might not all fit in one book, but here are ten simple ways to jazz up your use of Illustrator.

Punching Holes

Take a close look at the two blue circles in Figure 18-1. The hole in the center of the left circle is actually a white circle that obscures the background. In Illustrator, white is a color that is really "there" — and it blocks anything behind it. In the circle on the right, the hole in the center really is a hole, revealing the image behind it.

Figure 18-1: Use Compound Paths to create a "hole."

How do you accomplish this remarkable feat? If you set the fill color for the white circle to None, just the little circle becomes transparent, revealing the blue circle behind it — so that won't work. The trick is to use compound paths. The Compound Paths command joins two or more paths in such a way that wherever the paths overlap, you get a hole revealing whatever lurks behind the paths. Incidentally, this is how the holes in letters, such as O and P, are created so that when you run type over an object, you see the object through the holes.

All you need to create a compound path is two objects — one to serve as a cutting tool and the other to serve as a place to put the hole. Then follow these handy do-it-yourself steps (no safety goggles required):

1. **Place the object that you'll be using to make a hole in front of the object in which you want to cut the hole.**

   In my example, the white circle is the cutter, and the blue circle is the cuttee.

2. **Select both objects with any selection tool.**

3. **Choose Object⇨Compound Path⇨Make.**

   Where the paths overlap, you get a see-through area — you know, a hole.

To make the paths behave normally again, select the objects and choose Object⇨Compound Path⇨Release.

Perform the same feat by using the Pathfinder panel and choosing the Subtract from Shape Area command from the Shape Modes section. For more details, see Chapter 4.

Use Photoshop Effects in Illustrator!

Photoshop Effects (accessed at the bottom of the Effect menu) are always "live" in Illustrator, meaning that you can change them at any time. In addition, you can always change the attributes of your Illustrator artwork, making the artwork fully editable. If you were to take that same artwork into Photoshop, it would be difficult to maintain the same level of editability and scalability as you have in Illustrator.

When White Isn't Nothing

Double negatives aside, here's a little tip that can save you *beaucoup* bucks whenever you use gradients and spot colors in artwork you're creating for print.

If you work with print publishing, you come to think of the color white as being *nothing*. In most of the familiar printing techniques, specifying the color white means *don't put down any ink* (or toner, or dye, or any of the methods for putting color on paper) for anything colored white. White ink doesn't exist except in rare situations (and no, correction fluid doesn't count). The white that you see in print publications is just the white of the paper.

This approach depends on an actual, tangible piece of paper to provide the white for the image. To save yourself untold woe, don't use the technique I describe here if your artwork is destined to live on the Web. It's strictly a hard-copy issue.

Suppose you're creating a two-color publication using black ink and a nice blue Pantone 9344 ink. The publication might be pretty dull in only two colors, but that's all you have a budget for, so you decide to spice things up by using gradients. You create lovely gradients by blending Pantone 9344 into white (assuming that white means *no ink*). Unfortunately, in terms of gradients, Illustrator thinks of a blend as a whole new CMYK (cyan, magenta, yellow, black) color (see Chapter 1), so the blend between white and a spot color (such as Pantone 9344) involves much more complicated instructions to the computer than you might have intended.

Sure, your graphics look perfect, but unbeknownst to you, your job has mutated from a two-color job to a five-color job. Usually, you discover this after your job is already at the printer, and then you have to pay hundreds of extra dollars for a mistake you didn't even know you made.

The trick is to use the same Pantone color for all steps of the gradient (see Figure 18-2). Just follow these steps:

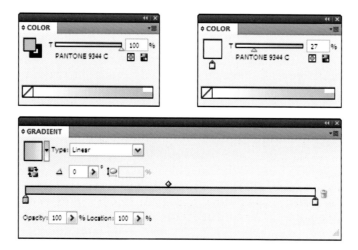

Figure 18-2: The same color is used at two different tint percentages, specified in the Color panel.

1. **Choose Window⇨Gradient.**

   The Gradient panel appears.

2. **Choose Window⇨Swatch Libraries⇨Pantone Coated (or another swatch library of your choice).**

   The Pantone swatch library opens.

3. **Click the color of your choice in the Pantone library and drag the color from the Library onto a color stop in the Gradient panel.**

   A *color stop* is the icon that looks like a little house; it represents a color in the gradient.

   Repeat this until all color stops in the Gradient panel are the same color. (See Chapter 10 for more information on gradients.)

   At this point, the gradient is one solid color. Not a gradient at all, really. But wait!

4. **Double-click a color stop in the Gradient panel.**

   The Color panel opens, showing the Pantone color set to 100%.

5. **Set the tint of the Pantone color to 27%.**

   This action gives you true, one-ink spot-color gradients that use the paper as "white" in that good old traditional way. See Chapter 10 for more info on gradients.

Expanding to Get to the Root of the Artwork

If you piled on the effects to some artwork, sometimes making adjustments to the end result is hard. If you're absolutely sure that you'll never need to go back and edit the original artwork, you can *expand* the artwork into "traditional" artwork that includes all the pieces necessary to create the appearance you see on-screen.

To expand an object, follow these steps and examine Figure 18-3, which shows the original object with a gradient fill (top left) is expanded (bottom left) to 20 objects (with paths showing) and the final object (bottom right):

1. **Select the object with any selection tool.**

2. **Choose Object⇨Expand.**

3. **In the Expand dialog box that opens, choose to expand the fill, the stroke, and the object (if you selected an object blend) by selecting those check boxes.**

   Select the Fill check box to expand the fill and simplify gradients. Select the Stroke box to create custom brushes, and select the Fill or Stroke box to create patterns — or just leave all three selected to cover all your bases. You can also specify what the gradient is expanded to: either a gradient mesh object or individual path objects.

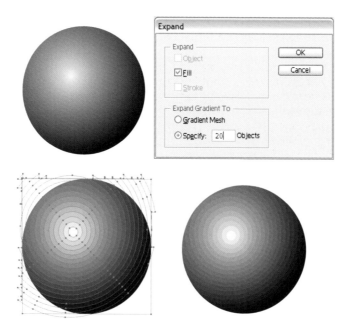

Figure 18-3: Expanding a Gradient fill object.

Quick! Hide!

Simply hiding things can greatly improve your productivity in Illustrator. Otherwise, you might have a hard time seeing your current creation with all the floating panels and interface elements in the way.

You can hide all open panels and the Tools panel by pressing the Tab key (unless the Type tool is selected and a blinking I-beam cursor is on your page — then you just insert a Tab into your text). Press the Tab key again to bring everything back.

If you're creating exclusively for the Web, hide the Artboard and the Page Tiling feature. These features show you the size of the page you're printing to and the printable area on that page. This information is useless if you're never going to print! Choose View⇔Hide Artboard and View⇔Hide Page Tiling to make them go away, respectively.

Have you ever made an object that contains so many points that after you select it you can't tell what the object *is* anymore for all the highlighted points and lines? You can hide these, too, while keeping the object selected. Choose View⇨Hide Edges to make the highlights disappear.

You can hide everything you have open on your computer (including your desktop) except for the current Illustrator document by clicking the Full Screen Mode with Menu Bar button in the Tools panel. To hide everything including the Menu bar, click the Full Screen Mode button. (You can toggle through these modes by pressing the F key on your keyboard; this works for both PCs and Macs.) To get a completely unobscured view of your artwork, switch to the Full Screen Mode view and press the Tab key to hide your panels. Real power-users work this way, using keyboard shortcuts to access all the tools and menu items.

Taking a Tip from Illustrator

Illustrator offers ToolTips as a very helpful feature. Hover your cursor over a tool for a moment, and a little yellow box of text pops up telling you what the tool is. If the tool has a keyboard shortcut, that shortcut appears in parentheses after the name.

ToolTips, despite their name, don't work with tools alone. (And they don't give you tips — just the names of things. Go figure.) They work just about anywhere in Illustrator that you can position a cursor. Hover over a color swatch, and the ToolTip tells you the name of that color. Hover over a brush, and it tells you the name of the brush. Not sure what a cryptic icon in the Pathfinder panel means? Just let the ToolTip tell you.

ToolTips are invaluable whenever you're using the program because there are just too many things to remember. With ToolTips, you don't have to!

To toggle ToolTips off or on, choose Edit⇨Preferences⇨General and select (check) or clear (uncheck) the Show ToolTips check box.

Changing Your Units Whenever You Want

Do you feel that no matter what you do, your units of measure seem to be wrong? Are they always set to points, for example, when you really want inches? (Sometimes centimeters are easier to work with.) Fortunately, Illustrator lets you change your mind on the fly.

To see your measurement options, choose View⇨Show Rulers and then right-click in Windows (Control-click on a Mac) any location on the rulers at the top and side of your screen. You get a drop-down menu that shows all the units of measurement that Illustrator understands. Choose the unit you desire; from that moment on, Illustrator uses that unit of measurement.

You can reposition rulers by clicking and dragging out from where the rulers meet at the upper-left corner. To reset them, double-click that corner.

However, you don't have to change your unit of measurement to use a different one. In any field where you specify an amount (such as the Height and Width options in the Rectangle dialog box), just type in the amount you want, followed by the abbreviation of the unit of measurement that you want to use. If you don't know the abbreviation, just use the whole name. Illustrator makes the conversions for you.

Want to impress your friends with a great power-user tip? You can cycle through the different measurement units by pressing Ctrl+Alt+Shift+U (⌘+Option+Shift+U on a Mac). It helps to have your rulers up when doing this so you can see what the current measurement system is.

Reusing Your Brushes, Swatches, and Libraries

Has this ever happened to you? You go through the trouble to create custom brushes, beautiful colors, and outstanding appearances; save them in the Styles panel; and later discover that they're all specific to the document that you created them in. Rats! To prevent that from happening to you again, you can open the swatches, brushes, and styles that you created in one document in any other document.

For example, to get the brushes from another document, choose Window⇨ Brush Libraries⇨Other Library. In the Open dialog box that appears, choose the document with the brushes that you want to add to the current document, as if you were going to open it. Click Open. Instead of opening that document, Illustrator opens the custom brushes in their own panel, ready for you to use. Follow the same steps, choosing Window⇨Swatch Libraries⇨Other Library or Window⇨Style Libraries⇨Other Library to add your swatches or styles.

Avoiding Russian Dolls

Have you ever seen those cute Russian dolls? You know, the hollow doll that you open to find another smaller doll inside? And then you open that one to find an even smaller doll inside? And then you open *that* doll. . . .

Illustrator enables you to create the digital equivalent of those Russian dolls. You place a Photoshop image into Illustrator, rotate the image, add text over the image, and save the whole thing as an Illustrator file. To add more, create a new document in Illustrator, placing the previously created Illustrator graphic (which also contains within it a Photoshop file) into the new document by using the File⇨Place command. You save this Photoshop file within an Illustrator file within another Illustrator file as an EPS file and place it within a page layout document. You have a Photoshop file now embedded four layers deep within the page layout document. (Dizzy yet?)

Although nothing prevents you from creating the digital equivalent of a Russian doll, editing the file is very difficult. A better method is to open Illustrator files and then copy and paste them into a document rather than placing them, especially if you want to do edits later on.

Subscribe to the KISS method: Keep It Simple, Silly Goose! Avoid going more than three places from the original file (such as a Photoshop file placed inside an Illustrator file, placed inside an InDesign document, with scaling happening in only one of those places). Two places are even better if you can limit yourself. If you need to bring Illustrator data from one Illustrator document to another, open both documents and copy and paste the info rather than place it.

Selecting Type When You Want

If you work with type and objects, you might discover how annoying it is to select an object that's lurking behind type. Even when you click where there's obviously no type, you still select the type instead of the object behind it. This happens because one of Illustrator's most annoying features is turned on. The Type Area Select feature automatically selects type when you click anywhere in its area — not just when you click directly on the type or its path.

Turn off this (ahem) feature by choosing Edit⇨Preferences⇨Type & Auto Tracing. In the Type & Auto Tracing Preferences dialog box, remove the check mark from the Type Area Select check box. Click OK. Breathe easier. Henceforth, type shall be selected whenever you click directly on a letter or on its path, and at no other time, by royal proclamation of the user.

Ten (Or So) Ways to Customize Illustrator

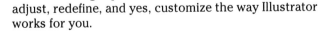

In This Chapter

> Telling panels where to go
> Setting up custom keyboard shortcuts
> Getting easier access to tools
> Changing the start-up documents
> Tweaking the default settings
> Editing preferences
> Creating Actions

*K*eyboard commands are great shortcuts — you gotta love 'em, finger cramps and all — but what if you could make them easier to use? Or maybe you have some styles that you use all the time and you want them to be (gasp) available all the time. And how about that quirky default page size that each new document shows up wearing? Well, if you itch to tinker, adjust, and fine-tune (but you misplaced your ball-peen hammer), you came to the right place. This chapter shows you how to adjust, redefine, and yes, customize the way Illustrator works for you.

Before you go on a feature-tweaking rampage, consider this: You're changing how Illustrator works globally. So a word to the wise: Read first. Then, if you like what you see, make a change and try it out for a while before you change anything else. Return to default settings if you make a mistake.

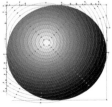

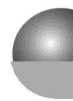

Positioning Panels

Illustrator saves all panel positions just as they were when you quit Illustrator. The next time you use Illustrator, the panels appear right where you left them. This structure is handy most of the time, but your panels can get a bit disorganized if you move them all over the place while chasing a creative inspiration. If you want to get them back to Square One with no fuss, read on.

You can save a set or sets of panel positions for later use by saving a Workspace, located at Window⇨Workspace⇨Save Workspace. Whenever you need to reset the panels to their convenient locations, just choose the workspace from the Window⇨Workspace list. If you'd like to get back to the original Illustrator "factory settings," choose Window⇨Workspace⇨Essentials.

The Flexible Tools Panel

Give each tool in the Tools panel its own keyboard shortcut. For example, pressing the V key brings up the Selection tool, and pressing the Z key brings up the Zoom tool.

To change the keyboard shortcut for a tool (or to add shortcuts for tools that don't have any), choose Edit⇨Keyboard Shortcuts. In the Keyboard Shortcuts dialog box, shown in Figure 19-1, choose Tools from the drop-down menu at the top left of the dialog box (if it's not already selected), find the tool you want to change (or add), and then highlight the current command. Type a new shortcut and then click OK to make the new shortcut available.

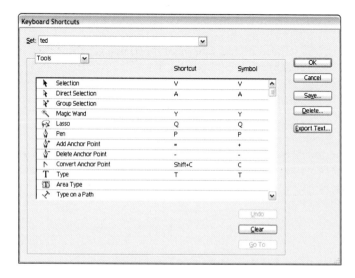

Figure 19-1: Use the Keyboard Shortcuts dialog box to customize tool commands.

If the shortcut has been assigned to another command, you'll see a warning message that there's a conflict, what the conflict is, and you'll have the ability to undo your proposed change at that time.

Changing the Items on the Menu

You can customize keyboard shortcuts to all Illustrator menu commands by using the Keyboard Shortcuts dialog box (refer to Figure 18-1). Go to this dialog box by choosing Edit⇨Keyboard Shortcuts.

You can redefine even the most common commands, such as Open and New, with different keyboard shortcuts. To add a new keyboard shortcut, follow these steps:

1. **Choose Edit⇨Keyboard Shortcuts.**

   The Keyboard Shortcuts dialog box opens.

2. **Choose Menu Commands from the drop-down menu at the top left of the dialog box (the default name is Tools).**

   A list of all Illustrator menus appears. Click the arrow beside the menu name to open the complete list of items under that menu. If the item already has a keyboard shortcut, you find it listed to the right of the menu item, in the Shortcut column.

3. **Change the keyboard shortcuts by highlighting the current keyboard shortcut, typing a new shortcut, and pressing Enter.**

   If the item has no keyboard shortcut assigned to it, you can give it one. To highlight the empty space, click in the Shortcut column (to the right of the menu item) and type in your shortcut there.

You can also print out a big sheet of all the keyboard shortcuts, even if you haven't changed any of them. To print out all the keyboard shortcuts, follow these steps:

1. **Choose Edit⇨Keyboard Shortcuts.**

   The Keyboard Shortcuts dialog box opens.

2. **Click the Export Text button at the middle right of the Keyboard Shortcuts dialog box.**

   A Save dialog box opens.

3. **Name the text file that you want to contain your keyboard shortcuts, specify a location for it on your hard drive, and then click OK to save the text file.**

4. **Open any word processing program on your computer, choose File⇨Open, open the text file you just created, and print it.**

You can always return to the original keyboard commands by choosing Illustrator Defaults from the Set drop-down menu in the upper-left corner of the Keyboard Shortcuts dialog box.

Changing the Default Settings

You can change how the entire Illustrator application works. Assuming that you have a plan (handy to have at a time like this), choose Illustrator (icon)⇨Preferences⇨General (Mac) or Edit⇨Preferences⇨General (Windows). Behold: The Preferences dialog box appears, as shown in Figure 19-2, with the General settings already displayed for you.

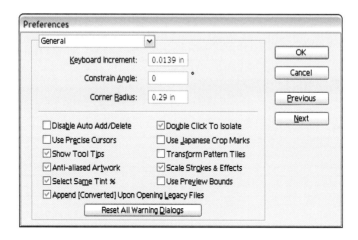

Figure 19-2: Set preferences here.

The General tab of the Preferences dialog box is just the first of several Preferences tabs containing a multitude of options for you to change. Each change affects how that the application works, and Illustrator saves these changes when you quit the program, regardless of the documents that you're working in.

WARNING!

Don't start changing preference settings all helter-skelter when you first stumble across this dialog box. Doing so might cause unexpected behaviors in the application, such as Illustrator printing your letterhead in hieroglyphics. A better idea is to look at the list of items and change only one at a time, testing each item after you change it, even writing down what you did so you can remember the changes. If the results of a change aren't up to snuff, then be sure to change the preference back to its original setting.

Changing Hidden Commands You Never Knew About

In addition to those nice, respectable, visible menu commands and tool shortcuts, all sorts of nifty shortcuts just hang around in Illustrator without a single menu item or tool associated with them. These shortcuts are handy commands, such as Increase Type Size: Ctrl+Shift (Windows)/⌘+Shift (Mac). Even better, every one of these commands can be customized. Simply scroll through the Keyboard Shortcuts dialog box to find every command that exists in Illustrator. (Choose Edit➪Keyboard Shortcuts to get there.) If you find one that looks as though it might prove useful, give it a new shortcut. Figure 19-3 shows some keyboard commands you might not have known about that you can change easily.

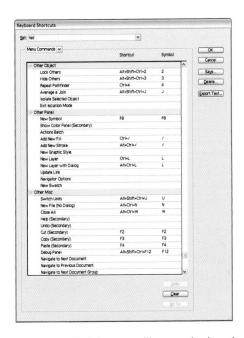

Figure 19-3: Find the secret Illustrator keyboard commands.

Action Jackson

Have you ever found yourself doing things again and again (such as typing the word *redundant* dozens of times)? Have you ever wished that your computer could do some of this tedious work for you? Well, that's where Actions come in. Actions make Illustrator do the grunt work while you get to do all the fun stuff.

Illustrator comes with hundreds of Actions although only a dozen are installed with the software. You can find the rest on your Illustrator application CD-ROM, which you'll have to insert and copy *after* you install. Better yet, you can make your own Actions! *Actions* can be virtually any series of Illustrator activities, such as scaling, rotating, changing colors, or bringing selections to the front. You can even use Actions to select objects if they have specific names.

One of the handiest uses for Actions is creating compound keyboard shortcuts. For example, you can perform a set of procedures at the same time — such as Create New Layer, Place, and Scale — without even wrenching your wrist. Instead of performing all three keyboard commands individually, you can easily set up an Action to do all three simultaneously. Result: One keyboard command does three tasks! You just smile and watch. Choose Window⇨Actions, and meet the friendly Actions panel in Figure 19-4.

To use any Action, click it in the Actions panel and then click the

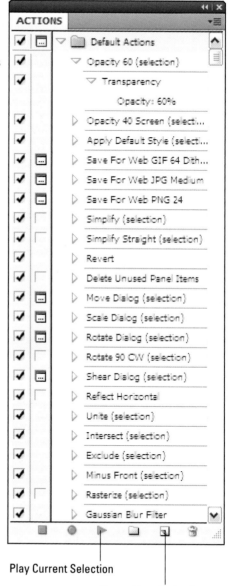

Play Current Selection

Create New Action button

Figure 19-4: The Actions panel puts power at your virtual fingertips.

Play Current Selection button (the right-pointing arrow) at the bottom of the panel.

Creating your own Action feels something like taping your voice or image and then playing it back. When you record an Action, Illustrator watches what you do and records every step as closely as possible. (This procedure is a lot like creating a macro in Word.)

Computers have no imagination; you have to tell them exactly what to do. Therefore, your recorded Actions must use precise values. Anything that requires a level of human interaction does not get recorded. In effect, Illustrator says, "That's not my department. So there." For example, creating a one-inch rectangle is a precise action. Drawing a squiggly line is not. You can't always know in advance whether Illustrator can record all the actions you perform — but you know for certain after you play it back. Hey, it's not a program; it's an adventure.

To create your own Action, just follow these steps:

1. **Open a new document in Illustrator and choose Window⇨Actions.**

   The Actions panel opens.

2. **Click the Create New Action button.**

   The New Action dialog box opens.

3. **Name the Action, click OK to close the New Action dialog box and then click the Record button on the Actions Panel.**

   For example, type the name **Red Rectangle** for the Action. After you click the Record button, the Action records everything you do, tapping your phone, and transmitting that information back to Adobe where they're keeping a file on you. Just kidding. Honest.

4. **Perform a series of actions with the keyboard or the mouse.**

   For the example, select the Rectangle tool and drag out a rectangle in the document. Then choose a red swatch from the Swatches panel for the Fill color.

5. **Click the Stop Playing/Recording button.**

   The Action shows up on the Actions panel, ready for, um, *action*. Great gung-ho attitude, eh? But hold on a minute. . . .

6. **Prepare to test your Action.**

   In this case, delete your original rectangle. This finishing touch prevents the Action from creating another rectangle of the exact same size, shape, color, and position.

7. **Test your Action by clicking the name of the Action and then clicking the Play Current Selection button.**

   If the Action does exactly what you planned, it's ready for duty.

The preceding example is a simple Action. With a bit of practice, you can create infinitely more complex Actions. This wonder results from a simple fact: An Action records (nearly) everything you do from the time you start recording to the time you click Stop. The Action can be a simple menu command or something as complex as the creation of some amazing artwork, as if by magic.

Sticky Settings

Some of the things that you do in Illustrator remain "sticky" until you quit the application. For example, if you create a rectangle that's 1 x 2 inches, the next time you click with the Rectangle tool, the values are automatically set to 1 x 2 inches. All the dialog boxes in Illustrator remember what you did last during your current Illustrator session. (But don't worry; they won't tell a soul.)

Between sessions, the entries in the Preferences dialog box and the positions of the panels are all that remain constant. Oh, well. At least *something* does.

Index

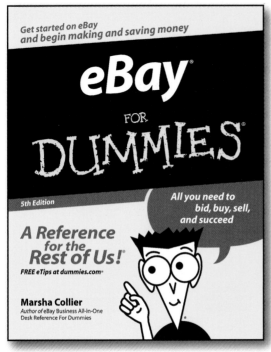
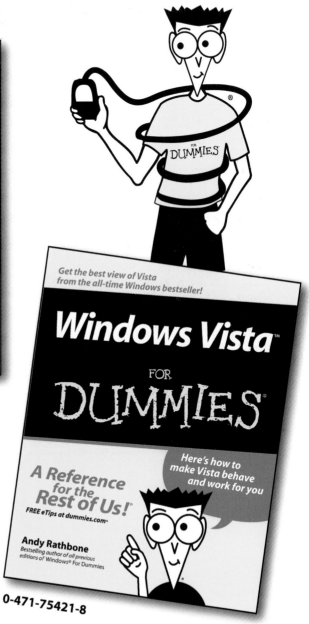

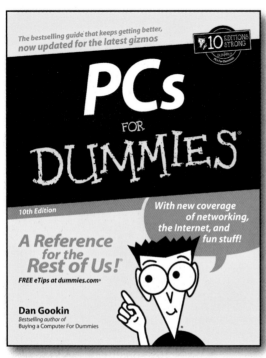

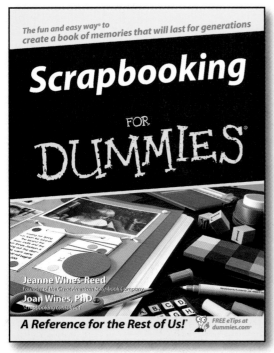